Beyond Skill

Beyond Skill

Institutions, Organisations and Human Capability

Edited By

Jane Bryson
Victoria Management School, Victoria University of Wellington

First published 2010 by
PALGRAVE MACMILLAN

Palgrave Macmillan in the UK is an imprint of Macmillan Publishers Limited, registered in England, company number 785998, of Houndmills, Basingstoke, Hampshire RG21 6XS.

Palgrave Macmillan in the US is a division of St Martin's Press LLC, 175 Fifth Avenue, New York, NY 10010.

Palgrave Macmillan is the global academic imprint of the above companies and has companies and representatives throughout the world.

Palgrave® and Macmillan® are registered trademarks in the United States, the United Kingdom, Europe and other countries

ISBN 978-0-230-23057-6   hardback

This book is printed on paper suitable for recycling and made from fully managed and sustained forest sources. Logging, pulping and manufacturing processes are expected to conform to the environmental regulations of the country of origin.

A catalogue record for this book is available from the British Library.

Library of Congress Cataloging-in-Publication Data
    Beyond skill : institutions, organisations and human capability / edited by Jane Bryson.
        p. cm.
    "The chapters in this book were based on invited papers presented at a symposium on 'Developing human capability in, and for, the workplace'"–
        ISBN 978-0-230-23057-6
      1. Organizational learning–Congresses. 2. Work environment–Congresses. I. Bryson, Jane.

    HD58.82.B495 2010
    331.25'92–dc22   2010011563

10   9   8   7   6   5   4   3   2   1
19   18   17   16   15   14   13   12   11   10

Printed and bound in Great Britain by
CPI Antony Rowe, Chippenham and Eastbourne

Contents

Acknowledgements

The chapters in this book were based on invited papers presented at a symposium on 'Developing human capability in, and for, the workplace'. Thanks are due, not only to the authors, but also to the policy officials, trade union representatives, business and other industry stakeholders who provided lively discussion of the papers at the symposium. Much of the New Zealand research reported in this book would not have been possible without the support of various agencies, in particular the Foundation for Research, Science & Technology, the Department of Labour, and our host universities. The research reported from Australia, the United Kingdom, Europe and the United States is likewise indebted to agencies with the foresight to fund this type of intellectual and practical enquiry into the larger world of work.

I am most grateful to all the workers, business owners, managers, consultants, union officials, industry associations, policymakers, and others who so generously took part in the developing human capability research which gave rise to the symposium and that I report on, in two chapters. This book is for you.

The editor and publishers wish to thank the following for permission to reproduce copyright material:

Department of Labour
Department of Labour (1999) *Human Capability: A Framework for Analysis*, Report by Department of Labour, Wellington: NZ Government. (Figure 2.1)

Institute for Employment Studies
Tamkin. P., Giles, L., Campbell, M. and Hillage, J. (2004) *Skills Pay: The Contribution of Skills to Business Success*, SSDA, Research Report 5. (Figure 2.2)

Ingrid Robeyns
Robeyns, I. (2000) *An Unworkable Idea or a Promising Alternative? Sen's Capability Approach Re-examined*, Discussion Paper Series 00.30, Centre for Economic Studies, University of Leuven. (Figure 2.3)

Russell Sage Foundation

Mason, G. and Salverda, W. Table 1, 'Incidence of low pay, 2003–2005', in Gautié, J. and Schmitt, J. (eds) *Low Wage Work in the Wealthy World*. © 2010 Russell Sage Foundation, 112 East 64th Street, New York, NY 10065. Reprinted with permission (Table 4.1).

Mason, G. and Salverda, W. Figure 1, 'Trends in the incidence of low pay, % of employees below the low pay threshold, 1973–2005', in Gautié, J. and Schmitt, J. (eds), *Low Wage Work in the Wealthy World*. © 2010 Russell Sage Foundation, 112 East 64th Street, New York, NY 10065. Reprinted with permission (Figure 4.1).

Bosch, G., Mayhew, K. and Gautié, J. Table 2, 'Bargaining coverage 1980, 1990, 2000', in Gautié, J. and Schmitt, J. (eds), *Low Wage Work in the Wealthy World*. © 2010 Russell Sage Foundation, 112 East 64th Street, New York, NY 10065. Reprinted with permission (Table 4.2).

Bosch, G., Mayhew, K. and Gautié, J. Table 3, 'Union and employer density and extension of agreements', in Gautié, J. and Schmitt, J. (eds), *Low Wage Work in the Wealthy World*. © 2010 Russell Sage Foundation, 112 East 64th Street, New York, NY 10065. Reprinted with permission (Table 4.3).

Sage Publications

Schmid, G. 'Is full employment still possible? Transitional labour markets as a new strategy of labour market policy', *Economic and Industrial Democracy*, 16(3): 429–456, © 1995 by SAGE Publications. Reprinted with permission (Figure 3.1).

Vandenberg, R.J., Richardson, H.A. and Eastman, L.J. 'The impact of high involvement work processes on organizational effectiveness: A second-order latent variable approach', *Group & Organization Management*, 24(3): 300–339, © 1999 by SAGE Publications. Reprinted with permission (Figure 7.1).

Notes on Contributors

Leda Blackwood is a Post Doctoral Fellow in the School of Psychology at the University of St Andrews, Scotland. From 2005–2008 she was a senior research fellow on the 'Developing Human Capability: employment institutions, organisations and individuals' research programme at Victoria University of Wellington. Prior to this she held positions in the Australian public service. Her research interests focus on intergroup and intragroup processes involved in (a) collective action and the politicisation of identity; and (b) social movement building.

Peter Boxall is Professor of Human Resource Management and Associate Dean for Research in the Business School at the University of Auckland. His research is concerned with the links between HRM and strategic management and with the changing nature of work and employment systems. He is the co-author with John Purcell of *Strategy and Human Resource Management*, co-editor with John Purcell and Patrick Wright of the *Oxford Handbook of Human Resource Management*, and co-editor with Richard Freeman and Peter Haynes of *What Workers Say: Employee Voice in the Anglo-American Workplace*.

Jane Bryson is a Senior Lecturer in the Management School at Victoria University of Wellington, New Zealand. She was one of two objective leaders in a recently completed research project 'Developing human capability: employment institutions, organisations, and individuals' which explored the range of influences on the development of human capability in, and for, New Zealand workplaces. This research was funded by the Foundation for Research, Science & Technology (FRST). She is now involved in another FRST funded research team investigating firm level productivity – in particular the impact of HRM and OD on productivity. Jane is an organisational psychologist, and prior to joining the University staff she worked for 15 years as a consultant in organisation development and HRM. Her research interests focus on the investigation of HRM, organisational and individual capability; and on professionals, managers and occupational change.

John Buchanan is Director of the Workplace Research Centre at the University of Sydney. Prior to his appointment at the WRC (ACIRRT), John was employed for seven years in the Australian Public Service. During this period he worked on issues as diverse as public sector job creation and local employment initiatives, the employment impact of cuts in barrier protection and labour dimensions of microeconomic reform. Between 1988 and 1991 he was part of the team that undertook the first Australian Workplace Industrial Relations Survey (AWIRS). His last position in the APS was as Director, Policy Research, in the Commonwealth Department of Industrial Relations. John also worked briefly for the trade union movement as a researcher examining the issue of performance pay amongst white collar, public sector employees.

Since joining the WRC John has lead a large number of research teams that have examined a wide range of issues concerned with the changing nature of work. He was one of the authors of WRC publication, '*Australia at work: Just managing?*' (1999). This text consolidated all the key findings arising from the Centre's first decade of research. Currently his major research interests are the demise of the classical wage earner model of employment and the role of the state in nurturing new forms of multi-employer coordination to promote both efficiency and fairness in the labour market.

Paul Dalziel is Professor of Economics at Lincoln University, a position he has held since 2002. His research focuses on New Zealand economic and social policy, which has produced more than 160 academic publications since 1984, including five books (two of which have been translated and published in Japan). He has undertaken commissioned research for the OECD and for a range of government agencies in New Zealand. Professor Dalziel is the science leader for a large five-year programme supported by the Foundation for Research, Science and Technology that is researching the way schools and communities can better support young people making choices about their education and employment as they leave school. He is the President of the Australia New Zealand Regional Science Association International and has twice received awards from Lincoln University for excellence in research and a third award for excellence in teaching.

Michelle Jakubauskas is a Research Analyst in the Workplace Research Centre (WRC) at the University of Sydney. Michelle began her career at the Australian Bureau of Statistics, before joining the WRC in 2007. After working on waves 1 & 2 of the longitudinal Australia at Work study, Michelle began focusing her research on skills, training and workforce development. Her research so far has covered industries as diverse as public libraries, primary industries, and community services and health.

Ewart Keep is Professor in the School of Social Sciences at Cardiff University and Deputy Director of SKOPE, an ESRC designated research centre on Skills, Knowledge and Organisational Performance. In the UK, Ewart Keep has acted as an advisor to the National Audit Office, H M Treasury, the Department for Trade and Industry, the Department for Education and Skills, the Cabinet Office, the Welsh Assembly Government, the Scottish Government, the Scottish Parliament's Life-long Learning Committee, and the UK Parliament's Select Committee on Education and Skills, and the Select Committee on Innovation, Universities, Skills and Science. He is a member of the UK Commission on Employment and Skills' Expert Panel, and of the Skills Committee of the Scottish Funding Council. He has also chaired conference sessions for the OECD, and worked with the governments of Queensland and New South Wales on skills policy. He has published widely on issues related to skills policy, higher education, and vocational education and training, in journals such as: the *Journal of Education and Work*, the *Journal of Education Policy*, the *Oxford Review of Economic Policy*.

Keith Macky is currently Associate Professor of Human Resource Management in the Department of Management at the Auckland University of Technology (AUT). He has previously held positions at both the University of Auckland and Massey University, as well as in the private sector including KPMG and Ernst & Young. His recent research publications have been in the areas of employee responses to high-performance work systems, organisational downsizing, why people do or don't join unions, and employee retention and turn-over. He is co-author with Gene Johnson of *Managing Human Resources in New Zealand* and editor of *Managing Human Resources: Contemporary Perspectives in New Zealand*.

Ken Mayhew is Professor of Education and Economic Performance, Department of Education, Oxford University; Fellow and Tutor in

Economics at Pembroke College, Oxford. He is also Director of SKOPE, an ESRC designated research centre on Skills, Knowledge and Organisational Performance. Founded in 1998, it is a multi-disciplinary centre based in the Oxford Departments of Economics and Education and in Cardiff University's School of Social Sciences. Ken was educated at Oxford and LSE. After graduate school he joined Her Majesty's Treasury before moving back to Oxford. In 1989 and 1990 he was Economic Director at the UK National Economic Development Office, and has worked as a consultant for many private and public sector organisations at home and abroad. His main research interests are in labour economics, human resource management and the economics of education and training. He is an editor of *Oxford Economic Papers* and of the *Oxford Review of Economic Policy*.

Paul O'Neil is a research associate of the Industrial Relations Centre at Victoria University of Wellington, New Zealand. He has recently been engaged as a Research Fellow with the just completed Developing Human Capability Project funded by the Foundation for Research Science and Technology. He has a background in political economy and in agricultural economics. His research interest is the interaction between globalising production and political processes and local labour market structures and policies.

Professor **Paul Spoonley** is the Research Director for the College of Humanities and Social Sciences at Massey University, New Zealand. He has been involved in the Labour Market Dynamics Research Programme since the mid-1990s and has led the programme for the last 10 years. The research team have been funded to examine the changing labour market in New Zealand, including non-standard work, employability, youth and Maori work transitions, by the Foundation for Research, Science and Technology. More recent funding ($3.2 million in 2007) is to examine the labour market outcomes and integration of immigrants to New Zealand. Paul Spoonley has edited or written 24 books on ethnicity and identity, labour markets and politics with publishers such as Oxford University Press, Pearson and Penguin. He is currently the co-editor of *Kotuitui*, the Royal Society's online social science journal. He is writing a book on immigration for Auckland University Press and has completed a biography on one of New Zealand's most pre-eminent Maori academics, *Mata Toa: The Life and Times of Ranginui Walker.*

List of Figures and Tables

Figures

Tables

1
Beyond Skill – An Introduction

Jane Bryson

This book discusses things of importance to many of us: work, employment, pay, work environments, learning, participation and voice. It discusses the impact of government policy, other institutional arrangements, organisational practices, collective and individual behaviour, on all these things. The chapters in this book are based on a series of invited papers given at an International Symposium on 'Developing human capability, in and for, the workplace', in June 2008 at Victoria University of Wellington, New Zealand. This symposium marked the end of a five year research programme investigating the impact of institutions, organisations and individuals on the development of human capability. The core task of the book is to critically analyse recent policy and practice pertaining to work and skills. It does this from a variety of perspectives, and it introduces (in Chapters 2 and 10) the concept of human capability as a way to constructively reorient our considerations of work, skill, and productive societies.

Why move beyond skill?

Labour market, work and economic development policy visions in many developed countries have been dominated in recent years by a fixation on skills. However, skill and skill development alone is not enough to harmonise societies, transform economies, galvanise organisations, and fulfil individual aspirations.

The whole notion of skill has become fraught. In recent years discussions of skill have experienced both a broadening and a narrowing of focus. On the one hand new institutional meanings of skill have extended to, for example, aesthetic skills (e.g., the skill of looking good) particularly in the service sector, and a greater emphasis on soft skills (interpersonal) over technical skills (see Warhurst and Nickson, 2007). On the other hand there has been a narrowing of policy views on skill acquisition, for instance that it largely occurs through training episodes or formal qualifications. This view fails to acknowledge that skills, knowledge and other attributes are also developed by 'doing', that is through the performance of work and engagement with the work environment and the design of the work (see Eraut and Hirsh, 2007).

The skill narrative tends to reduce discussion to short-term actions (training, recognition of prior learning, employer determined competency frameworks) but does not clarify policy objectives. Skill, whilst important, distracts attention from a more complex bigger picture. That picture includes society as whole, the place and aspiration of the individual (and groups) within it, the role of work and employment, and the influence of capitalist and democratic institutions. Thus reality is far more complex than the somewhat linear vision of the high skill pathway.

Challenges of moving beyond current notions of skill

We live in societies, not just economies. We aspire to live lives we have reason to value, that is to be capable humans not just skill sets for the workplace. This bigger picture has been the traditional concern of academic debate. Philosophers, political economists, sociologists, and others (from Marx and Weber to Giddens and Sen) have reflected and theorised on the connections between humans, work, society and well-being. The academic and policy challenge in moving beyond current notions is, as it has always been, to generate better or different understanding of the settings in which we operate.

Our current settings also present challenges. Globalisation, mobility and migration, have made our communities and economies more complex. In many developed countries changes to collective bargaining (such as: lower coverage, decreased union density) and minimum employment standards, and changed modes of employment (such as: non-standard, low paid, precarious, contractors and non-employees) have undermined more traditional views of citizenship and industrial citizenship (Fudge, 2005). As a result some have observed tension in developed economies between 'the promise of citizenship equality and the harsh inequalities generated by capitalist markets' (Brodie, 2002, cited in Fudge, 2005, p.635). There are two recent examples of attempts to rethink the big picture in order to respond to growing tensions. One is work in the European Union (EU) which links human capabilities, economic policy and social policy (see Salais and Ville-neuve, 2004). The EU work drew on the human capability approach of Amartya Sen, and likewise in this volume Bryson and O'Neil and the research project they report (Chapters 2 and 10) employ capability to reconfigure understandings. The second example is the skills eco-systems approach. First explored by Finegold (1999) this approach acknowledges the broader institutional context and the inter-dependency of a network of factors that underpin business success. It's starting point and central focus is skill and workforce development across an industry or region. Buchanan et al (2001) recommended adopting a skills ecosystem approach in Australia, noting that 'policy on work and skills needs to repositioned. While skills are not "the answer", there can be "no answer" without skills…this requires opening up the policy system…and accommodating the "cross-cutting" character of policy initiatives on work and skill' (p.1). In Chapter 3 of this volume Buchanan and Jakubauskas revisit skill eco-systems in the light of the developing human capability research.

Beyond skill

The chapters in this book take the debate and critical analysis another significant step forward by: i) looking beyond current notions of skill, and ii) acknowledging the complex interaction of institutions, organ-isations and individual behaviour in shaping our societies, workplaces and ourselves. The chapters report new research from New Zealand, Australia, the United Kingdom, Europe and the United States of America. They provide a series of insights to the complexity of creating work institutions which allow people to be capable.

In particular several chapters introduce and explore the notion of developing human capability. Human capability, described by Sen (1999) as the ability to lead lives we value and have reason to value, provides a much needed counterpoint to the largely organisationally instrumental and human capital assumptions that have dominated debates on work and skills. Workplaces, employers and workers are complex and unique, but all exist within a larger social system. This collection of chapters reflects on the complex range of influences on experiences of employment impacting on human capability. Connections are drawn between government policy, institutions, organisational practices and individual experiences.

Whilst acknowledging the high skills visions of economic development favoured by many western economies, this book takes a critical stance reporting on practical issues encountered by employers and workers in pursuing this vision. It also takes a broader alternative view by connecting to notions of human capability and by exploring the range of influences on societal, organisational and individual outcomes.

The lot of today's worker is not just a function of acknowledged or accredited skill, but is a complex mix of institutional arrangements, organisational strategies and practices, and human responses. Hence the book is organised in three parts.

Part I comprises chapters which address a range of institutional influences and workplace effects. The first of these, Chapter 2 (Bryson and O'Neil), draws on the work of Sen to introduce the concept of human capability for use in reconfiguring prevailing views of skill and work. Sen's (1999) original formulation of the capability approach provided a different way to examine economic development in developing countries. This approach placed positive freedoms and the capabilities to function at the centre of analysis and policy consideration rather than economic outcomes. As Bryson and O'Neil point out, translating this approach to the world of work permits a systemic analysis of the impact of the social arrangements which facilitate or constrain human capability development. In addition, significantly, it reorients focus onto human capability – how people can achieve lives of value to them – (for instance, as citizens, community members, workers or family members).

Drawing on several recent large scale Australian studies John Buchanan and Michelle Jakubauskas in Chapter 3 reflect on changing conditions of labour supply and demand, and processes of matching them. They use the concepts of transitional labour markets and of skill eco-systems to aid this reflection. They combine their insights with those of the Developing Human Capability framework (Chapter 10), in particular the observation in the framework that 'good people are (often) custodians of bad policy/practice'. In conclusion they propose a reconceptualisation of occupation and vocational streams as public goods which may provide a better way to aid human flourishing.

In Chapter 4 Ken Mayhew reports on research examining low end work in five European countries – the UK, France, Germany, Denmark and the Netherlands. He discusses major differences between these countries and also America. He shows how the dismantling of various institutional protections in the 1980s stimulated the growth of low paid work in the United Kingdom. Comparison to changing practices in other countries provides convincing evidence that the differences in their low pay profiles are due to the nature of their pay setting institutions. Mayhew also explores the role of skill acquisition in ameliorating misfortune in the labour market.

In Chapter 5 Paul Spoonley explores the impact of the significant growth in various forms of non-standard work. Using the New Zealand context he examines the changing institutions that have underpinned and reflected this growth, for example, changes in: labour markets, labour market engagement, employment contracts, and the organisation of the labour process.

The chapters in Part II focus on organisational influences and individual effects. The first of these, Chapter 6 by Ewart Keep, reports on workplace learning research and its implications for national skills policies across the Organisation for Economic Cooperation and Development (OECD). Keep reflects on recent research acknowledging the embeddedness of learning in workplace practices, hence the complex connection between good jobs, good learning and positive economic performance, rather than an overly simplistic path between qualifications and economic growth. In the final analysis he concludes that recognising this complexity suggests the need for a more holistic approach which reconnects skills policy with employment relations policy.

Moving further into the 'black box' of the organisation Boxall and Macky in Chapter 7 investigate high performance work systems and employee well-being. They discuss the issues associated with assessing organisational performance and with quantifying the managerial practices of high performance work systems (HPWSs). They note that some of the HPWSs lauded in the US are basic institutional requirements in other countries (for example through labour laws or policies), and thus in those countries they are not recognised as sources of high performance. They argue for greater emphasis on high involvement work processes and report on research in New Zealand workplaces looking at worker responses to such processes. Central to worker experiences are good reported levels of empowerment but these are not matched by their experiences of information, rewards and training.

In Chapter 8 Paul Dalziel examines employer-led channels for helping young people make good education to employment linkages. The chapter reviews economics literature in the area, and in particular recent research which has adopted dynamic choice modelling techniques to understand youth transition. It also introduces research into education employment linkages that Dalziel and his team will be conducting over the next few years. Key to that research programme is the recognition that young people do not make a single, static career choice at one point in time. Rather, that decisions change, are sequential, and are influenced by information available and other factors. Young people are in the process of discovering capabilities, discovering the things they value, the lives they do and don't want to lead. Dalziel comments on potential weaknesses in the employer-led channels in New Zealand's system of helping young people make good education employment linkages.

Leda Blackwood in Chapter 9 provides a social psychological perspective on workers and their capability as expressed in collectives such as through trade union membership. The chapter highlights the individualised nature of discourse around workers, and the employment relationship. In particular she argues that the dynamic interactions between individuals, organisations, and the institutions that structure the employment relationship give rise to our aspirational goals and so to the requisite capabilities. She challenges the thinking about the role of unions in developing human capability, both at work and in society.

Part III presents the final chapter concluding discussions on developing human capability. Chapter 10 by Jane Bryson and Paul O'Neil reports on the findings of empirical research into the conditions for the optimal development of human capability in New Zealand workplaces. The analysis of these findings operationalises Sen's capability approach in a framework aimed to assist workplace practitioners in shaping social arrangements which develop human capability. It also serves to remind us that skill and work are just one, albeit important, part of the fabric of our lives as capable humans.

Individually these chapters each tell an interesting story. Collectively the themes they have in common are far more powerful. First, they demonstrate the importance of institutions – and not single institutions but the multiple overlapping regulations, policies, practices, customs and habits. How the labour market and work environments are regulated matters (refer Buchanan Chapter 3, Mayhew Chapter 4, Spoonley Chapter 5). Second, the specific strategies and practices of industries, organisations, and unions, also matter. And finally, the practices and behaviour of managers, supervisors, and workers matter – they impact work environments, aspirations and opportunities (refer Keep Chapter 6, Bryson and O'Neil Chapter 10).

Indeed, the time is ripe to move beyond skill to envision societies that enhance human capability.

References

Buchanan, J., Schofield, K., Briggs, C., Considine, G., Hager, P., Hawke, G., Kitay, J., Meagher, G., Macintyre, J., Mounier, A. and Ryan, S. (2001) *Beyond Flexibility: Skills and Work in the Future*, Report to NSW Board of Vocational Education and Training, Sydney, Australia.

Eraut, M. and Hirsh, W. (2007) 'The significance of workplace learning for individuals, groups and organisations', *SKOPE Monograph*, Cardiff, Cardiff University, SKOPE.

Finegold, D. (1999) 'Creating self-sustaining high skill ecosystems', *Oxford Review of Economic Policy*, 15(1): 60–81.

Fudge, J. (2005) 'After industrial citizenship: Market citizenship or citizenship at work?', *Relations industrielles/Industrial Relations*, 60(4): 631–656.

Salais, R. and Villeneuve, R. (eds) (2004) *Europe and the Politics of Capabilities*, Cambridge: Cambridge University Press.

Sen, A.K. (1999) *Development as Freedom*, Oxford: OUP.

Warhurst, C. and Nickson, D. (2007) 'Employee experience of aesthetic labour in retail and hospitality', *Work, Employment & Society*, 21(1): 103–120.

Part I

Institutional Influences and Workplace Effects

2
Exploring Social Arrangements for Developing Human Capability

Jane Bryson and Paul O'Neil

Over the past decade most governments have emphasised the importance of work related skills, and by proxy the increase of qualifications, as one of the keys to economic growth. In this chapter, and in Chapter 10, we argue the importance of broadening the debate from these narrow understandings of skill to the wider concept of human capability. We believe this widening of focus is important for a number of reasons, some of which are ably demonstrated in other chapters of this volume. For instance, it permits us to consider: learning rather than counting credentials (also refer Keep's Chapter 6); the utilisation (and not just development) of skills, knowledge, and other attributes; the purpose of work (both paid and unpaid) in society beyond narrow organisational and economic ends; and the impact of regulation and social arrangements on the capabilities of organisations, individuals and communities (also refer Buchanan's Chapter 3, Mayhew's Chapter 4 and Spoonley's Chapter 5).

As well as widening our focus, this chapter also introduces the search for clues to the optimal social arrangements for developing human capability at work. By this we mean institutional and organisational infrastructure, and the practices and processes through which individuals access and realise the opportunities to live lives of value (whatever that may be). We commence the chapter by briefly outlining the aims and objectives of the 'Developing Human Capability' research project. The background policy environment that gave rise to our interest in human capability at work is discussed. We then review a selection of literature addressing organisational practices which impact on workers and their capability. This reflects our search for a definition of human capability. It includes a summary of relevant themes from the vast literatures addressing learning organisations, human resource development, human resource management (HRM), workplace learning and adult education. Discussion of wider debate centred in the literature on high performance management in workplaces follows. The discussion draws attention to the inherently narrow instrumental assumptions of many management and HRM practices in the pursuit of organisational goals and competitive advantage. Ultimately we introduce Sen's capability approach, originally used for economic development, to explore social arrangements in the world of work and their impact on the development of human capability. We propose human capability as a concept that facilitates a more holistic view of organisations and workers, and enables organisations to fill a broader wealth creation role in society as capability enhancing institutions.

Researching human capability development

In 2003 the New Zealand Foundation for Research, Science and Technology funded a five year project investigating human capability development. The overall aims of the Developing Human Capability research project were 'to identify and foster conditions for the optimal development of human capability in New Zealand organisations'. To this end, the principal objectives were: 1) to analyse the structure and operation of existing labour market institutions in terms of their influence on the development of capability; 2) to examine associations between workplace practices, and a range of organisational outcomes related to capability; 3) to investigate how institutional structures and organisational practices shape the development of individual capability. There was also a Maori research strand running through these objectives looking at how Maori organisations approach developing human capability, and capability development issues for Maori workers.

It was intended that the research project would result in New Zealand specific information about the institutional, organisational and individual levels of human capability development and be used to inform both workplace practice and government policy. In particular the project was designed to result in frameworks and/or models of superior people management practice tailored to New Zealand institutional, organisational, social and cultural environments. It was conducted through case study analysis across four sectors in New Zealand, followed by a series of targeted discussion groups with managers and workers, and analysis of New Zealand policy documentation.

This chapter provides a selective overview of the international literature underpinning our field research and conclusions.

Human capability and the background policy environment

This research project is historically placed in New Zealand at the time of a change of policy direction for labour market initiatives following the election of a Labour-led government in 1999. Ryan (2007) provides a useful background to the shift by the Labour-led government from 2000, from market-led solutions to economic growth towards a more active state role in industry and regional development. These initiatives aimed to find new ways to reproduce the conditions for economic growth and the distribution of the benefits of this growth to all New Zealanders. It has been described as a 'third way' between the increasingly interventionist Keynesian-welfare state of the post-second world war period until 1984 and the neo-liberalised state which succeeded it in the period from 1984 to 1999 (Chatterjee, 1999). Such a view however presupposes an *a priori* coherent set of economic and social policies. This was not the case, however, and political pragmatism may be a better explanation for the adoption of a third-way mode of political governance (Chatterjee, 1999). At the time that the Government took office in 1999, the operation of neo-liberal approaches to economic and labour market policy had resulted in a massive restructuring of the economy. This had resulted in historically high levels of unemployment, and particularly of long-term unemployment. The Department of Labour, as the Government's advisor on labour market policy had viewed this with concern throughout the 1990s, both because of the concerns about the loss of productive potential within the economy, but also because of the linkages between unemployment and social exclusion.

In an attempt to analyse the root causes of the problem, and to identify how the process of labour market adjustment could be speeded up, the Department developed a Human Capability Framework. This attempted to provide an ' ...integrated view of key economic and social objectives, and understanding the role of the labour market in achieving them' (Department of Labour, 1999, p.4). It was based in an analysis that placed equal emphasis on the need to increase growth in the economy as a whole, and to ensure that significant groups in the community (and in the New Zealand context, particularly Maori) did not miss out on the economic and social benefits of labour market participation.

The original human capability framework is presented diagrammatically in Figure 2.1 below. In this framework, human capability is broadly defined as the ability of people to advance their well-being. It is conceptualised as comprising capacity ('what people are able to do'), opportunity ('the options available for people to get financial and personal reward from using their capacity'), and matching ('the process of matching capacity with opportunity'). Implicit in this framework is that well-being, although not well-defined, is achieved through labour market participation (or human capability development).

Figure 2.1 Elements of the New Zealand Department of Labour Human Capability Framework

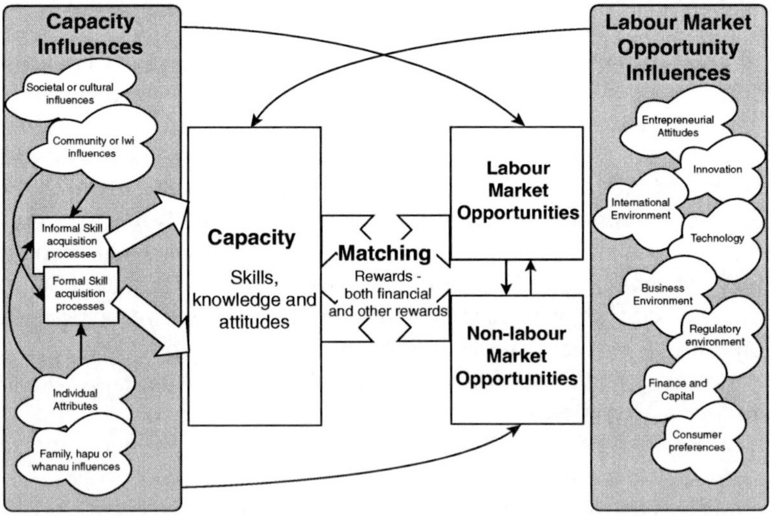

Source: Department of Labour (1999), p.19

When applied to the labour market, the human capability framework, pulls together standard analyses of labour market functioning drawn from mainstream economics. There is a demand-side (opportunities), a supply-side (capacity) and an equilibrating process (matching). The model does, however, acknowledge the reality of the complex social and economic processes (such as concentrations of disadvantage in some groups) behind these mainstream labour market concepts. Despite recognising imperfections in labour market operation, this human capability framework largely reduces back to the utilitarianism of mainstream economics. For example, while recognising that labour capacity is socially constructed, influences on capacity are reduced to processes such as education and training which give labour value to employers as a commodity – that is, to participate in the labour market. This ignores influences on capacity development which may result from other non-market activities – such as activities taking place in the home. On the demand-side, the complexity of the economic environment within which the demand for labour is derived is acknowledged. However, the key process determining labour demand, the process of production, is ignored. Lastly, labour market 'imperfections' that occur in the matching process (such as the imprecise nature of labour 'contracts', search costs and uncertainty) are acknowledged. Despite this, such imperfections are expressed as relative to the 'ideal' world of perfect competition.

Although largely drawing on mainstream economics concepts of labour market structures and functioning, the conceptualisation as human capability in this way represented the beginnings of new thinking about workforce development, particularly in its relationship with the direction of future economic growth. Learning from the experiences of European social democracies, a new approach to New Zealand's preferred future economic growth and development was through substantial economic transformation towards high-value end production. Further, it was recognised that this transformation could not be achieved through state fiat or through unfettered market regulation, but required social dialogue and the leadership and discipline that peak social organisations (notably the state and those agencies representing the interests of workers and of capital), respectively give and expect of their constituents. The concepts within the human capability framework closely corresponded with this new approach: on the supply-side with the skills capacity needed for high-value end production; on the demand-side with the production and delivery of high-value goods and services; and in the matching process with the right for unions to collectively bargain subject to the requirement of 'good faith' bargaining, and with an active labour market policy that favours labour market participation, as the means to enjoy the fruits of this economic development path.

The three objectives of our research project broadly correspond with the connections the Department of Labour human capability framework has with the economic transformation agenda. In the first objective is an examination of the process of 'matching' through the institutional framework surrounding and shaping bargaining, particularly collective bargaining. Some examination of 'matching' within the firm is also evident in the second objective, however, it is also concerned with the demand or labour market opportunities side of the human capability framework. The third objective is primarily concerned with the supply or capacity side of the framework.

Whilst our research objectives can be seen as broadly corresponding with this policy conception of human capability, there is some departure from it as well. Firstly, we question the assumption of 'free' exchange in the labour market as an equilibrating process. For instance, our research recognises that institutions matter because they provide a social context within which labour bargains are made and held. Secondly, the realm of production and workplace practices are considered, a realm which economics largely treats as a 'black box'. Implicit here it is recognised that labour market opportunities and the matching process result from complex social relations within the firm. Thirdly, the research recognises that individuals have differing opportunities and choices in response to institutions, workplace practices and social relations to which they are exposed.

From this starting point, we now turn to the literature. Here we recount a limited selection of themes which have informed our search for clarity around the concept of human capability.

Informing human capability

Notwithstanding the policy background, one of the central challenges for the research has been defining human capability. As Bryson et al (2006) note, the notion of capability is a contested one. Various literatures refer to diverse aspects such as organisational capability, economic capability and individual human capability. There are also varied meanings attached to capability, with the concept portrayed in diverse ways as an outcome (a capable nation, a capable worker, an informed citizen), an output (productivity, performance) and as an input (knowledge, competency, ability to perform). The particular focus of this chapter is on human capability at the level of the organisation and of the individual. We view the various meanings attached to capability at these levels reflecting on a wider debate centred within the literature on high performance management. This literature discusses the factors which lead to improved organisational performance in the uncertain external environments which organisations face.

We started our explorations of human capability from a broad base in the literatures on learning organisation, human resource development, human resource management, workplace learning, and adult education. We found burgeoning and overlapping interests in these literatures, largely underpinned by an implicitly instrumental view of human capability as a tool for the achievement of organisational goals. However, the small but growing critical strands of these literatures (particularly in workplace learning and adult education) show us that workplaces can be characterised as more or less supportive of learning. Various factors are influential in this including: job design, the context in which workplace learning takes place, access and opportunity, and particular organisational strategies and goals (Billett, 2002a, 2002b, 2004; Fuller and Unwin, 2004; Keep, 1997). A persistent gap between the haves and have-nots in access to development opportunities has also been noted (Rainbird, Munro and Holly, 2004), and our own cases (Bryson et al, 2006) confirm the suggestions in the literature that development opportunities may be differentially experienced according to level in the organisational hierarchy or type of job.

This critical perspective in the literature has seriously questioned the assumed mutuality of purpose and outcome of learning activity for the individual and the organisation (Fenwick, 1998; Thomson et al 2001). The amount of choice and self-direction individuals have in their own learning and career is arguable (Grimshaw et al, 2002) and the assumption that individual learning and knowledge are commodities, useable for organisational competitive advantage is still pervasive (Bryson, 2006, Casey, 2003; Gherardi, 2000). In a trenchant critique of learning organisation and the knowledge-based economy, Casey (2004) argues that 'economic discourses of work and organisations, and of adult education, have precluded significant attention to the cultural dimensions of work – the non-material, personal and relational aspects of productive activity – which defy economic and productivity measures' (p.620). She appeals for education and skill acquisition to be directed towards goals of self and community development needed for living and working in participatory democracy. In turn we argue in this chapter that a rebalancing in favour of a more holistic view of developing human capability is a much needed antidote to the economic rationalist assumptions dominating current debate.

The literature pertaining to high performance workplaces and their management is also highly influential. This literature debates the emergence and shape of new forms of work organisation which have appeal to various social actors as the high-wage, high-skill productive base upon which contemporary social and economic development aspirations can be met. We contend that in this literature, capability is largely focused on the organisation and its ends, with little regard for individuals other than as instrumental to achieving the organisation's goals. Ramsay, Scholarios and Harley (2000) note the unchallenged assumption in this literature that the 'causal link which flows from practices through people to performance' (p.503) has positive outcomes for workers. They go on to suggest that high performance management systems may enhance workplace performance through some increase of employee discretion but that the trade-off may be increased work intensification, job insecurity and stress for workers.

As Butler et al (2004) note, commentators on new forms of work organisation fail to present a coherent holistic view into how factors and practices combine to produce outcomes within organisations. In order to provide greater conceptual clarity they develop a taxonomy of the rather diverse high performance literature. The categories for this classification of the literature are drawn from the work of Bélanger, Giles and Murray (2002). This identifies three interrelated spheres of changing workplace practice: production management, work organisation and employment relations. Production management concerns the logic of the overall organisation of the systems and processes through which goods and services are produced (for example, batch or unit production), the ways in which the production process is laid out (for example, assembly lines or modular groups) and which parts of the process are internal to or external to the production process (such as the degree of outsourcing). Work organisation relates to the ways in which jobs are defined and configured within the overall organisation of the production of goods and services. For example, the degree of discretion in the way workers do their jobs, whether work is organised individually or in teams, and the degree or form of supervision. Lastly, employment relations are the policies and practices which govern the employment relationships of individuals and groups involved in production. These include the broad range of HRM practices such as recruitment, remuneration, training and promotion that are designed to direct workers skills and motivations towards the achievement of employers' goals, and the negotiation and application of rules such as collective agreements.

Butler et al (2004), and more recently Hughes (2008), use these three categories to review existing research on high performance and identify their dominant focus. For example, a production management focus is typified in 'high performance work systems' studies of Appelbaum et al (2000); a work organisation focus in 'high involvement work systems' studies such as Edwards and Wright (2001); the employment relations focus of 'high commitment management' studies like those of Whitfield and Poole (1997). Butler et al argue that none of these formulations are necessarily wrong but need to be recognised as reflecting both the particular interest and emphasis of the researcher(s) concerned and of the varying degrees and forms of actual practice. Bélanger et al (2002) argue that it is crucial to consider all three spheres of the workplace in order to make sense of the diverse array of workplace practices. The work of Tamkin (2005) integrates examination of all three spheres by utilising the construct of capability. This is illustrated by the '4A' model of workforce capability (Tamkin et al, 2004) which is reproduced in Figure 2.2.

As with Bélanger et al's (2002) conceptualisation, Tamkin's (2005) model draws upon the diverse literature on workplace change and considers the elements which constitute the effective deployment of the workforce within an organisation. She identifies two dimensions of workforce capability: the development and deployment of the workforce on the one hand, and the interplay between the individual and organisational capability on the other. Putting these dimensions

Figure 2.2   A Model of Capability

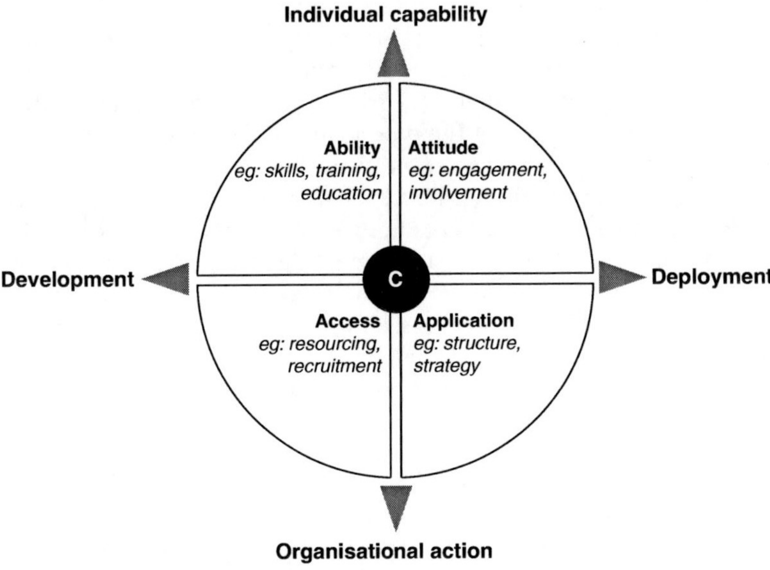

Source: Tamkin et al, 2004, Figure 9, p.44

together she arrives at four quadrants: access; ability; attitude; and application. Access refers to those policies and practices to do with the entry of workers into the organisation or into new roles within the organisation. Such policies and practices include recruitment policies and practices, and the existence or otherwise of an internal labour market. Ability encompasses the existence and development of workplace skills and competencies and includes both the existing skill and competency of the workforce, and the way in which skill is developed through training and other formal and informal means of development. Attitude refers to the motivational and psychological side of capability, including processes for employee engagement and the way people are kept informed as to what is expected of them. Lastly, application is the way in which skills and engaged workers are utilised by the organisation through the jobs they do, the resources they have available to them and the strategy that the organisation pursues. Together, these quadrants constitute workforce capability. In the left side quadrants of the model are factors which primarily contribute to the development of capability: worker capacity in terms of worker experience and education; the investment organisations put into training and development and the decisions organisations make about recruitment and job placement. In the right side quadrants are the deployments of capability, the efforts the workforce is willing to put in, the resources such as physical capital the organisation makes available, the organisation of work and the overall business strategy.

Capability as used in this sense by Tamkin (2005) recognises the various elements which constitute the ability of the workforce to perform. It is a useful device to capture diversity and complexity in the organisation of production; and opens the space to accommodate developments and debates within these elements, such as the relative importance of workplace learning to formal learning. It must also be recognised that it is a construct that is instrumental and management-driven and concerns how management can make use of human capability to control and direct worker effort. Human capability in this instrumental sense is in part about the use of workplace practices to manage the hearts and minds, as well as the labour power, of an organisation's workforce towards organisational goals. There is little in this model of capability that explicitly recognises agency other than that of management and it places emphasis on the employment relations/HRM sphere in work organisation.

Thus this model (Tamkin et al, 2004, 2005) helps to reinforce that the high performance work system literature is underpinned by assumptions of capability as the ability of a workforce to perform activities which contribute towards organisational outcomes. Additionally, that there is a tendency in these constructs to exaggerate the rationality and effectiveness of HRM practices to 'create a social system in support of the technical system' (Butler et al, 2004) and to underplay the management and worker agency in resolving the social tensions and technical constraints that occur in production. Hughes (2008) notes that how issues are discussed in the literature 'encourages theorists, practitioners, indeed, policymakers, to think of high performance work practices as in themselves ready-made solutions that might be injected into a range of different contexts' (p.46). This rather linear or 'billiard-ball model of causality' (p.46) underplays and does a disservice to the complex nexus of relationships which impact performance in workplaces.

Defining 'human' capability

Although the Developing Human Capability research began with a working definition of capability as 'the sustained ability of workers to perform', this review of the literature and our field interviews (reported in Chapter 10) highlighted the inadequacies of such a definition. It was on the one hand too broad, and on the other hand implied a too narrowly instrumental view of human capability serving only organisational or work ends. In interviews of workers in a range of different industries and workplaces (see Bryson et al 2006; Bryson, 2007; Bryson and Merritt, 2007; O'Neil and Bryson, 2007) we observed a serious contradiction with respect to the purpose for which capability was being developed. Does human capability refer to the capability of people within organisations to meet or serve the goals of the organisation? Alternatively does human capability go beyond the organisation and refer to workers themselves and how they live or would like to live their lives? The relevance of the two questions is important in respect of the scope of the research questions around 'developing' human capability. If capability is defined largely around work processes, then development is largely concerned with questions related to training and skill formation. If, alternatively, the concept of capability is wider than work, then the focus of analysis becomes workers themselves, and their individual and collective aspirations, where work is but part of a broader capability to live and enhance personal well-being.

Human capability in the sense of competence to meet organisational ends was important in the interviews we conducted but such capability was part of a wider endpoint which related to the ability to lead a good life of one's own choosing. Capability to 'do the job' was merely part of how people defined themselves and what they could do with their lives. For example, through the skills and training 'to do the job' of assisting patients recover from their illnesses, mental health workers were also purposefully developing their personal interest towards self-knowledge and self-awareness. For Maori mental health workers, capability 'to do the job' also encompassed the capability to have a valid and legitimate life and existence as Maori (O'Neil, Bryson and Lomax, 2008). There was also diversity in the reasons why people entered a job or profession, diversity in what people brought into a job, and diversity in what people took out of a job. This led us to think of human capability as the freedom to achieve things. This sense of capability as a positive freedom is one which resonates with the 'capability approach' of Amartya Sen, and helped inform an emergent meaning to attribute to developing human capability which the interviews exposed.

Sen's use of the concept of capability originates in debates within welfare economics and is principally applied in the context of economic development. Sen's thought has been widely summarised and presented in the literature (for example: Gasper, 2002; Osmani, 1995; Pressman and Summerfield, 2000). Sen himself has provided many summary accounts of his thoughts (see: Sen, 1984, 1985, 1987, 1992, 1995, 1999). Whilst Sen's capability approach raises complex philosophical issues and is developed out of a detailed critique of mainstream economic approaches to welfare, the essential point of departure of Sen's work is his focus upon human well-being and within that his arguments that the purpose of development is the expansion of people's well-being and freedoms so that people have the opportunity to expand their achievements.

As Sen himself (1993) and other commentators (Robeyns, 2000; Sehnbruch, 2004) emphasise, the capability approach operates at three levels. First it is primarily a framework of thought or a mode of thinking. Second, Sen stresses 'the plurality of purposes for which the capability approach can have relevance' (Sen, 1993, p.49), below which is a critique of other welfarist approaches in welfare economics. On a third level is the capability approach as a formula for interpersonal comparisons of welfare.

The capability approach involves 'concentration on freedoms in general and the capabilities to function in particular' (Sen, 1995, p.266). The major constituents of the capability approach are the concepts of functionings and capabilities. In *Development as Freedom*, Sen offers a set of definitions of functionings and capability:

> the concept of 'functionings'... reflects the various things a person may value being or doing. The valued functionings may vary from elementary ones, such as being adequately nourished and being free of avoidable disease, to very complex activities or personal states, such as being able to take part in the life of a community and having self-respect... A capability [is] a kind of

> freedom: the substantive freedom to achieve alternative function-
> ing combinations (Sen, 1999, p.75).

Functionings are thus the 'beings and doings' of a person, whereas a person's capability is the various combinations of functionings that a person can achieve. The two concepts are related but distinct in that:

> a functioning is an achievement, whereas a capability is the ability to achieve. Functionings are, in a sense, more directly related to living conditions, since they are different aspects of living conditions. Capabilities, in contrast, are notions of free-dom, in the positive sense: what real opportunities you have regarding the life you may lead (Sen, 1987, p.36).

A key point that Sen is making out of his critique is that the avail-ability of a commodity (such as a money wage or a job) does not necessarily or automatically imply that people can achieve an intended act or state of being. With the concept of 'functionings', Sen is trying to capture the notion that what 'doings and beings' a person achieves depends upon command over a particular set of commodities, individual circumstances, the physical and social environment one lives in, and all other factors that may impact on the conversion of commodities into achievements.

Following Robeyns (2000), a schematic representation of the capa-bility approach is presented in Figure 2.3. By introducing the con-cept of functionings Sen is concentrating on what an individual can achieve with a particular set of commodities given that person's circumstances. In this process, they have to make choices and take decisions. Capabilities capture this notion of choice by considering what people *could* achieve given a certain set of commodities. Capa-bilities thus refer to the ability of a person to do or be something, whereas functionings refer to the actions or states of people. The capability of a person thus corresponds to the freedom that a person has to lead one kind of life or another, chosen from a range of options.

In recognising agency, crucial to the capability approach of Sen, is what Browne, Deakin and Wilkinson (2004) refer to as the con-version factors which facilitate freedom or capability. These conver-

Figure 2.3 A Schematic Representation of the Capability Approach

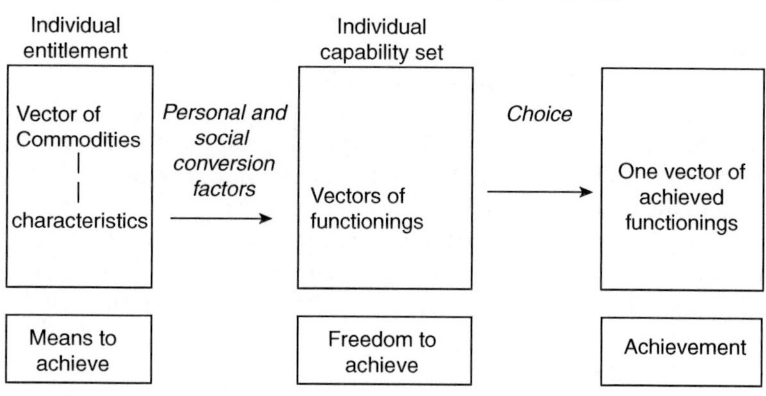

Source: Robeyns, 2000, p.5

sion factors are the characteristics of people, the society and the environment they live in, which together determine a person's capability to achieve a given range of functionings. Personal characteristics in this sense include such things as a person's metabolism, age and gender. Societal characteristics would include such things as societal norms, legal rules and public policies. Environmental characteristics would include such things as climate, physical surroundings, infrastructures and legal-political institutions.

The capability approach of Sen thus provides an alternative framework of thought or lens through which to identify the factors that lead to the optimal development of human capability in organisations. It asks, what are the social arrangements or conversion factors that lead to the ability of people to do or be something? Viewed through this lens, our research becomes an end-based approach: in organisations focusing on workers as ends-in-themselves, their ultimate well-being, rather than merely as a means-based approach focusing on the income workers earn, the skills they have or the type of job they hold.

Whilst there are few studies which apply Sen's capability approach to work and employment in developed nations such applications, where they exist, focus upon inequality in employment and employment outcomes. A notable example is the work of Sehnbruch in her study of the Chilean labour market (Sehnbruch, 2004). Sehnbruch's starting point is that in the Chilean case, economic liberalisation in the 1980s may well have led to a reduction in unemployment, the creation of more jobs and rising income levels per capita compared to state responses to earlier crises, but ignores the fact that the benefits of such economic development have been very uneven and have not spread to the lower income groups. Mirroring Sen and his capability approach, Sehnbruch argues that economic growth should 'focus upon how and whether the benefits of growth are passed onto the individual through employment' (Sehnbruch, 2004, p.6). In other words, it is the quality of employment that matters as much as the quantity of employment when considering the benefits of economic development.

In New Zealand, whilst employment has grown and unemployment has fallen since market de-regulation began in the 1980s, such de-regulation has caused increased income inequality (Weeks, 2005). One response to such inequality, based in assumptions about the question of perfectly competitive markets, is that such inequality, if it persists, occurs as a result of 'external influences' such as trade unions preventing market adjustment. In a similar vein, inequality is argued to reflect the human capital endowments of the labour supply.

It is however difficult to reconcile this response with the persistent and chronic inequalities characterising the distribution of work. The burden of labour market risks continues to be borne by ethnic minorities, women, the disabled, the old and the young. The mainstream response is that such discrimination occurs before such groups enter the labour market (that is, in the education and training system) and the labour market subsequently reflects those inequalities in an even-handed way. The evidence however suggests that patterns of inequality are not simply inherited but are in fact magnified by the labour market. Firstly, individuals of equal human capital endowments continue to experience different levels of exposure to labour market risks, and secondly, the magnitude of income inequalities in the labour market continue to exceed those associated with virtually all measures of human capacity (Thurow, 1975).

Sociologically-based and historically grounded accounts of labour market dynamics point to social regulation of labour markets, the forms of which vary enormously, ranging from formal labour law to socially embedded work norms (O'Neil, 2005; Peck, 1996). These institutions and social forms are conceived as endogenous to labour markets and are deeply implicated in their structures and dynamics and which segment labour – that is, 'separate the labour market into different segments within which workers are treated differently' (Villa, 1986, p.257). Contemporary labour market segmentation theory thus argues that labour market structures and dynamics do not derive from a fully coherent inner logic. Rather, the labour market is a complex, composite structure bearing the imprints of a diverse range of influences. Some of these influences are grouped together in the spheres of labour demand, labour supply and the state. Labour demand often takes primacy as an explanation of segmentation. Here a diversity of demand-side causes: factionalised industry structures, imperatives for labour control, workplace struggles, variable product market conditions, technological development, which can take institutionally and socially variable forms, are recognised. On the supply-side, it is recognised that the structure and dynamics of the sphere of social reproduction exert relatively autonomous influences on forms of segmentation. Social restructuring is not reducible to demand-side factors, but are related to a range of relatively autonomous factors, in particular, the role of the household division of labour in shaping labour market participation, the stigmatisation of certain social groups as secondary workers, processes of occupational socialisation, and the influence of unions in restricting labour supply to certain occupations. Also state actions and institutional forces are afforded a central causal role, where sources of segmentation are traced to the structure of education and training systems, industrial relations regimes, and welfare systems (Mayhew, Chapter 4 of this volume; Peck, 1996; Rubery, 1992).

Each causal sphere has its own characteristic structure and dynamic and each brings with it different tendencies towards segmentation. Segmentation thus arises as 'the outcome of the contingent and dialectical interaction of several causal tendencies: the state, the sphere of social reproduction and demand-side factors' (Peck, 1996, p.75), the precise form of which cannot be determined purely by a priori reasoning (Wilkinson, 1983).

The central point of this discussion on segmentation theory is that there are arguments which point to causes *within* labour markets that cause persistent inequalities in labour market outcomes. From the perspective of the capability approach of Sen, for those for whom such structures lead to poor quality employment relative to those who obtain good quality employment, their capability to lead lives they value has been compromised by factors which have disadvantaged them relative to others. There is thus an ethical argument that such inequalities are unfair, and in a 'fair society', for the existence of social arrangements which address differences in equalities in employment. Sen's broader notion of human capability not only allows one to focus on the worker as an end rather than solely instrumental to organisational goals, but also, importantly, it enables consideration of the influence of institutions as well as that of organisations and individuals themselves.

This chapter has documented the range of thinking in the Developing Human Capability research project as it grappled with how to arrive at a more expansive view of human capability. This was necessary in order to ultimately explore the influence of institutions, organisations and individuals on human capability, that is, the range of factors which enable and constrain people from living lives they value. From the literature we know that institutions matter, production and workplace practices matter, and people matter, that they are all influential on human capability in positive and negative ways. We also know that social arrangements created in and by organisations (such as, hierarchies; teams; role delineations; communication or voice mechanisms, etc.), and by government policy (such as, labour market institutions, education infrastructures, etc) are highly influential on the freedoms and opportunities individuals have to develop their capability.

In Chapter 10 we present a framework which summarises the conditions we identified as driving and undermining the development of human capability in New Zealand workplaces.

References

Appelbaum, E., Bailey, T., Berg, P. and Kellberg, A. (2000) *Manufacturing Advantage*, Ithaca: Cornell University Press.

Bélanger, P., Giles, A. and Murray, G. (2002) 'Towards a new production model: Potentialities, tensions and contradictions', in Murray, G., Bélanger, J., Giles, A. and Lapointe, P. (eds), *Work and Employment Relations in the High-Performance Workplace*, London: Continuum.

Billett, S. (2002a) 'Workplace pedagogic practices: Co-participation and learning', *British Journal of Educational Studies*, 50(4): 457–481.

Billett, S. (2002b) 'Toward a workplace pedagogy: Guidance, participation, and engagement', *Adult Education Quarterly*, 53(1): 27–43.

Billett, S. (2004) 'Learning through work: Workplace participatory practices', in Rainbird, H., Fuller, A. and Munro, A. (eds), *Workplace Learning in Context*, London: Routledge, pp.109–125.

Browne, J., Deakin, S. and Wilkinson, F. (2004) 'Capabilities, social rights and European market integration', in Salais, R. and Villeneuve, R. (eds), *Europe and the Politics of Capabilities*, New York: Cambridge University Press.

Bryson, J. (2007) 'Human resource development or developing human capability?', chapter 10 in Bolton, S. and Houlihan, M. (eds) *Contemporary Human Relations in the Workplace: Searching for the Human in Human Resource Management*, Basingstoke: Palgrave Macmillan.

Bryson, J. (2006) *Human Capability at Work: Property Right or Human Right?*, Proceedings of the 6th International Conference of the Human Development and Capability Association, Groningen, Netherlands.

Bryson, J. and Merritt, K. (2007) 'Work and the development of human capability', *Formation Emploi: Revue Française de Sciences Socials*, Numero Special: Pour une approche par les capacites avec Amartya Sen, 98, 41–53.

Bryson, J., Pajo, K., Ward, R. and Mallon, M. (2006) 'Learning at work: Organisational affordances and individual engagement', *Journal of Workplace Learning*, 18(5): 279–297.

Butler, P., Felstead, A., Ashton, D., Fuller, A., Lee, T., Unwin, L. and Walters, S. (2004) 'High performance management: A literature review', *Learning as Work Research Paper No. 1*. Leicester, Centre for Labour Market Studies, University of Leicester.

Casey, C. (2003) 'The learning worker, organisations and democracy', *International Journal of Lifelong Education*, 22(6): 620–634.

Casey, C. (2004) 'Knowledge-based economies, organisations and the socio-cultural regulation of work', *Economic and Industrial Democracy*, 25, 607–627.

Chatterjee, S. (ed.) (1999) *The New Politics: A Third Way for New Zealand*, Palmerston North, N.Z.: Dunmore Press.

Department of Labour (1999) *Human Capability: A Framework for Analysis*, Report by Department of Labour, Wellington, NZ Government.

Edwards, P. and Wright, M. (2001) 'High involvement work systems and performance outcomes', *International Journal of Human Resource Management*, 12(4): 568–585.

Fenwick, T. (1998) 'Questioning the concept of the learning organisation', in Scott, S., Spencer, B. and Thomas, A. (eds), *Learning for Life*, Toronto: Thompson Educational Publishing, pp.140–152.

Fuller, A. and Unwin, L. (2004) 'Expansive learning environments: Integrating organizational and personal development', in Rainbird, H., Fuller, A. and Munro, A. (eds), *Workplace Learning in Context*, London: Routledge, pp.126–144.

Gasper, D. (2002) 'Is Sen's capability approach an adequate basis for considering human development?', *Review of Political Economy*, 14(4): 435–461.

Gherardi, S. (2000) 'Practice-based theorizing on learning and knowing in organizations', *Organization*, 7(2): 211–223.

Grimshaw, D., Beynon, H., Rubery, J. and Ward, K. (2002) 'The restructuring of career paths in large service organizations: "Delayering", upskilling and polarization', *Sociological Review*, 50(1): 89–116.

Hughes, J. (2008) 'The high-performance paradigm: A review and evaluation', *Learning as Work Research Paper No. 16*, Leicester, Centre for Labour Market Studies, University of Leicester.

Keep, E. (1997) '"There's no such thing as society...": Some problems with an individual approach to creating a Learning Society', *Journal of Education Policy*, 12(6): 457–471.

O'Neil, P. (2005) *Contemporary Form and Dynamic of the International Division of Labour*, unpublished Ph.D. thesis, Centre for Labour Studies, Department of Societies and Cultures, Hamilton, University of Waikato.

O'Neil, P. and Bryson, J. (2007) 'Developing human capability', *Employment Agreements: Bargaining Trends & Employment Law Update 2007*, Wellington, Industrial Relations Centre, Victoria University of Wellington.

O'Neil, P., Bryson, J. and Lomax, H. (2008) *Maori Organisations*, Discussion Paper, Developing Human Capability Research Project, Industrial Relations Centre, Wellington, Victoria University of Wellington.

Osmani, S. (1995) 'The entitlement approach to famine: An assessment', in Basu, K., Pattanaik, P. and Suzumura, K. (eds) *Choice, Welfare and Development: A Festschrift in Honour of Amartya Sen*, Oxford: Clarendon Press, pp.253–294.

Peck, J. (1996) *Work-place: The Social Regulation of Labour Markets*, New York: Guilford Press.

Pressman, S. and Summerfield, G. (2000) 'The economic contributions of Amartya Sen', *Review of Political Economy*, 12(1): 89–113.

Rainbird, H., Munro, A. and Holly, L. (2004) 'The employment relationship and workplace learning', in Rainbird, H., Fuller, A. and Munro, A. (eds), *Workplace Learning in Context*, London: Routledge, pp.38–53.

Ramsay, H., Scholarios, D. and Harley, B. (2000) 'Employees and high-performance work systems: Testing inside the black box', *British Journal of Industrial Relations*, 38(4): 501–531.

Robeyns, I. (2000) *An Unworkable Idea or a Promising Alternative? Sen's Capability Approach Re-examined*, Discussion Paper Series 00.30, Centre for Economic Studies, University of Leuven.

Rubery, J. (1992) 'Productive systems, international integration and the single European market', in Castro, A., Méhaut, P. and Rubery, J. (eds), *International Integration and Labour Market Organisation*, London: Academic Press, pp.244–261.

Ryan, R. (2007) *Why Workplaces Matter; the Role of Workplace Practices in Economic Transformation*, Report for Department of Labour, Wellington, Athena Research Ltd.

Sehnbruch, K. (2004) 'From the quantity to the quality of employment: An application of the capability approach to the Chilean labour market', *Centre for Latin American Studies*, Berkeley, CLAS Working Paper No. 9.

Sen, A.K. (1984) 'Rights and capabilities', in Sen, A.K., *Resources, Values and Development*, Oxford: Blackwell.

Sen, A.K. (1985) 'Well-being, agency and freedom: The Dewey lectures 1984', *The Journal of Philosophy*, 82(4): 169–221.
Sen, A.K. (1987) 'The standard of living', in Hawthorn, G. (ed.) *The Standard of Living*, Cambridge: Cambridge University Press.
Sen, A.K. (1992) *Inequality Re-examined*, Oxford: Clarendon Press.
Sen, A.K. (1993) 'Capability and well-being', in Nussbaum, M. and Sen, A.K. (eds), *The Quality of Life*, Oxford: OUP.
Sen, A.K. (1995) 'Gender inequality and theories of justice', in Nussbaum, M. and Glover, J. (eds), *Women Culture and Development: A Study of Human Capabilities*, Oxford: Clarendon Press, pp.259–273.
Sen, A.K. (1999) *Development as Freedom.* Oxford: OUP.
Tamkin, P. (2005) *The Contribution of Skills to Business Performance*, Brighton, U.K.: Institute for Employment Studies.
Tamkin, P., Giles, L., Campbell, M. and Hillage, J. (2004) *Skills Pay: The Contribution of Skills to Business Success*, SSDA, Research Report 5.
Thomson, A., Mabey, C., Storey, J., Gray, C. and Iles, P. (2001) *Changing Patterns of Management Development*, Oxford: Blackwell.
Thurow, L. (1975) *Generating Inequality*, New York: Basic Books.
Villa, P. (1986) *The Structuring of Labour Markets: A Comparative Analysis of the Steel and Construction Industries in Italy*, Oxford: Clarendon Press.
Weeks, J. (2005) 'Inequality trends in some developed OECD countries', *DESA Working Paper No. 6*, SOAS, University of London.
Whitfield, K. and Poole, M. (1997) 'Organizing employment for high performance: Theories, evidence and policy', *Organization Studies*, 18(5): 745–764.
Wilkinson, F. (1983) 'Productive systems', *Cambridge Journal of Economics*, 7, 413–429.

3

The Political Economy of Work and Skill in Australia: Insights From Recent Applied Research

John Buchanan and Michelle Jakubauskas

One of the major legacies of the 'new right' ascendancy was the denial of choices about the future. As Margaret Thatcher asserted frequently in the early 1980s: 'there is no alternative' (TINA) to increased reliance on market mechanisms. What once had to be asserted subsequently became conventional policy wisdom. We call this the TINA syndrome (see Watson et al, 2003). Authors such as Thomas Frank (2000) have shown this is now part of wider 'market populism' with deep roots in civil society.

The Global Financial Crisis (GFC) has revealed the limitations of this legacy. While comprehensive analyses of the crisis are yet to be completed, the essential facts are agreed. Global financial flows froze following the collapse of the large US investment bank, Lehmann Brothers, in September 2008. This event was widely accepted as being symptomatic of major vulnerabilities in financial institutions, primarily as a result of their exposure to bad debts. The closely integrated nature of world capital markets meant crisis in the US quickly became global. Fearing that the closure of further leading financial institutions would trigger a collapse of the world financial system, governments around the world took unprecedented action. These measures were aimed at stabilising or restoring liquidity levels, boosting industrial production and international trade and helping to mitigate rising unemployment. The timing and degree of intervention varied from country to country. Generally, however, it involved government guarantees for banks (sometimes involving nationalisation or partial nationalisation, as was the case in the US and the UK) and direct stimulatory measures by governments. These initially provided direct payments to consumers and, in the longer term, allocations for large scale government expenditure, primarily for public works. It is estimated that these interventions will amount to the equivalent to 18% of global GDP in 2010 and 2011 (Rudd, 2009).

These facts have had two profound implications. The first concerns the allegedly immovable nature of 'economic reality'. Reality in 2008, and especially in the weeks surrounding the collapse of Lehmann Brothers, appeared very hostile. But as the crisis deepened the clearer the need for action became. During this period 'economic reality' shifted from being a 'constraint' that had to be accepted to a 'problem' that had to be solved. Second, the response by Government's around the world broke totally with the TINA syndrome. Throughout the crisis few players argued 'there was no alternative' to market solutions. On the contrary, there was widespread agreement that letting 'the market' take its course would turn a crisis into a catastrophe.

Arguably the greatest strength of the Developing Human Capability (DHC) project (see Bryson and O'Neil, Chapters 2 and 10 of this volume) is its consideration of policy objectives. In a post-GFC world this is very important. Clarifying objectives is no easy matter. If we are to overcome the legacies of the recent past, however, we need more than this. How are clarified objectives to be achieved? In particular, how can the insights of this project avoid the usual fate of good quality, critical policy research: being either ignored altogether or 'absorbed' into the policy regime generating current problems? The project provides some pointers on this matter. For example, it identifies the 'conditions which promote and undermine human capability development' (see Chapter 10 of this volume). These are presented primarily as a series of observations arising from the case study research and focus groups undertaken for the project. In this paper we contribute to this dimension of the project's analysis. In particular, we build on a very simple, but powerful, observation provided by a manager during the project field work. This person observed that one of the key barriers to developing human capability is that:

> Good people are [often] custodians of bad policy/practice. (Bryson and O'Neil, 2008, p.40)[1]

We now live at a time where there is no excuse for 'good people to be custodians of bad policy and practice'. The recent crisis has highlighted this fact. A significant problem in moving forward, however, is addressing what Robert Kuttner (2008) has called the problem of policy 'undertow'. While the orthodoxies of recent decades have been exposed as flawed their grip in the minds of many people, especially business and public officials, has loosened little. The GFC is commonly defined as merely necessitating a 'rebooting' of the system. As such the challenge, according to this narrative, is to get back to where we were before the crisis – not how to prevent the re-emergence of another. This context underlines the importance of ensuring the findings of the DHC project are neither marginalised nor absorbed in the political 'rip tide' of recent orthodoxy morphing into something acceptable in a post-Lehmann Brothers world.

The fact 'good people are [often] custodians of bad policy and practice' occurs for two reasons. The DHC project helps overcome the 'TINA' notion that the only way to organise human affairs is on the basis of markets. In this sense it helps overcome the 'subjective' barrier to moving forward. What we also need is a rigorous understanding of objective conditions – the constraints – that define the limits of what is possible. Unless these are properly understood 'good people' are likely to either seek to achieve too little or too much change – whether they are custodian of 'good' policy or 'bad'.

This chapter contributes to this endeavour by summarising the insights from recent applied research undertaken by ourselves and colleagues at the Workplace Research Centre at the University of Sydney on the changing nature of work and skill in contemporary Australia. We define the issue of interest as the political-economy of work and skill because it is politics and economics that profoundly determines what is possible. In the realm of work and skill the predominant way of defining the issues is in terms of the dynamics of labour supply and labour demand. Critiques of orthodoxy at the level of concepts are well developed (e.g., Botwinick, 1993; Fine, 1998; Kaufman, 1988). In this chapter, we highlight what our recent empirical work reveals are the key challenges in labour supply, labour demand and the mechanisms linking them of relevance for taking the findings of the DHC project forward. Armed with better empirical information 'good people' can become custodians of good policy informed by the DHC project. It gives them a robust understanding of the settings in which they operate. For it is only by engaging with reality as it is that policy, no matter how well intentioned, can succeed.

Our chapter is comprised of four sections. The first summarises the key issues concerning labour supply. In this we build on the idea of transitional labour markets as a framework that gets beyond the traditional breadwinning and individualist frames of reference associated with much policy orthodoxy. The second deals with labour demand. This draws on our work concerned with skill eco-systems. This concept allows us to move beyond traditional notions of labour demand as something 'derived' from output demand – a core assumption of orthodox economic policy at both the micro and macro levels. The third section summarises our work on how labour supply and demand are linked. In orthodox theory this is a function of 'price'. Our work on employment agreements shows the limitations of this and highlights the wider array of forces at work shaping the evolution of labour contracts. The chapter concludes by noting the need to continue working on both 'subjective' and 'objective' dimensions of working life policy and practice if we are to avoid the very real problem of 'good people being custodians of bad policy/practice' in the future.

Understanding labour supply: fragmentation in transitional labour markets[2]

As in most advanced industrial societies the underlying assumptions and realities of labour supply have changed profoundly in recent decades in Australia. For much of the past century policies on working life in Australia have been shaped by a variant of the traditional model of breadwinning. This has been called the 'Harvester Man' model of employment and domestic relations (Watson et al, 2003). This model was never fixed and evolved dramatically over time (Nolan, 2003). The key precepts of this model are well known. Males were assumed to work in full-time, full year jobs and accrue a wide range of entitlements associated with 'standard' employment. These were accrued against longstanding employers at rates of pay that allowed a man and his family to live a civilised life in 'frugal comfort' (Justice Henry Bournes Higgins quoted in Macintyre, 1985). Women were assumed to be financially dependent on men and primarily responsible for looking after households. From at least the 1960s onwards, however, this model declined in significance as both an account of labour market reality and aspiration for many citizens. Since the 1980s another policy model has steadily emerged. In the realm of economic and labour market policy neo-liberal precepts have become increasingly influential (ACIRRT 1999; Pusey, 1991, 2004). At the core of this model is the vision of individuals as free contracting agents making choices about the role of work, leisure and family life in their lives. As opposed to the 'status'-based notion of social relations in the 'Harvester Man' model, this model is firmly based in a 'contract' vision of social relations. Like the 'Breadwinner Model' before it, this notion of labour supply is partial at best and at worst misleading in the issues it highlights as important for analytical and policy priorities.

Reality is very different. Since at least the mid-1990s there has been a growing literature which highlights the power of a more open analytical framework for understanding workers' labour supply preferences and behaviours. Gunther Schmid and colleagues (Schmid, 1995, 2002a, 2002b) have devised what they call the 'transitional labour markets' (TLM) framework for this purpose. They argue modern working life is best understood as involving changes in the links between paid employment in four key transitions over the life course. These are: employment and education, family formation,

Figure 3.1   The Transitional Labour Markets Framework

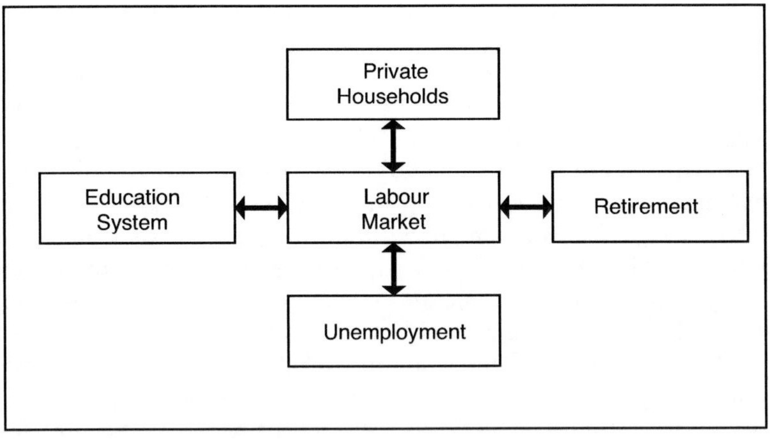

Source: Schmid, 1995, Figure 4, p.442

spells of unemployment and retirement. A diagrammatic presentation of this framework is provided in Figure 3.1.

Whereas the traditional breadwinner model defined these flows
in relatively fixed, status-based terms, the 'TINA' model holds that
navigating these transitions is a matter of individual choice. The
TLM researchers are, however, interested in understanding patterns
in such flows and how such flows can be improved for the benefit of
citizens, firms and society. In recent years research at our Centre has
shown that many working life transitions now occur in the context
of a decaying 'breadwinning model' co-existing with the fictions
of a 'TINA' policy regime. As a result transitions in working life are
often difficult, with people's capacity to navigate them highly unequally
distributed.

In the following paragraphs we report on the key developments
affecting labour supply in Australia, organised on the categories derived
from the TLM model. Central to our findings is that in Australia in
recent times TLMs have evolved in an era where free market ideology
has been in the ascendancy at the level of ideas, and where employers have been in the ascendancy in the economy and the workplace.
Politics has ensured that the state has actively buttressed this ideological and economic ascendancy. The significance of this ascendancy – a deepening and reconfiguration of inequality – is evident
in every dimension of transitions highlighted as important in the
TLM framework.

Developments within the labour market

At the core of the TLM framework is paid employment. This is where
the majority of people get the wherewithal to live. It is also where
many of the improvements in productivity occur. Rising productivity
is important as it provides economic surplus vital for economic and
social renewal. Figure 3.2 summarises movements in labour productivity growth and movements in real wages in Australia for the last
25 years. While output per unit of labour has increased dramatically
over this period, real wages have hardly improved.

Unsurprisingly wages share of GDP has fallen and profit share has
risen significantly during this period. This reverses the shift to earners
that occurred in the 1970s. Both trends are evident in Figure 3.3.

Complementing this economy-wide restructuring of earning has
been deepening fragmentation in wages and hours of work. Between

Figure 3.2   Labour Productivity and Growth in Real Wages, 1984–2008

Source: ABS, cited in Rafferty and Yu, 2009

Figure 3.3   Profit Share and Employee Share of GDP, 1959–2006

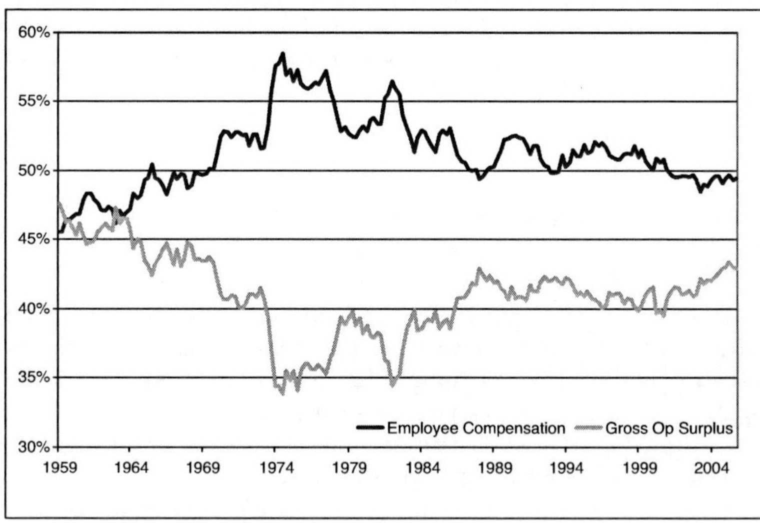

Source: ABS, cited in Rafferty and Yu, 2009
Note: Gross Operating Surplus includes mixed income of unincorporated enterprises

Table 3.1   Hours Actually Worked, Australia, 1979–2009

October:	1–15	16–34	35–40	41–49	50+	Total
1979	1.9	15.8	43.8	15.0	23.4	100
1989	2.5	16.0	37.0	16.1	28.4	100
1999	3.0	15.7	32.5	16.0	32.9	100
2009	3.5	21.0	33.6	14.7	27.4	100

Source: ABS, Labour Force Survey, Cat. No. 6291.0.55.001.

2005–6 and 2007–8 the ratio of median earnings between those in the top and bottom deciles increased from 2.86:1 to 3.15:1. Even more dramatic has been the change in working hours. These are summarised in Table 3.1. Over the last 30 years the proportion of people working 35–40 hours a week fell from 44% to 34%. Those working less than 35 hours a week rose from 18% to 25%. Those reporting that they actually worked more than 50 or more hours per week rose from 23% to 27%.

Closely allied to the change in hours has been the rise in non-standard work. Whereas in the early 1980s less than 10% of employees were engaged on a casual basis, today just on one in five (20% are so employed). Given that around another one in five are self-employed, this means just over half (51.5%) are employed as full-time, 'permanent' employees (ABS, 2009a). These shifts in earnings, working time and job quality have pervaded each of the four key labour market transitions involving paid employment and changing life courses.

Employment, unemployment and under-employment

Trends in unemployment and underemployment between 1978 and 2009 are summarised in Figure 3.4. Unemployment follows a cyclical pattern with increases during recessions eventually subsiding to pre-recession levels with the passing of time. Underemployment, on the other hand, increases during economic downturns and remains at those levels – until the next downturn where it increases again. Moreover, detailed data taken during the recession of the 1990s revealed that the 'employed' and 'unemployed' are not different stocks of workers. In 1996 when average unemployment hovered in the range of 8–9%, nearly a quarter of all workers (24%) reported a spell of unemployment during that year (Watson and Buchanan, 2001).

Figure 3.4   Total Number Unemployed and Underemployed ('000), 1978–2009

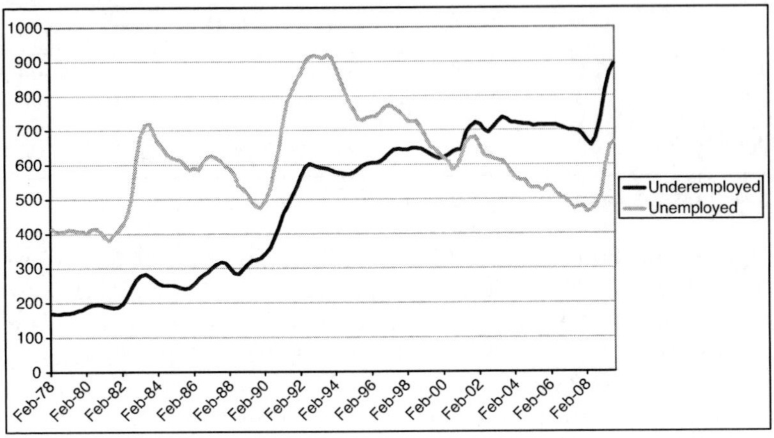

Source: ABS 2008b, Underemployed Workers, Cat. No. 6202.0

Underemployment is part of such flows. The primary reason people desire more hours is to increase income (ABS, 2008a). There is also a strong gender dimension to underemployment: of the 687,000 part-time underemployed workers in 2008, 447,000 were women. During the recent downturn, however, the most rapid growth in underemployment has been amongst men.

Employment and life (especially care work) beyond it

One of the greatest changes in life courses has arisen from dramatic increases in women's workforce participation. This represents a huge gain for women who had, as recently as the late 1960s, been actively driven from the workforce when they married. Rising levels of female workforce participation have also coincided with the longer hours noted earlier. These long working hours appear even more intense for heads of households. In 2007, over half of all employed men were working more than 40 hours a week, while one third were working over 50 (ABS, 2008b). Unsurprisingly, growing numbers of households now report major pressure on balancing work and care responsibilities. This is not just a function of increased hours of work reported by individuals earlier. It is, rather, a function of the combined hours provided by dual earner households. The dramatic shift here is evident in Figure 3.5.

In recent years this problem has been defined as one necessitating increased flexibility in the hours worked by employees. Given the

Figure 3.5 Weekly Hours Worked per Household

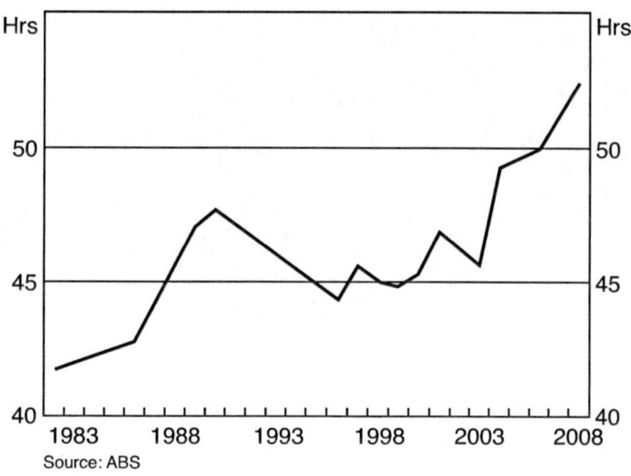

Cited in: Richards (2009)

scale of the change in household hours, however, it is just as much a problem of the absolute number of hours worked – not just a question of when they are worked.

Employment and education

Where once there was a clear demarcation between work and study for 15 to 24 year olds, the line between the two statuses is becoming blurred. The issue is no longer just the blending of work and education. Rather, it's about the subordination of the education experience to the needs of the economy. Figure 3.6 shows the numbers of young people in employment and their student status. The numbers of younger people employed full-time and not studying have fallen from around 1.2 million in 1986, to around 950,000 in 2009. While the numbers working part-time and studying have increased from just over 200,000 in 1986 to just below 600,000 in 2009. Although students working full-time have not increased radically, they have doubled from around 20,000 to 40,000.

Even when people choose to go into full- or part-time employment without studying, there is still an increased chance that they are engaged in vocational workplace-based training. Figure 3.7 shows the

Figure 3.6 Whether Attending School or Tertiary Education, by Part-Time/ Full-Time Employment Status, 15–24 year olds ('000), 1986–2009

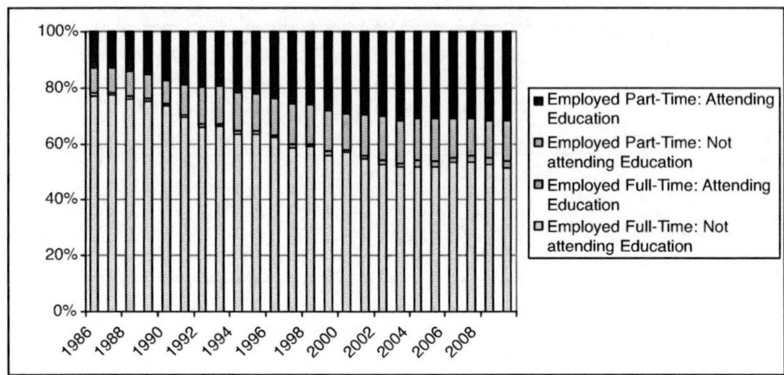

Population: All employed 15–24 year olds
Source: ABS, 2009b – Labour Force Survey, Cat. No. 6291.0.55.001

increase in the number of apprentices and trainees between 1970 and 2008. During the 1980s there were, on average around 150,000 apprentices in training per annum. Today there are over 400,000 apprentices and trainees. As a percent of young workers their proportion has only slightly increased from 8% to 9% between 1986 and 2008. This implies

Figure 3.7 Apprentices and Trainees In-training, 1998–2008 ('000)

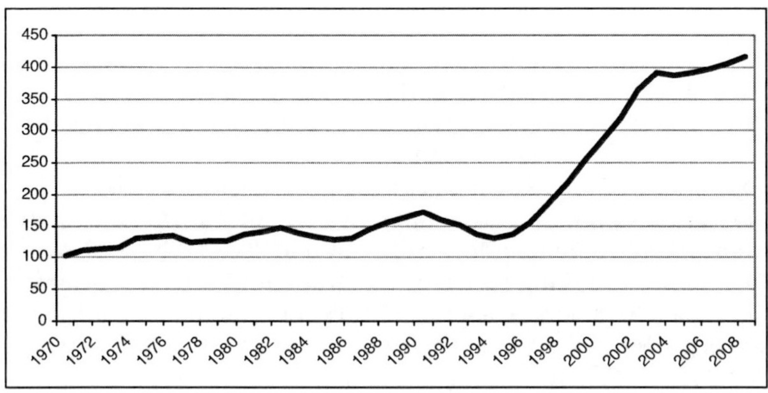

Source: Data from 1970–2002, Watson et al, 2003; Data from 2002 onwards NCVER, 2008

that most of the growth in employment-based training has come from the 25 plus workforce. This indicates a major transformation in how transitions between work and learning are evolving today.

Employment and retirement

While the transformation of the work/education nexus is recasting the early and middle stages of the life courses, changes in employment and retirement income support are defining how and when people exit working life. Workers are expected to provide for an increasing proportion of their retirement income. This is exacerbated by the government's decision to lift the eligibility for the pension from 65 to 67 years. The result of this is that people will have to stay in the workforce longer. Currently, the median superannuation balance for those aged 65–69 still accumulating super is $80,000 – a long way off the $250,000–$500,000 commonly assumed as needed to fund a decent retirement.[3] Table 3.2 provides details of current savings levels.

Over the last three decades we have witnessed a shift in quasi-'status-based' transitions to ones which are more 'commercially' defined. That is, these changes are indicative of the commodification of growing parts of social life. The key indicator of this is women's status. Their role is changing dramatically. While they are still not equal, they are being treated significantly more equally than in the past. The problem is the character of the equality that is emerging. Down market men are being treated like women and up market women are being treated like men. This is starkest in the hours issue: there are growing numbers

Table 3.2   Median Superannuation Balance by Age Group, 2007 ($)

Age	Accumulation Accounts	Defined benefit accounts	Hybrid accounts	Total superannuation balance
45–54	31,762	91,379	36,006	45,525
55–64	56,195	110,629	51,000	71,731
65–69	80,000	np	**36,566	80,000

Population: All persons with superannuation accounts in the accumulation phase
Source: ABS Survey of Employment Arrangements, Retirement and Superannuation, Cat. No. 6361.0
**Estimate has a relative Standard Error greater than 50% and is considered too unreliable for general use

of under-employed part-time, casual men and increasing numbers of involuntary, extended hours women (Watson et al, 2003). Moreover, for many people in Australia today navigating the key working life transitions can only be achieved by working on a casual, part-time basis and/or significantly compromising the subjective quality of life as discretionary time is squeezed out of households. Hence, while fragmentation of the older model has provided the potential for increased diversity – it has primarily resulted in a deepening and reconfiguration of inequality. In particular, this new policy mix has been most successful in shifting many of the costs and risks of working life away from employers and the state and increasingly onto households in general, but especially more marginal participants in the labour market (Watson et al, 2003). Low- and middle-income households where women are the secondary earner have been particularly big losers (Apps, 2004, 2006). This shift in the dynamics of labour supply is also evident in the dynamics of labour demand.

Understanding labour demand: unsustainable skill eco-systems

Within mainstream analysis labour demand is treated as a derived variable. At the micro level it is defined as arising from decisions made at enterprise level. The key determinants are demand for the firm's product/service and the production function specifying various capital-labour ratios associated with producing that output. The final balance in utilising capital and labour is determined by the relative price of each. At the macro level the issue is primarily about the quantum of labour actually deployed in production. If firms lack effective demand for their output there will be insufficient demand for labour. Effective demand can be increased by changing fiscal, monetary and wages policy. Orthodox economic notions of production define the problem as one of deploying labour efficiently: allocating it between competing uses at the micro level, utilising it fully at the macro level.

This approach has a number of major limitations which result in significant policy and practical blind spots. The most profound arises from the fact that labour is not a commodity which only needs to be deployed efficiently and fully. Rather, it is a factor of production that needs to be developed as well as utilised. This is the starting point for wider analysis of labour demand. In Australia such analysis is loosely characterised as the 'skill eco-system' or 'workforce development' approach. (See for example Buchanan et al, 2001 which builds on Briggs and Kitay, 2000; Crouch et al, 1999; Finegold, 1999. Skills Australia 2009a, b and c provide the comprehensive recent formulation of this approach).

At the core of this approach is an understanding of humans as a distinctive factor of production. Labour is usefully conceived as a standard commodity – indeed, it is not a commodity at all. When considered as an economic input the human element is comprised of two components:

(i) its underlying competence which sets the limits to a person's potential to perform (this is acquired on and off the job, formally and informally). This is referred to as the *'development'* aspect of labour productivity,

(ii) and the application of this potential in the workplace (i.e., the performance of work on the job). This is referred to as the *'deployment'* aspect of labour productivity.

When considering skills matters the key dynamic of interest is the balance between the development and deployment of labour. This balance is determined by the skill eco-system in which work and skill formation is embedded. A skill eco-system is comprised of:

- business settings (i.e., relevant product and capital markets)
- institutional and policy frameworks
- pre-dominant mode of engaging labour (e.g., 'casual' employment)
- the structure of jobs, including job design and work organisation
- the level and type of skill formation (e.g., apprenticeships).

In a healthy (i.e., sustainable) skill eco-system the development and deployment of labour are in balance. An unsustainable one is usually characterised by a pre-occupation with deploying labour (e.g., work overload) squeezing out the space for the orderly, systematic rounding out of skills on the job. Alternatively underutilisation of skill on the job results in 'under-employment' or 'wasted skills'.

The power of the skill eco-systems approach is best illustrated by analysing a particular region or sector. A study of Victorian manufacturing undertaken in the early 2000s provides a good example of the application of this approach (Buchanan et al, 2002).[4] The key finding was that Victorian manufacturers had actually articulated quite clearly what their requirements were for more highly developed cognitive and behavioural skills, and they had, moreover, identified particular skill shortages. However, they lacked the ability to meet new and emerging skill needs. Excess productive capacity, intense competition and pressures on margins were leading them down a blind alley. Because of these pressures they had reduced their intakes of apprentices, and had become increasingly reliant on an aging workforce for their skills needs. At the same time, they had turned to new forms of business organisation, such as outsourcing, and had increased their use of non-standard labour, both of which further reduced their internal capacity to reproduce skills. The links between economic context and their impact on work and skill are summarised in Figure 3.8.

As Figure 3.8 shows the research identified four key dimensions to this problem of inadequate skills formation arising from the dynamics of labour demand. First, the capacity of workplaces to conduct skills development was being undermined by work intensification and a preoccupation with ensuring labour was fully deployed on-the-job. The stock of skills required for growth and long-term survival were diminishing in a fashion akin to 'farmers eating their seeds'. The reliance on an aging workforce was particularly notable in the various sub-industries studied, with the decline in the proportion of younger workers particularly strong in chemicals and plastics. Whereas in 1984, 19% of its workforce was younger than 24, by 2001 this had fallen to 3%.

Secondly, systemic approaches to on- and off-the-job training were breaking down. For example, head office pressures had seen one food processing plant – which had formerly been an industry leader in broad-based training – restrict itself to training only in those competencies directly relevant to the job. This limited the capacity of workers to be re-deployed when machines broke down or when others were unexpectedly absent from work due to illness. Another prosperous workplace with expanding markets was pre-vented by head office from employing additional apprentice stain-less steel welders, even though this was one of the key skills required in that workplace, and was a skill in chronic short supply. These were typical of many examples the researchers found in sectors as

Figure 3.8 An Unsustainable Skill Eco-system – Victorian Manufacturing, Early 2000s

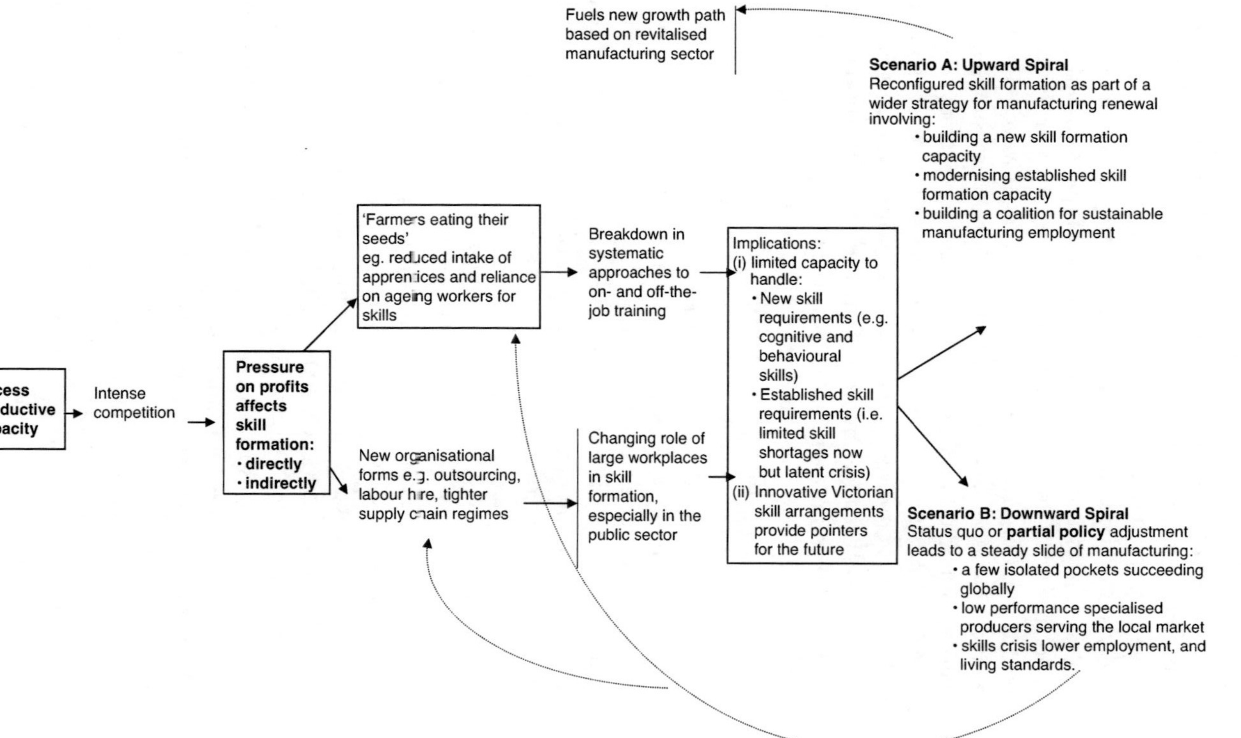

diverse as biotechnology, engineering, chemicals and plastics where short run management strategies were undermining the conditions for long run growth (Buchanan et al, 2002).

Thirdly, declining skill formation capacity was linked to new forms of business organisation and the increased use of non-standard employment. In the 1960s and 1970s firms made use of labour hoarding as a way of responding quickly to market upturns. However, during the 1980s and 1990s this was replaced by lean workforces, supplemented by casuals, contractors and labour-hire workers as required.

Fourthly – and this is a more general point which goes beyond Victorian manufacturing – there are some important changes in the distribution of apprentices by workplace size. The proportion of workplaces with 100 or more employees engaging in four-year apprenticeships fell from 26% to 14% between 1990 and 1997. While this may reflect a changing distribution in workplaces overall – that is, a reduction in the number of large workplaces – other evidence suggests that large firms have reduced their commitment to apprenticeships. This is particularly so among large public sector workplaces, such as railways, public works and electricity authorities.

Dynamics of this nature are not confined to manufacturing. There is a growing research literature and realm of policy development examining workforce development based on these ideas. It has examined sectors as diverse as dairy farming, community services, public hospital emergency departments and Victoria's prison industries (Buchanan and Considine, 2008; Buchanan and Hall, 2003; Cole, 2004; GMCT, 2005; Skinner et al, 2006). Initiatives directed at improving workforce development by improving the operation of skill eco-systems have been piloted in an even more diverse range of industries, sectors and regions (Alcorso and Windsor, 2008; Skills Australia, 2009b).

The key finding from these studies and pilots is that it is often the dynamics of demand, especially labour demand, driving problems in skill formation and use. In hospital emergency departments, for example, chronic under-funding has resulted in deepening work overloads, problems in the recruitment, development and retention of junior doctors and inadequate approaches to managing 'unstreamed' doctors. This has resulted in a now chronic dependence on locums and declining numbers of registrars in emergency medicine (GMCT, 2005; Skinner, 2005). The challenge of moving to a carbon constrained future requires more than new competencies standards or training providers.

It requires a new way of linking innovation, on-the-job learning and new approaches to increasing energy efficiency.

Beyond price: agreement making and the reality of coordination

Within conventional policy discourse labour supply and demand are coordinated by changes in the relative price of labour. This variable bears a heavy analytical and policy weight. Within labour supply the price of labour (i.e., the wage and bundle of associated work related earnings) shapes the calculus surrounding investments in education and the work/leisure choice of the individual. Within labour demand it affects decisions taken at enterprise level concerning the capital and labour intensity of production. Armed with these analytical priors, much mainstream policy asserts that the best way for 'price' to perform its magic in coordinating labour supply and demand is to remove 'barriers' to its free movement. That is to 'deregulate' and let the parties settle their own employment contracts. The ideal arising from this model is that individual workers and their employers settle customised agreements that meet their unique requirements. This was the vision behind the neo-liberal/neo-conservative *Work Choices* reforms to Australian labour law that ran from March 2006 to July 2009. The impact of this model was the subject of two large scale studies run by our Centre. The first involved a comprehensive quantitative study of major agreements from the retail and hospitality sectors (Evesson et al, 2007). The other assessed how the changes affected over 8,000 randomly selected workers (van Wanrooy et al, 2007). Both studies revealed that the reality of agreement making in the contemporary Australian labour market is a long way from the orthodox conception of the process. The key findings from these studies can be summarised as follows.

The reality of enterprise bargaining has not been increased customisation of employment arrangements, but rather a redefining of labour market standards. The most empirically novel study involved detailed, comprehensive analysis of agreements registered under *Work Choices* (Evesson et al, 2007). Traditionally agreement analysis has been based on samples and rarely made reference back to the relevant awards. This study undertook full enumerations of agreements in retail and hospitality in 2006. The major conclusion of the project was that the instruments could not be regarded as 'agreements' in any meaningful sense of the term. Rather they were the mechanism that enabled employers to move their workers off award standards and onto the lower statutory entitlements. What was particularly stark was the level of 'template' agreements. Amongst all retail and hospitality non-union collective agreements registered in the first nine months of *Work Choices*, just under one in four (24%) were identical and had been 'brokered' by the one consultant – Enterprise Initiatives. As Evesson et al (2007) conclude:

> In understanding the decline of enforceable rights at work under *Work Choices* in sectors where workers have limited bargaining power the key dynamic at work appears to involve **policy induced, consultant facilitated employer determination of collective contracts.** (p.47, emphasis in original)

The inequality of bargaining power is neither uniform nor non-existent.[5] The *Australia at Work* study examined the employment contract, wages and working conditions of 8,143 randomly selected workers in March 2007 who had been in or looking for work in March 2006 (van Wanrooy et al, 2007). One the key findings noted in the first, benchmark report was that there needs to be a more nuanced understanding of unequal bargaining power in the labour market. The study occurred at a time of strong labour demand. However, the recent surges in demand had not been uniform. To understand the impact of changes in economic and industrial relations policies the study confirmed the need to pay close attention to the different realities of power for different groups of workers. While strong economic growth and skill shortages have strengthened many workers' bargaining power, for many others a lack of power in negotiation remained a grim reality. An increase in labour demand did not overcome deep-seated inequalities of bargaining power that are still a defining feature of the Australian labour market. Researchers and policymakers who focus primarily on the aggregates miss this simple, but profound reality. But equally an undifferentiated view of the inequality of bargaining power needs to be reconsidered. The issue that needs to be grasped is not just that there is inequality of bargaining power between employers and employees – there are also significant differences in the form this inequality takes among different groups of workers (van Wanrooy, 2007).

Individual and collective arrangements are complements, not substitutes. The *Australia at Work* study also found that Australians' working arrangements are governed by a subtle blend of collective and individual arrangements. Too often in public debate it is asserted that workers' individualistic outlook is incompatible with allegedly outdated collectivist arrangements. *Work Choices* went further than any other set of labour laws in the western world to allow individual agreements to override collectively determined and publicly enforceable labour standards. This conflict between individualism and collectivism was, however, an artefact of the legislation – not modern life. The key finding by the researchers about the nature of different legal instruments governing life at work was clear. In understanding pay determination we need to distinguish between the formal instruments codifying enforceable rights and the processes involved in setting and improving pay and conditions. The formal instruments are defined on an individual or collective basis, but the formalities should not be assumed to reflect the actual process involved in setting wages and conditions. Pay and conditions for employees on individual statutory contracts – known as Australian Workplace Agreementes (AWAs) – were often determined on a group or collective basis involving commonality across the workplace. Equally, many of those on collective agreements and awards have individual factors shape the final level of their pay and conditions. In short, elements of individual- and collectively-based arrangements co-exist and work as complements, not rivals, in shaping structures, practices and outcomes in working life (van Wanrooy et al, 2007).

The findings of these studies provide important pointers for the future. Clearly on the issue of agreement making the issue is not 'agreements' or 'regulation' – rather it is how do the two co-exist. Similar to bargaining, employers as much as workers coordinate their claims. Again the issue is not either individual or collective bargaining – rather it is how can bargaining between different levels be best connected?

Conclusion: public goods at work

Over the last three decades major problems in labour demand, labour supply and the way they are connected have emerged. The risks associated with navigating the life course often occur in an inefficient and unfair way. Wage inequality and problems with working time mean the transitions involving employment and education, family formation, spells of unemployment and retirement are often pressured, unpleasant experiences. The preoccupation with deploying labour has squeezed out time for its orderly development, especially on the job. Coordination between labour supply and demand is often haphazardly organised, with the focus down market on reducing labour standards. Is there no alternative to this state of affairs? Since the early 1980s it has commonly been assumed that there is none. Deepening and reconfigured inequality has been portrayed as the necessary price for a world that could only flourish if market principles reigned supreme. Developments since September 2008 have shattered the credibility of this narrative. Given these developments, the finding of the recent New Zealand work on developing human capability are very important. They provide a robust basis for reformulating enterprise and national priorities in a post-Lehmann Brothers world. If the project's insights are to inform effective change they need to be supported by an allied set of understandings. In particular, how constraints are understood profoundly shapes what is defined as possible and what it is that needs to be reformed. This chapter has summarised some of the key findings from our Centre's research into how the dynamics of fragmentation are operating in contemporary Australia. The analysis provides pointers on priorities for improvement.

Many of the areas identified for change primarily concern organisational arrangements. They neglect the 'subjective' substance of what all this change is for. Work is about more than 'transitions', 'development' and 'agreement making'. For most people in advanced industrial economies paid employment is about more than the extrinsic rewards, such as money. As the Developing Human Capability focus groups on this point noted, building on a much larger literature, it is also about social support and networks and the ability to undertake challenging (or at least valued) activity. For us, this is the most underdeveloped aspect of our Centre's analysis of the political economy of work and skill to date. The Developing Human Capability Framework offers critical leads on content here. The idea of letting individuals live lives they value – at, through and beyond – work is especially important here.

We need, however, to go further. An observation we have made from our wide range of applied research projects in the last two decades is that in analysing labour flows it is important to move beyond the categories traditionally used to make sense of how work is evolving. For flows between work and life beyond it we have shown the power of the transitional labour market framework. In our latest research on workforce development we have identified the limitations of mainstream approaches to skill for understanding flows within the labour market. These are defined on the basis of either totally fragmented atoms of skills embodied in competency standards or in tightly defined occupational categories. In reality, most people gain clusters of competence, often cohering in various vocational streams. This broader, more open concept of occupation appears to be very important for making sense of how people deepen their capabilities over time (Buchanan et al, 2009). As we move forward we need to think more about how we can help define and nurture such vocation streams – i.e., a broader notion of occupation. This gets us beyond the narrow world of demarcations associated with the guilds of a previous age. Equally it gets us beyond the vacuous notion of skill underpinned by notions of dismembered units of competence and 'choice of work' through individual contract. This broader notion of occupation as vocational streams sees the development of more structured career and skill development for individuals over time as a public good. How this public good is nurtured needs considerably more analytical and policy attention than it is currently getting.

Devoting attention to a broader notion of occupation has the major advantage of reframing approaches to understanding both the 'objective' and 'subjective' dimension of work. The former concerns issues like wages, hours of work and rights to time for care, education and retirement. The latter goes to notions of identity and perceived well-being. In recent decades subjective preferences about economic life have been profoundly shaped by what Thomas Frank has called 'market populism'. This defines life projects – not just the efficient allocation and deployment of resources. A focus on the development of human capability gets us a long way from the assumed virtue of a commercial life embedded deep within current orthodox policies – but as the New Zealand project has highlighted the capability framework itself needs deepening in the realm of work/paid employment. Here the notion of vocational streams or a broader notion of occupation is very important.

The New Zealand work on human capability offers important leads on objectives in policy and practice about work. Our research offers powerful leads that help guide the implementation of these objectives. The challenge is to open up new realms of inquiry and policy research around the notion of occupation and vocational streams as public goods. Achievement in this area offers real prospects of getting beyond the policy 'dead end' we find ourselves in and offers the potential of finding significantly better ways of helping individuals and societies flourish in the future.

Notes

1   This quote is taken from 'Organisational Factors', sub-heading dealing with 'Workplace [industrial] relations and cultures' and included in 'factors that undermine human capability development'.
2   This section draws heavily on material contained in two syntheses of our Centre's research: Watson et al, 2003 and Buchanan et al, 2006.
3   Robust definitions of 'adequate' levels of savings for retirement are hard to come by. The estimates provided in the text are based on norms commonly used by financial advisers who recommend that a comfortable retirement can be had with $20,000 per person per year. We have assumed a life expectancy of around 15–20 years following retirement at age 65.
4   The following summary draws heavily on the account of this project provided in Watson et al, 2003 Chapter 10. The findings of this study were supported by a subsequent study undertaken by NSW Manufacturing. See Buchanan and Briggs, 2004.
5   This and the following section reproduce parts of the conclusion to the first Australia at Work report: van Wanrooy et al, 2007: 92–95.

References

ABS (2008a) *Survey of Employment Arrangements, Retirement and Superannuation,* Cat. No. 6361.0, Australian Bureau of Statistics, Canberra.
ABS (2008b) *Underemployed Workers*, Cat. No. 6202.0, Australian Bureau of Statistics, Canberra.
ABS (2009a) *Forms of Employment, November,* 2008 Cat. No. 6359.0, Australian Bureau of Statistics, Canberra.
ABS (2009b) *Labour Force Survey*, Cat. No. 6291.0.55.001, Australian Bureau of Statistics, Canberra.
ACIRRT (1999) *Australia at Work: Just Managing?*, Sydney: Prentice Hall.
Alcorso, C. and Windsor, K. (2008) *Skills in Context: A Guide to the Skill Ecosystem Approach to Workforce Development*, NSW DET and Department of Education, Employment and Workplace Relations, Sydney.

Apps, P. (2004) 'The high taxation of working families', *Australian Review of Public Affairs*, 5(1): 1–24.

Apps, P. (2006) 'Family taxation: An unfair and inefficient system', http://heifer.ucc.usyd.edu.au/law/FMPro?-db=lawstaff.fp5&-format=academic-staff_detail2.htm&-lay=web&StaffID=PatriciaApps&-find accessed 9 May.

Botwinick, H. (1993) *Persistent Inequalities: Wage Disparity under Capitalist Competition*, Princeton: Princeton University Press.

Briggs, C. and Kitay, J. (2000) *Vocational Education and Training, Skill Formation and the Labour Market: Overview of Contemporary Studies*, NSW Board of Vocational Education and Training Changing Nature of Work Working Paper, Sydney.

Bryson, J. and O'Neil, P. (2008) *Developing Human Capability: Employment Institutions, Organisations and Individuals*, Discussion Paper – Overview of findings on developing human capability, Wellington, Industrial Relations Centre, Victoria University.

Buchanan, J. (2006) *From 'Skill Shortages' to Decent Work: The Role of Better Skill Ecosystems*, NSW Board of Vocational Education Research Policy Research Paper, Sydney, http://www.skillecosystem.net/data/files/general/Buchanan_Report_Lowres_single.pdf

Buchanan, J. and Briggs, C. (2004) 'Not with a bang but a whimper?', *Skills and the Future of NSW Manufacturing and Engineering*, Sydney, NSW TAFE Commission.

Buchanan, J. and Considine, G. (2008) *From Labour to Work: An Evaluation of, and Options for, Victoria's Prison Industries*, Melbourne. http://www.justice.vic.gov.au/wps/wcm/connect/DOJ+Internet/Home/Prisons/Prisons+in+Victoria/Prison+Industries/JUSTICE+-+Review+of+Prison+Industries+-+From+Labour+To+Work

Buchanan, J., Evesson, J. and Briggs, C. (2002) *Renewing the Capacity for Skill Formation: The Challenge for Victorian Manufacturing*, Victorian Department of Education and Training, April (published at http://www.otte.det.vic.gov/publications/Knowledgeandskills/pdf/project7-manufacturing-FinalReport.pdf).

Buchanan, J. and Hall, R. (2003) *Beyond VET: Skills and the Future of Victorian Service Industries* (Executive summary provided http://www.vsc.vic.gov.au/__data/assets/word_doc/0004/9346/BeyondTAFEExecutiveSummary.doc).

Buchanan, J., Schofield, K., Briggs, C., Considine, G., Hager, P., Hawke, G., Kitay, J., Meagher, G., Macintyre, J., Mounier, A. and Ryan, S. (2001) *Beyond Flexibility: Skills and Work in the Future*, Board of Vocational Education and Training (NSW), Sydney, 2001 (published at http://www.bvet.nsw.gov.au/pdf/beyondflex.pdf).

Buchanan, J., Marginson, S., Wheelahan, L. and Yu, S. (2009) *Education, Work and Economic Renewal: An Issues Paper Prepared for the Australian Education Union*, Workplace Research Centre, Sydney.

Cole, M. (2004) *Dairy: Employment for the Future – Towards an Employment Strategy*, ACIRRT [now WRC] Sydney, 2004 (published at http://www.wrc.org.au/documents/WP92.pdf).

Crouch, C., Finegold, D. and Sako, M. (1999) *Are Skills the Answer? The Political Economy of Skill Creation in Advanced Industrial Countries*, Oxford: Oxford University Press.

Evesson, J., Buchanan, J., Bamberry, L., Frino, B. and Oliver, D. (2007) *'Lowering the Standards': From Awards to Work Choices in Retail and Hospitality Collective Agreements*, September 2007 (published at http://www.industrialrelations. nsw.gov.au/resources/lowering_the_standards_13sept2007.pdf).

Fine, B. (1998) *Labour Market Theory: A Constructive Reassessment*, London: Routledge.

Finegold, D. (1999) 'Creating self-sustaining high-skill ecosystems', *Oxford Review of Economic Policy*, 15(1): 60–81.

Frank, T. (2000) *One Market Under God. Extreme Capitalism, Market Populism and the Economic Democracy*, London: Vintage.

GMCT (Greater Metropolitan Clinicans' Taskforce) (2005) Locum Working Group, *Meeting the Medical Locum Challenge: Options for NSW Public Hospitals*, North Ryde, GMCT (published at http://www.health.nsw.gov.au/gmct/pdf/locum_issues.pdf).

Kaufman, B.E. (ed.) (1988) *How Labor Markets Work: Reflections on Theory and Practice*, Lexington: Lexington Books.

Kuttner, R. (2008) *Obama's Challenge: America's Economic Crisis and the Power of a Transformative Presidency*, Melbourne: Scribe.

Macintyre, S. (1985) *Winners and Losers: The Pursuit of Social Justice in Australian History*, Sydney: Allen and Unwin.

NCVER (2008) *Australian Vocational and Education Training Statistics*, National Centre for Vocational Education Research, Adelaide.

Nolan, M. (2003) 'The high tide of a labour market system: The Australasian male breadwinner model', *Labour and Industry*, 13(3): 73–92.

Pusey, M. (1991) *Economic Rationalism in Canberra*, Melbourne: Cambridge University Press.

Pusey, M. (2004) *The Experience of Middle Australia: The Dark Side of Economic Reform*, Melbourne: Cambridge University Press.

Rafferty, M. and Yu, S. (2009) *The Economic Crisis and Working Lives of the Future – A Report for the Australian Council of Trade Unions*, Workplace Research Centre, University of Sydney.

Richards, T. (2009) *Housing Market Developments*, Reserve Bank of Australia, Sydney.

Rudd, K. (2009) 'Pain on the road to recovery', *Sydney Morning Herald*, 25 July.

Schmid, G. (1995) 'Is full employment still possible? Transitional labour markets as a new strategy of labour market policy', *Economic and Industrial Democracy*, 16(3): 429–456.

Schmid, G. (2002a) 'Transitional labour markets and the European social model: Towards a new employment contract', in Schmid, G. and Gazier, B. (eds), *The Dynamics of Full Employment: Social Integration Through Transitional Labour Markets*, Cheltenham, UK: Edward Elgar, pp.393–435.

Schmid, G. (2002b) 'Towards a theory of transitional labour markets', in Schmid, G. and Gazier, B. (eds), *The Dynamics of Full Employment: Social Integration Through Transitional Labour Markets*, Cheltenham, UK: Edward Elgar, pp.151–195.

Skills Australia (2009a) *Overview Paper*, Workforce Futures. Papers to Promote Discussion towards an Australian Workforce Development Strategy, Canberra.

Skills Australia (2009b) *What Does the Future Hold? Meeting Australia's Skill Needs*, Background Paper One of Workforce Futures. Papers to Promote Discussion Towards an Australian Workforce Development Strategy, Canberra.

Skills Australia (2009c) *Powering the Workplace: Realising Australia's Skill Potential*, Background Paper Two of Workforce Futures. Papers to Promote Discussion Towards an Australian Workforce Development Strategy, Canberra.

Skinner, C., Riordan, R., Fraser, K., Buchanan, J., Goulston, K. (on behalf of the GMCT Metropolitan Hospitals Locum Issues Group) (2006) 'The challenge of locum working arrangements in New South Wales public hospitals', *Medical Journal of Australia*, 185(5): 276–278.

van Wanrooy, B., Oxenbridge, S., Buchanan, J. and Jakubauskas, M. (2007) *Australia at Work. The Benchmark Report*, University of Sydney, October (published at http://www.wrc.org.au/O01P002/A01/V01/_Assets/_Documents/ Australia@Work%20The%20Benchmark%20Report.pdf).

Watson, I. and Buchanan, H. (2001) 'Beyond impoverished visions of the labour market', in Fincher, R. and Saunders, P. (eds), *Unequal Futures: Rethinking Poverty, Inequality and Disadvantage in Australia*, Sydney: Allen and Unwin.

Watson, I., Buchanan, J., Campbell, I. and Briggs, C. (2003) *Fragmented Futures: New Challenges in Working Life*, Sydney: Federation Press.

4
The Future of Low Paid Work in Europe and the US

Ken Mayhew

Introduction

In 2003 the New York-based Russell Sage Foundation published *Low Wage America*. This book explored the position of workers at the low end of the US labour market. It was concerned not just with relative pay but also with other monetary and non-monetary rewards and with working conditions more generally as well as with prospects for escaping into better jobs. A fairly grim picture emerged and one which appeared to have worsened over time.

Certain functions have to be performed in any modern economy – cleaning hotel rooms and hospitals, serving customers in shops, working on assembly lines. But does this have to imply, as it does in the US, that the workers who undertake these functions inevitably have to be condemned to dead-end, low paid jobs with poor working conditions? Or do other countries, with different histories, cultures, institutions and policies, 'construct' better jobs to perform these functions? With this question in mind, the Foundation commissioned teams from five European countries (the UK, France, Germany, Denmark and the Netherlands) to work to a common research design and to produce studies for each of their countries. The UK team was organised and led by the National Institute for Economic and Social Research and SKOPE. Books for each country were published in 2008 (Bosch and Weinkopf; Caroli and Gautié; Lloyd, Mason and Mayhew; Salverda, van Klaveren and van der Meer; Westergaard-Nielsen, all 2008). A volume comparing Europe and the US will be published in 2010 (Gautié and Schmitt, 2010).

The research was a mixture of standard 'desk work' and case studies. For the latter, low end occupations in five sectors were chosen. These were: cleaners and nurse assistants in hospitals, room attendants in hotels, operatives in food processing, agents in inbound call centres and salespersons in retail. The Foundation entered the project with two presumptions as to what the European research would produce. The first was that many jobs in Europe would be designed differently and better than their counterparts in the US, yielding higher productivity and therefore allowing better pay and conditions. The second was that, where jobs were not designed differently, better pay and conditions in Europe would come at a price in terms of lower employment rates. Neither presumption was confirmed by the research. A few jobs were designed differently – for example, food processing in Denmark, cleaners and nurse assistants in Germany and the Netherlands. But, by and large, the jobs studied looked much the same on both sides of the Atlantic. Yet employment consequences were surprisingly hard to find. The comparative book has attempted to explain these findings. The key to understanding differences between countries in the incidence of low pay appears to lie in how inclusive or exclusive pay setting institutions are. The next section of this chapter describes the extent and nature of low pay in the six countries and how it has changed over time. The UK is one of the countries where the incidence of low pay increased rather dramatically and the chapter analyses why this happened in order to illustrate the central role of pay setting institutions. We then turn to a more general discussion of the nature of pay setting institutions and of their influence on the incidence of low pay in all of the six countries in the study. Following this the chapter argues that other potential explanations of low pay are subsidiary to the role of pay setting institutions and also covers the issue of pay/employment trade-offs. Finally the chapter considers whether the more benign institutions of some countries are stable and draws policy conclusions.

The extent and nature of low pay

Workers are categorised as low paid if they earn less than two thirds of hourly median earnings. Table 4.1 compares the incidence of low pay in the six countries.

Table 4.1   Incidence of Low Pay, 2003–2005

	Denmark	France	Germany	Nether-lands	United Kingdom	United States
% employees below low pay threshold	8.5	11.1	22.7	17.6	21.7	25.0
Year	2005	2005	2005	2005	2005	2003–05
Source	CCP/ IDA	Enquête Emploi	German Socio-Economic Panel	Loonstruc-tuuronder-zoek	Annual Survey of Hours and Earnings	Current Population Survey

Source: Mason and Salverda (2010)

The highest incidence of low pay was found in the US. The UK and, surprisingly to many, Germany were close behind. At the other extreme, Denmark had a very low incidence, whilst France and the Netherlands fell between the two extremes. As Figure 4.1 demonstrates the trends over time also vary significantly across countries.

In the countries at the two extremes, Denmark and the US, no trend has been evident in the incidence of low pay since the mid-

Figure 4.1   Trends in the Incidence of Low Pay, % of Employees Below the Low Pay Threshold, 1973–2005

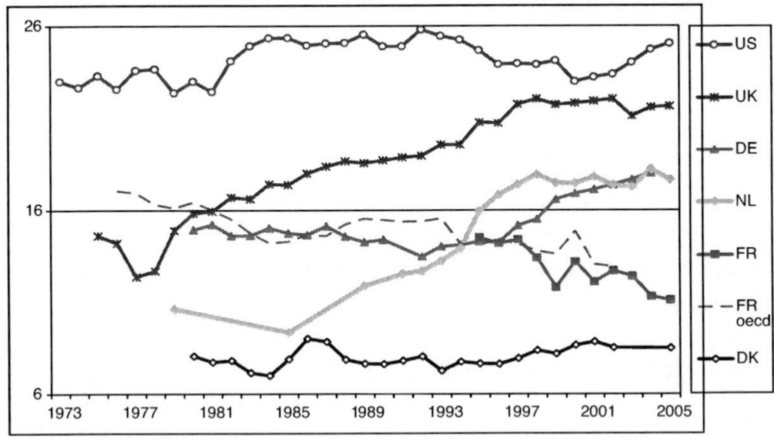

Note: DK = Denmark, DE = Germany
Source: Mason and Salverda (2010)

1970s, though the US had experienced a striking rise in earnings inequality shortly before then. Incidence increased in the UK from the mid- to late 1970s until the mid-1990s, since when it has stabilised. Incidence in the Netherlands increased from the mid-1980s until the late 1990s, whilst in Germany the increase in low pay came after the mid-1990s and is continuing.

In all countries, women, the young, part-timers, irregular workers (for example those in temporary or seasonal jobs) and the less educated are most exposed to low pay, but the degree of this exposure varies from country to country. Many low paid workers remain in that state for considerable periods of time, although mobility out of low pay is generally higher in Europe than in the US. Such mobility is especially high in Denmark where, more than in any other country, low pay tends to be a rite of passage for young people.

The case study sectors were chosen by the Foundation as ones containing significant numbers of low paid workers in the US. By and large this was the case in the European countries. However there were some exceptions, notably food processing in Denmark where there were no low paid workers. More generally the incidence of low pay within a given sector differed massively from country to country, as did the extent of low pay (measured relative to median earnings). Nevertheless the jobs were usually designed and structured in much the same way as in the US. As we have already noted, there were a few exceptions, but in general European employers were not taking 'the high road' (as it was termed in *Low Wage America*) compared to their American counterparts, and yet, at least in some countries, the same production strategy involved much less low pay than in the US.

The growth of low pay in the UK

The three decades after the end of the Second World War were characterised by extensive and growing protection for workers at the bottom end of the UK labour market. Trade union density (the percentage of the workforce unionised), for example, was 44.5% in 1950 and at roughly the same level in 1960. By 1970 it had risen to 48.5% and peaked at 55.8% in 1979. Unskilled and semi-skilled workers were often well represented. The percentage of the workforce covered by collective bargaining was even higher, being, for example, over 75% in 1979. There were two reasons for the gap between density and coverage. First, in workplaces where unions bargained, non-members benefited from negotiations. Second, in most of private manufacturing and in some parts of private services there was multi-employer bargaining. For example, in the engineering sector the employers' association, the Engineering Employers Federation, negotiated annually with the relevant unions to set minimum terms and conditions of employment for the sector. Members of the employers' association, whether or not they recognised unions within their own establishments, were obliged to offer at least these minima, whilst non-member firms also tended to respect them. Thus there was a sort of industry minimum wage in many areas of economic activity.

There were also various forms of statutory low pay protection. Wages Councils were established in sectors where unionism was weak. The sectors could be very large, like agriculture in England and Wales, or very small, ladies hosiery for example. Each Council consisted of a union representative, an employer representative and an independent chair. It set minimum pay rates for different categories of workers, together with things like standard weekly hours and minimum holiday entitlements. It was open to individual firms to offer more, but not less. An official body called the Wages Inspectorate was charged with monitoring and enforcing Wage Councils' orders. Dating in its modern form back to the early post- Second World War years, the Fair Wages Resolution applied to all firms tendering for government contracts. A condition of tendering was that fair wage was paid. Where a relevant multi-employer national agreement existed, a fair wage was defined as the minimum laid down in that agreement. Otherwise it was defined as the going rate for comparable work in the relevant geographical area. The 1975 Employment Protection Act extended the Fair Wages Resolution to the whole of employment. This effectively allowed unions to make claims based on comparability.

A Conservative Government entered office in 1979. Prime Minister Thatcher's supply side reforms were an integral expression of her free market philosophy. Central to this was a belief that economic efficiency was best served by private, competitive markets, as free as possible from the intervention of monopoly groups and from the dead hand of government regulation and control. The emphasis was on individual economic units rationally pursuing their own self-interest, which, in competitive markets, would maximise the efficient use of the country's resources. Trade unions were an obvious target of her reforms and successive pieces of legislation introduced by the Thatcher and Major governments were aimed at making it more difficult for unions to attract and retain members. The legislation also made it more difficult for them to call and successfully prosecute strikes. What is clear is that the balance of power between worker and employer massively changed in favour of the latter.

What is less clear is the contribution to this of the legislation as opposed to other factors. These other factors were many. An unusually severe macroeconomic downturn at the beginning of the 1980s, which contributed to an extremely slack labour market until 1986, proved very harmful both to union membership and union bargaining power. Changes in the composition of the workforce were away from the traditional union heartlands in manufacturing and blue collar work. Probably even more important were the changing attitudes of management. The 1970s was a decade of turbulent industrial relations and of abuse of union power in a number of well-publicised cases. At the same time attempts to make the industrial relations model of the employment relationship work were judged by the majority of employers to have failed. In making this judgment they often pointed to poor productivity growth in that decade. Therefore employer disillusionment with collective bargaining had set in before Mrs Thatcher entered Downing Street. The strains of dealing with the consequences of the coincident recession meant that management was prepared to deal more ruthlessly with unions not just in formal negotiations but in day-to-day matters at the shop floor level. Thus many apparently impregnable restrictive practices, such as those concerning job demarcation, entirely disappeared or were massively weakened. At the same time business school gurus had unveiled 'modern' human resource management techniques as an alternative way of managing the employment relationship and of capturing the collective voice. Unions were and remain relatively strong in public sector employment. Therefore the waves of privatisation from very early in the Conservative years contributed to the weakening of the union movement as a whole, as did the greater exposure of UK product and financial markets to global competition.

Whatever the relative importance of these various factors, the decline of unions, both in terms of representation and power, was particularly harshly felt in the lower reaches of the labour market.

Hostility to the collective was a salient aspect of new official philosophy. Encouraged by anti-collective rhetoric, employers dismantled multi-employer agreements, so that by the end of the 1980s bargaining took place only at the level of the individual organisation. The implications for lower paid workers were extensive. These multi-employer agreements had acted like sector- or industry-wide minimum wages and accordingly had provided significant low pay protection.

At the same time official protections were also removed. Shortly after entering office, the Conservatives abolished the Fairs Wages Resolution and repealed the Employment Protection Act. Wages Councils were severely restricted in scope in 1986 and abolished altogether in 1993.

As a result of this array of developments the inclusiveness of UK pay setting institutions massively declined and by the mid-1990s the incidence of low pay, accompanied by a large increase in earnings inequality, had risen to more or less today's levels. Since then the incidence of low pay has remained more or less constant. The policies of the Labour Government, which entered office in 1997, appear to have succeeded in stabilising the incidence of low pay but not in reducing it. The incoming government thought in terms of a 'contract' between itself and the electorate. The government owed a duty of care to each citizen, part of which was to ensure that people were protected from poverty. But a contribution to society was expected in return. In theory this contribution could take on many forms including paid work, engaging in charitable activities or looking after the family. However, the government put especial stress on the contribution being made through employment. One of the reasons for this was the belief that bringing people back into contact with the world of work, even in humble and ill rewarded jobs, meant them regaining a foothold on the employment ladder. Subsequently they would clamber up it into better jobs and thus be no longer dependent on state support. In a series of New Deals for different groups, most importantly for the young and adult unemployed, the government insisted that people who had been receiving out-of-work benefits for more than a certain period of time, the length of which depended upon the group concerned, attended for interview and advice at a JobCentre Plus. Once this process was completed an individual would preferably receive the offer of a regular job. If one was not found, then he or she would be offered a subsidised job, or a place on a charitable or community programme, or a place in full-time education or training. All of these options offered, to varying degrees, higher weekly income to the person concerned. Failure to take up an offer could lead to the withdrawal or reduction of benefits. The aim was to get people into work even at low wages and, following the first foot on the employment ladder argument, hopefully this would lead to progression to better and higher paid employment.

Meanwhile if low pay caused an individual to be in poverty, which would depend on his or her household circumstances, then generous in-work social security benefits were available to relieve the situation. Indeed the Labour Government accelerated a change in emphasis in social security policy away from out-of-work towards in-work benefits. The former became less generous compared to the latter and were more harshly administered in terms of duration and conditionality.

This labour market strategy was also motivated by a strong belief in 'flexible' and competitive labour markets, flexibility having many dimensions including financial, temporal and functional. In this sense Blair was very much the heir of Thatcher. Unions were no longer able to resist such flexibility and it was believed that this was a good thing. By 2006 union density had fallen to 28.4%. Workers were no longer empowered in the workplace via collective bargaining – the need to be competitive in the global economy, it was contended, made that undesirable and impossible. Instead the aim of the government was to empower them in the labour market via education and training.

At first sight the introduction of a National Minimum Wage in 1999 appears to sit oddly with this strategy. In fact this is not the case, as will be explained in the next section. Meanwhile the important point to note is that the Labour Government did little to restore the pay setting institutions which had been dismantled under the previous Conservative government. This erosion of a range of pay setting institutions had been accompanied by an increase in the incidence of low pay in the UK. In the next section we turn to the importance of such institutions in explaining the contrasting experiences of the six countries in the Russell Sage study.

Pay setting institutions

In explaining low pay profiles, the key difference between countries lies in the inclusiveness or exclusiveness of their pay setting institutions.

Pay setting institutions are defined as 'the formal and sometimes informal mechanisms used to determine wages and benefits received by workers in different industries and occupations within each country' (Bosch, Mayhew and Gautié, 2010). By one mechanism or another, in inclusive systems the gains achieved by the most powerful workers are shared with the less powerful. In this respect the proportion of the workforce covered by collective bargaining seems to be more important than union density per se.

Table 4.2 gives data on coverage, whilst Table 4.3 gives details on union and employer density.

Union density fell in all the countries in our study, but to very different extents and from very different starting points. The fall was biggest in the UK and least in Denmark. However at the beginning of the period covered by the table, UK union density had been high compared with all the other countries except Denmark, so that despite the large fall its density remains comparatively high. Coverage also fell in the US, Germany and the UK and particularly strongly so in the last two of these countries. By contrast it actually rose in the other three and very significantly so in Denmark, where it now stands at 90%. Coverage is also 90% in France and is 80% in the Netherlands. These three countries with the highest coverage have the lowest incidence of low pay.

High coverage is achieved in a number of ways. In Denmark high union density is the main driving force and inclusiveness is increased by a strong tradition of solidaristic wage bargaining. In France and the Netherlands coverage has increased despite falling union density. This is because collective agreements are extended by law to the rest of the

Table 4.2   **Bargaining Coverage 1980, 1990, 2000**

	1980	1990	2000	Change 1980–2000
USA	26	18	14	−12
UK	70	47	30	−40
DE	91	92	68	−24
FR	85	95	90	+5
NL	76	81	80	+4
DK	69	69	90	+21

Source: Bosch, Mayhew and Gautié (2010)

Table 4.3   Union and Employer Density and Extension of Agreements

	Trade Union density 1980	Trade Union density 1990	Trade Union density 2003	Change 1980–2000	Employer density* 1994–1996	Employer density 2000	Change 1994/6– 2000	Extension of agreements by the state
USA	22	16	12	–10	0			No
UK	50	39	29	–21	54	40	–14	No
DE	36	33	23	–13	72	63	–9	Few and decreasing
FR	18	10	6	–12	74	74	–	Very high and stable
NL	35	26	26	–9	79	85	+6	Very high and stable
DK	76	71	71	–5	39	52	+	No

*measured by employees covered by employer peak organisations

Source: Bosch, Mayhew and Gautié (2010)

sector concerned. Key is bargaining at the multi-employer level and the influence and power of employers' associations which are committed to this form of bargaining. France is a particularly interesting case. Union density there was never high and is now very low indeed, lower even than in the US. Yet a small number of bargains have an impact which is levered through to other workers via legal extension arrangements in which employers' associations play an important role. From an Anglo-American perspective it is easy to underestimate the importance of employers associations. They have never been a significant feature of the scene in the US whilst, with the decline of multi-employer bargaining, their role in the UK has diminished. The figures (derived from Organisation for Economic Cooperation and Development (OECD) indicators) in Table 4.3 still indicate quite a high employer density in the UK, but this is misleading in that it reflects membership of 'overarching' organisations, especially the Confederation of British Industry, which do not engage in collective bargaining. The table shows that employer density is particularly high in France and the Netherlands.

It is still relatively high in Germany but has diminished. Multi-employer bargaining used to dominate the German labour market, resulting in over 90% coverage. In recent years coverage has declined to about 60% and this is largely because of the weakening of employers' associations and the attendant refusal of many employers, who are feeling the pressures of cost competition, to follow industry agreements. The US has never had any higher level bargaining. As we have seen, multi-employer bargaining disappeared in the UK in the 1980s. Therefore today, as in the US, bargaining, such as it is, is at the company or even establishment level. As a consequence in these two countries the decline in union coverage closely tracked the decline in union density. Though the decline in coverage has been less in the other low paying country, Germany, the pattern of decline there has had a disproportionate effect on the low paid end of the labour market, occurring especially in labour intensive sectors such as the ones covered in the Russell Sage project.

In one of the countries in our study, France, inclusive collective bargaining on its own would not have been sufficient to prevent a high incidence of low pay. Some of the negotiated rates were actually below the low pay threshold and low pay was avoided only by the existence of a national minimum wage that was set at relatively high levels. In mid-2003 it stood at 95% of the low pay threshold and it was received by over 16% of employees.

By contrast the National Minimum Wage in the UK, introduced in 1999, was initially set at a very low level – less than 50% of median hourly earnings. Though there were subsequently substantial up-ratings, by the mid-2000s it still stood at less than 80% of the low pay threshold. It was part of the Labour government's welfare to work strategy which was described in the previous section. As we saw, the philosophy behind the New Deals was to get the unemployed and inactive into work, even at low rates of pay. By getting them back into contact with the world of work, individuals would be on the first rung of the employment ladder and would have the opportunity to climb up it and out of low pay. If, in the meantime, low pay caused house-hold poverty, the state would intervene with generous in-work social security benefits. At first sight a national minimum wage has no role to play in such a strategy. Why not let nature, red in tooth and claw, take its course and simply ameliorate unfortunate consequences with the use of social security payments? In fact the National Minimum Wage had an important, albeit restricted, role to play. Set at a low level, it was likely that it would bite largely on monopsonistic employ-ers who could afford to pay more but who were using their mono-poly power over their workers to pay them less than they were worth. Without minimum wage legislation, the social security system, and ultimately the tax payer, would end up subsidising such employers and indeed encouraging them to exploit their monopsonistic position even more ruthlessly. Monopsony power is likely to be held over workers who are relatively immobile, and in this context it is striking that a large proportion of the low paid in the UK are married women.

Two other countries in our study have a national minimum wage – the Netherlands and the US. In recent years it has not much helped those at the bottom end of the labour market in either country.

In the case of the US, the Federal minimum wage is extremely low and was not up-rated between 1996 and 2007, thus falling in both real and relative terms. In the mid-2000s it stood at only 54% of the low pay threshold and only 1.3% of American employees were at the minimum wage level. Some states set their own minima at higher levels but this does not fundamentally alter the picture. The Dutch minimum wage is significantly higher relative to the low pay thresh-old, 84% of it. But over the years the social partners agreed to various phases of wage restraint with the consequence that the bite of the minimum wage has been reduced. These agreements were components of macroeconomic packages to deal with the consequences of the Dutch Disease and the attendant high unemployment and inactivity levels. The Dutch Disease describes the apparently perverse economic impact of the discovery and exploitation of a valuable natural resource – North Sea gas. Success in this sector pushed up the Dutch exchange rate, which, in turn, massively reduced the international competitiveness of other sectors of Dutch production. Periodically from the early 1980s the minimum wage was sometimes lowered in nominal terms or frozen in real terms. As a consequence its real purchasing power fell by nearly 25% between 1979 and 1997. Some countries have lower minimum rates for young workers, thus reducing its inclusiveness effect. This is particularly striking in the Netherlands where youth rates can be as little as 30% of the adult rate.

Two other components of pay setting institutions are important in determining the extent of inclusiveness or exclusiveness. These are product market regulation or deregulation and employment protection legislation.

In the last 20 years or so product market regulations have been removed or weakened in all developed economies. World Trade Organisation agreements are part of the story. So is EU policy towards creating a single, competitive European market. Agreements within the EU to deregulate the utilities and transport and communications industries were and are being accompanied by various forms of privatisation. In the last five years or so similar deregulatory drives have been more deliberately directed towards services than before. All five European countries have shared such experiences but, if we are to trust OECD indicators, today the UK has the most deregulated product markets followed by the US, Denmark, Germany and the Netherlands. France has experienced the least deregulation. Monopolistic employers might well be better disposed towards unions and offer better terms and conditions than employers exposed to product market competition since they earn higher profits and monopoly rents. Ceteris paribus, therefore, deregulation is threatening to collective organisation and action by stimulating product market competition. A similar threat to union effectiveness is posed by privatisation, given that historically public sector employers have generally been more tolerant of unions than employers in the private sector. The impact of privatisation on industrial relations in the UK is a dramatic case in point. Most importantly, however, the impact of deregulation is heavily 'filtered by the national institutions and attitudes regulating the labour market' (Bosch, Mayhew and Gautié, 2010). Thus it has had significantly less impact on pay and conditions in the Netherlands, Denmark and France than in the UK, the US and Germany.

Employment protection legislation (EPL) could strengthen the bargaining power of workers because, in making it more difficult to dismiss them, it makes labour more of a 'fixed' factor of production. The six countries differ massively in the extent of EPL. The distinction between 'standard' and 'non-standard' work is important here. By 'non-standard' we mean such forms of work as part-time, temporary contract or temporary agency employment. For 'standard' workers employment protection is high in France, Germany and the Netherlands, very low in the US and somewhere in-between in Denmark and the UK. The difference between countries is even more pronounced in the treatment of 'non-regular' workers. In France, for example, it is very difficult to replace regular workers with fixed-term or agency ones in order to evade employment protection law – at least if employers obey the law. It is much easier in the UK and US. If EPL is high and the gap between EPL for standard and non-standard workers is significant, as arguably it is in Germany, then there is a strong incentive for employers to replace the former with the latter, who have little bargaining power and who are therefore likely to obtain poor pay and conditions.

This raises the more general issue of what the Russell Sage researchers called 'exit options' which might allow employers to diminish inclusiveness by treating certain categories of workers less well than others. The European Commission has been well aware of this danger, issuing Directives prohibiting such behaviour with regard to part-time workers and those on fixed-term contracts. As recently as 2008 a third Directive covering agency work was issued. Notwithstanding these European-level developments, practice differs from country to country. Even in France there are two forms of temporary contract which offer little protection against unequal treatment. Since about 30% of unskilled manual workers are temporary, potentially this provides a significant exit option. To give another example, the Germans use mini-jobbers, agency workers and posted workers to attempt to avoid or diminish the impact of formal regulations. The two countries in which such unevenness of treatment is least are the US and Denmark. In the former case this reflects the fact that there is so little protection even for standard workers.

We have described the formal institutions and their importance in each of the countries. Also of importance is the extent to which institutional arrangements and legal requirements are actually enforced or evaded. This is where the power of trade unions may well come into play. In Germany powerful works councillors are central players. In large establishments their influence is considerable, which means that the formal institutions have their full effect. In smaller establishments low wage workers are often not represented and regulations and collective agreements are often not enforced. Similarly in the Netherlands there is considerable evidence that works councillors are not adequately representing low wage workers. In France low trade union density means that there are real problems of enforcement at the establishment or company level. Beyond simple enforcement, lack of union power also means that many French employers may adhere to, for example, minimum wage requirements but compensate by massive work intensification. In contrast to all of the other countries in our study, high union density in Denmark has meant that the formality of inclusiveness is pretty fully reflected in the actuality of the workplace. Interestingly the European Social Survey suggests a very strong negative correlation between the incidence of low pay and the strength of workplace union representation.

To summarise our argument thus far, in the US and the UK pay setting arrangements are not inclusive. Union power is weak and does not stretch much beyond those who are union members. The national minimum wage is low compared to average earnings. Job security is limited. The upshot is that the fortunes of workers are closely related to their individual bargaining power. An important difference between the two countries is in what might be termed the social wage. In the UK workers at the bottom end of the labour market can at least rely on paid holidays, sick leave and maternity leave as well as upon free health care. These benefits are usually not available to workers at the bottom end of the US labour market. In the four continental European countries, pay setting institutions are more inclusive. The extent of inclusiveness is strongly related to the incidence of low pay. The decline of inclusiveness in Germany was accompanied by the emergence of a low pay problem, as it was in the UK.

Other potential explanations of low pay and the issue of employment trade-offs

The substantial differences between countries in the incidence of low pay and in its trend exist despite the fact that all six countries have been facing many of the same external pressures and developments. Their companies have been exposed to significantly greater competition because, inter alia, of globalisation, summarised as the increased share of international trade in national income, and because of massively greater capital mobility between countries. At least in Europe, competition has also increased because of deliberate government policy, such that Europe has moved closer to America in this respect. Such developments have altered the balance of power between unions and employers in favour of the latter. Increasing European integration, specifically progress towards a single market, has been accompanied by the liberalisation and deregulation of capital and product markets. The impact of this upon both the intensity of competition faced by companies and on the bargaining power of workers has been intensified by the accession of central and eastern European countries in 2004. Yet these common pressures seem to have had different implications for those at the bottom end of the labour market in the different countries.

The Russell Sage researchers found that what they called 'country-specific, long run economic structural factors' (Gautié and Schmitt, 2010) had no discernible systematic impact on differences in low pay incidence. Amongst such factors they included the GDP growth rates, levels and rates of growth of productivity, various demographic forces such as the participation rates of women, and labour-capital shares. The one thing which was significant was the dispersion of earnings generally. The wider this was, the greater the incidence of low pay. The greater was the tendency of earnings inequality to increase, the more likely was the incidence of low pay to rise.

It would be absurd to deny some role for macroeconomic forces. For example, the unification of Germany had consequences for the macro economy which helped to weaken the traditional structures of collective bargaining and therefore contributed to a consequential increase in low wage work. In the US the incidence of low wage work is positively related to the business cycle. However, notwithstanding these examples, the more general finding was that similar macro-economic events were mediated in different ways by different national institutions. The same is true for microeconomic and institutional developments. We have already argued that whilst product market deregulation had significantly deleterious impacts on low end workers in the UK where pay setting institutions had become less and less inclusive, more inclusive and stable pay setting institutions in Denmark and the Netherlands meant that such deregulation was accompanied by greater protection for the workers. Similarly the impact of immigration was mediated in different ways in different countries. In 2004 immigrants comprised between 4% and 6% of the labour force in Denmark, France, the Netherlands and the UK. Yet the labour market fortunes of the immigrants and their impact on indigenous low end labour varied according to the inclusiveness of pay setting institutions (Gautié et al, 2010).

A potentially important influence on the extent of low pay is the social security system. Conventional economic analysis tells us that the generosity of out-of-work benefits influences the 'reservation wage' – the lowest rate of pay at which someone is prepared to take a job. The greater the generosity of such benefits, the higher the reservation wage. Generosity has two dimensions. The first is the replacement ratio – the ratio of income whilst out of work to net income in work. The second is the duration of benefit entitlement – that is whether or not there are time limits on the drawing of benefit and how strictly applied those time limits are. The Russell Sage research found some real effects here. For example, it is no accident that Denmark has a very generous out-of-work benefit system and the lowest incidence of low pay. The case of the UK introduces some complexity into any discussion of the role of benefits. Specifically it illustrates the need to make a careful distinction between in-work and out-of-work benefits. As we have already seen, the post-1997 Labour Government developed its social security policy as an integral part of its broader welfare to work strategy. This involved constructing a system of generous in-work benefits. The impact of these, as part of a broader labour market strategy, was to establish a low reservation wage in the UK.

However, despite these two examples, what was striking in the research was that very often changes in the generosity of benefits within individual countries had little apparent impact on the incidence of low pay (Gautié et al, 2010). A case in point is Germany since the mid-1990s. Another is the Netherlands between the mid-1980s and the mid-1990s.

Turning to the apparent lack of wage and employment trade-offs, the methodology employed in the Russell Sage project did not allow for systematic exploration of this issue. However, the comparative data presented in the study at the very least suggest that more careful thought is needed about the existence of such trade-offs. For example, Denmark and the Netherlands have much more generous social security systems than the UK and the US, but Denmark does better than both of the Anglo-Saxon countries on employment and unemployment rates, whilst the Netherlands does no worse. More generally the researchers found little evidence of systematic employment costs within any country when generosity towards the low paid improved. The experience of France is the most supportive to those who believe in pay employment trade-offs. Debate within that country has often been concerned with the adverse employment effects of the national minimum wage. In general, however, our findings suggest that the heterodox view merits further exploration. At this stage one can only speculate on why there is no obvious trade-off. One possible reason the researchers considered has already been mentioned – employers taking the high road in job design. However examples of this are limited in number. A second possibility that was considered was that in some countries wage compression can be thought of as providing a subsidy to workers at the low end of the labour market. A striking example of this would be the tradition of solidaristic wage bargaining in Denmark.

The issue of job design and job quality merits further discussion. In much of the literature on the 'high road', job quality is dependent on production strategy. The basic idea is that for any well defined product the producer can decide on the specification (spec) of that product, along a spectrum from low to high spec. The product becomes higher spec the more characteristics it possesses, the more readily its producer is willing to customise for different segments of the market and the more frequently the characteristics change. The production of a low spec product is closely associated with Fordist methods, which depend on achieving competitive advantage via economies of scale derived from long production runs. Because much the same thing is produced year after year, management can bundle the tasks that need to be performed into jobs which are predominantly low skilled. Price is the key – the producer with the lowest price wins. Price depends on unit labour costs, which in turn depend upon productivity and labour costs broadly defined. By contrast the high spec product cannot rely upon long production runs because its nature is frequently changing. For the same reason skill and capability cannot be designed out of the jobs involved. Workers need to be capable, adaptable and innovative. Thus the skill content of production will be higher and competitiveness will not be dependent simply upon the price but upon the nature of the product itself – the product niche. Thus the greater the percentage of production, in any economy, which is high spec, the greater the proportion of jobs which are higher skilled and better paid. The 'high skills vision' espoused by all governments in the developed world is based upon this argument. In the modern world economy, developing countries will compete effectively at the low spec end. A country which wants to be internationally competitive and, at the same time, have a relatively low dispersion of earnings needs to move as much of its production as possible to the high spec end.

This suggests an escape route for the low paid. Yet one wonders how realistic this is. Inevitably some areas of production will be low spec even in developed economies. More worryingly, some of the Russell Sage case studies suggest that higher spec products do not necessarily lead to higher spec jobs. The hotel industry is a case in point. Job quality in the higher grade hotels was not noticeably better than in the low grade ones. This is not to say that policymakers should not attempt to lever up the quality of production. Such moves are important both for distributional reasons and to boost international competitiveness. However, we are arguing that they may have little impact on those at the very bottom of the labour market.

Conclusions

The most important conclusion to be drawn from the Russell Sage study is that institutions, broadly defined, do matter. It is not single institutions that are decisive but the entire package. Historically some countries have had more inclusive pay setting institutions than others. Inclusivity is negatively related to the incidence of low pay.

Recall that one of the central questions posed by the Russell Sage Foundation was whether workers who performed essential functions like cleaning hotels or hospitals or serving in shops necessarily have to perform them in jobs which have poor pay and conditions and negligible prospects. What this study reveals is that workers in such activities get a much better deal in some countries than others. It also shows that this is not necessarily 'paid for' by different job design leading to higher productivity. And yet it is not obvious that the employment consequences usually expected in conventional economic analysis are inevitably present.

This raises an obvious question. Are benign institutions sustainable or have we been observing a 'disequilibrium' situation? Will global economic forces preside over a form of institutional Darwinianism, where national systems converge on the Anglo-American model? Two national systems have become noticeably less inclusive during the last 30 years – the German and the British. Both systems started to totter in unfavourable macroeconomic climes. In the case of Britain, this was the early 1980s recession. In the case of Germany it was in the period after unification. What is unclear is whether these crises inevitably led institutional disintegration or whether the mediation of a new dominant political and socio-economic ideology was the critical factor. In other words were there viable alternative responses to what were undoubtedly major macro and structural dilemmas in both countries? The experiences of France and Denmark suggest that the answer to this question is possibly 'yes'. But both countries had to accept trade-offs. In the case of France it probably was lower employment rates than otherwise. In the case of Denmark, it was the apparent acceptance of stronger labour market players that the relative rewards for this strength were less than in some other countries. Only time will tell whether their systems are stable. But what the Russell Sage study has demonstrated is that it is much easier to destroy benign institutions than it is to construct them.

Writing this chapter in the UK, the obvious question occurs about possible UK policy responses to the low pay problem in that country. The starting assumption is that there is a desire to improve the lot of the low paid. The next is that it would be absurd to expect wholesale changes in ideologies and systems. Therefore we are engaged in a perhaps limited art of the possible. We are not going to witness a reconstruction of inclusive collective bargaining institutions or even a significant revival of union power. The two most promising routes are probably via public sector employment and via the national minimum wage. Public sector employers could be charged with improving job quality and improving pay and conditions. However, this is not as easy as it sounds; not only because of budgetary considerations but also because of knock-on effects to the private labour market. The danger of increasing the national minimum wage are that it will start to impact on larger and larger numbers of employers who are not monopsonists and therefore start to have unfavourable employment consequences. Nevertheless, used carefully, it is the most promising avenue. It is no coincidence that debate about the merits of introducing a national minimum wage has only recently reached Germany, as their formerly benign pay institutions started to unravel.

References

Appelbaum, E., Bernhardt, A. and Murnane, R. (eds) (2003) *Low Wage America: How Employers are Reshaping Opportunity in the Workplace*, New York: Russell Sage.

Bosch, G., Mayhew, K. and Gautié, J. (2010) 'Industrial relations, legal regulations and wage setting', in Gautié, J. and Schmitt, J. (eds) (2010) *Low Wage Work in the Wealthy World*, New York: Russell Sage.

Bosch, G. and Weinkopf, C. (eds) (2008) *Low Wage Work in Germany*, New York: Russell Sage.

Caroli, E. and Gautié, J. (eds) (2008) *Low Wage Work in France*, New York: Russell Sage.

Gautié, J. and Schmitt, J. (eds.) (2010) *Low Wage Work in the Wealthy World*, New York: Russell Sage.

Gautié, J., Westergaard-Nielsen, N., Schmitt, J. and Mayhew, K. (2010) 'The impact of institutions on the supply side of the low wage labour market', in Gautié, J. and Schmitt, J. (eds) (2010) *Low Wage Work in the Wealthy World*, New York: Russell Sage.

Lloyd, C., Mason, G. and Mayhew, K. (eds) (2008) *Low Wage Work in the UK*, New York: Russell Sage.

Mason, G. and Salverda, W. (2010) 'Low pay, living standards and employment', in Gautié, J., and Schmitt, J. (eds) (2010) *Low Wage Work in the Wealthy World*, New York: Russell Sage.

Salverda, W., van Klaveren, M. and van der Meer, M. (eds) (2008) *Low Wage Work in the Netherlands*, New York: Russell Sage.

Westergaard-Nielsen, N. (ed.) (2008) *Low Wage Work in Denmark*, New York: Russell Sage.

5
New Ways of Working: Changing Labour Markets in 21st Century New Zealand

Paul Spoonley

The late twentieth century heralded some significant changes in the nature of production and ownership in the New Zealand economy as well as labour market regulation and the employment contract. By the turn of the century, various forms of non-standard employment had begun to edge out what had constituted standard work through the mid-part of the century. Salaried or waged work which occurred in a five day working week and which involved an expectation of ongoing employment in an industry or occupation over a working life dominated from the late 1940s until the substantial economic changes that occurred from the mid-1980s. Increasingly, a variety of non-standard forms of work – part-time, contract, temporary, casual, portfolio – grew in significance as more New Zealanders engaged in the labour market via these forms of employment. This raised questions about the nature of labour market engagement: ('good' versus 'bad' jobs); the precariousness of employment; returns on labour; the effects of these new forms of work on particular groups (youth, ethnic minorities, women); whether entry into the labour market via non-standard options contributed to labour market scarring; and whether the nature of the engagement was a matter of choice or a forced option. In many respects, these questions remain unanswered in a New Zealand context, as does the issue of whether the labour market reforms of the 1980s and 1990s has produced the intended flexible workforce or provided economic benefits, especially given poor labour productivity and the impacts of low waged work on individuals and households.

If a concern with labour flexibility characterised the 1990s, it changed as labour supply became an issue. Between 2000 and 2008,

New Zealand experienced significant shortages of labour, both in terms of the quantum available but also in terms of the quality of the human capital pool relative to labour demand. The mismatch of supply and demand was underlined by the significant skills shortage and highlighted issues concerning the appropriateness of education and training, the ability of employers (especially in small and medium sized companies) to recruit and retain appropriate labour and the nature of information flows between industries/employers and job seekers. Labour market adjustments, both as a product of informal shifts in behaviour as well as modifications in policy, have partially addressed these new circumstances but there remain major gaps or pressures, further complicated by the extensive changes that accompanied the global economic crises from 2008. These ongoing issues include: the role of immigrant labour in meeting New Zealand's skill requirements and the reluctance of employers to see immigrants as desirable employees; the appropriateness of education and training given changing labour demand; generational gaps in attitudes towards employment; debates about the nature of generic or soft skills and who is responsible for ensuring that such skills are available in terms of labour supply; the strategies of both job seekers and employers; and a policy lag between changes and labour market activation policies and strategies.

These shifts in the nature of labour market engagement and the employment contract raise some fundamental questions about the transformation of economic production and labour. As Castells (1996) has noted, the evolution of new forms of a globalised capitalism combined with a technology revolution have prompted a new organisational logic:

> ...the technological and managerial transformation of labour... [has become] the main lever by which the process of globalization affect[s] society at large (Castells, 1996, p.201).

While the nature of these broader societal changes are not explored in any depth here, there is an interesting debate concerning how best to describe what we are witnessing in relation to New Zealand's domestic labour markets. The standardised labour contract and conditions of a mid-twentieth century Fordism is being replaced by the more individualised and flexible employment of the twenty-first century, giving rise to the arguments that a flexible specialisation (Spoonley and Davidson, 2004) of a reflexive modernity (Beck, 1992; Castells, 1996) is in evidence. The transformation of employment reflects a more fundamental societal transformation. Lifetime employment is replaced by a 'disposable labour force that can be automated, and/or hired/fired/offshored depending upon market demand and labour costs' (Castells, 1996, p.267).

> In common with the disaggregation and individualisation of labour described by Castells, Beck's account of 'reflexive modernity' is derived in part on the temporal destandardisation of labour based on part-time and temporary employment (Doogan, 2001, p.420).

Doogan (2001) is one of those who is not convinced that there is such a transformation, and he argues that there are major continuities in labour market engagement, and that some of the new forms of working actually increase attachment, rather than lead to insecurity or a set of common experiences amongst a labour periphery. What follows is an exploration of the nature and growth of non-standard work. The extent of these changes suggest that there is a transformation occurring in how New Zealanders work although Doogan is correct to the extent that not all are impacted – there are still many standard workers – and that not all non-standard workers are part of a peripheral workforce that experience insecure and low paid employment. Non-standard work is a preferred and profitable option for some.

Non-standard work: Definitional challenges

The variety of forms of non-standard work share little in common except that they depart from the nature and conditions expected of standard work. In this sense, it is an inadequate categorisation because it implies a residual grouping of highly variable employment situations and contracts. Further, 'non-standard labour is not a neutral expression...because it implicitly assumes that a common notion exists of what standard labour is' (Dekker and Kaiser, 2000, p.1) and that non-standard work is a less desirable option. However, the power of the description lies in the way that it signals a departure from the post-war social contract that was built around guarantees of employment stability. It reflects new demand-led concerns to minimise labour costs and to maximise labour flexibility. For some, it is a preferred option; for many, it is the only option and it represents a number of unsatisfactory characteristics: insecurity, low pay, poor career options. Non-standard work is inevitably 'variable, and often uncertain, discontinuous and episodic' so that the employment protection and employment regulation of the twentieth century which were built around an assumption of 'stable work temporality' (Gottfried, 2008, p.194) has been progressively displaced to enhance labour flexibility.

Non-standard work is not new. Options such as part-time, casual or portfolio working have long existed. And they were not a minor part of labour market engagement in the early parts of the twentieth century, especially given the highly mobile population of males involved in itinerant employment from the late nineteenth century in an economy that was dominated by primary production. In the case of Maori, most were involved in waged labour as non-standard workers until the Second World War as secondary, rural labour. But standard work employment dominated through the mid-decades of the twentieth century. Since 1987, what has changed in many western societies is the fact that 'nonstandard employment reflect[s] a quantitatively larger share of total employment and mark[s] a qualitative shift in expectations about the rules governing contractual rights, risks and responsibilities deviating from the norms established as part of the post-war social contract' (Gottfried, 2008, pp.179–180).

It is difficult to know how best to categorise these more significant forms of labour market engagement; by reference to the fact that they are different to what occurred before ('standard' versus 'nonstandard') or in relation to the characteristics of this employment ('insecure', 'precarious', 'casualised'). For the moment, the term 'nonstandard' work is retained, in part because it does represent a widely used description, but also because it is able to be disassembled into quite specific categories of employment. The major forms of nonstandard work include:

- Part-time work, in New Zealand's case defined as those working less than 30 hours in any given week. There are distinct gendered patterns to part-time work although the dominance of a particular gender varies across the working life-course (Gottfried, 2008).

- Temporary or casual work which might include both direct-hires as well as via an agency (although this might be specifically identified as third party employment). The defining characteristic is that there is 'neither explicit nor implicit contractual commitments for continuous employment' (Gottfried, 2008, p.186). This can vary from fixed-term contracts where there is an explicit but still limited contract of employment through to various forms of casual employment which might or might not entail an explicit contract and which could include variable hours on a daily, weekly or monthly basis. Casual workers are those who are hired on a periodic basis as need arises, temporary workers are those who are hired for relatively short but unspecified periods while fixed-term are those who are hired for a specified period with an end date or for a particular project (WEB, 2004).
- Portfolio or multiple job holding. This includes any employment, of whatever nature (casual, fixed, permanent), that involves two or more employers or businesses. It might be as a waged or salaried employee but there are growing numbers of self-employed involved in multiple employment, especially on a contract for service.
- Own account self-employment. This includes those who are self-employed but have no employees. Self-employment as a generic option has increased through the 1990s but the own account form has seen particularly strong growth, particularly as older workers struggle to re-enter the labour market and own account self-employment becomes the only option.

Good jobs or bad jobs

The literature demonstrates two very different approaches to the question of whether non-standard employment is, by definition, precarious work, and therefore a departure from the post-war social contract that guaranteed high levels of employment protection, which saw the state mediate the employment relations of industries or specific workplaces and which produced relatively high levels of employment stability.

Nonstandard work means that fewer workers qualify for protections and more workers risk uncertain economic futures. The ubiquity of nonstandard employment threatens the security of standard employment. This changing nature of work renders old systems of social protection and welfare as inappropriate to new realities (Gottfried, 2008, p.181).

The tension between these century-old (in some instances, such as arbitration and conciliation) systems and employer/industry concerns with labour flexibility became apparent during the 1980s and the 1990s. Bururu (1999) noted that there were concerns through the 1990s in New Zealand at the impacts of labour market regulation on matters such as the ease of hiring and firing, the increase in non-wage compliance costs and the rigidity of working arrangements (Butcher, 2002, p.5). There was increasing pressure to alter the nature of the employment contract and of workplace protection, and the initial moves came from a reforming Labour Government in the late 1980s, and then were significantly expanded by a National Government in the early 1990s. The question then, and now, is whether these moves to enhance labour flexibility contributed to an increase in 'bad' jobs, jobs that were defined by their precariousness and/or poor returns. Before turning to the issue of precariousness, it is important to acknowledge that change was not simply driven by employer demand; there are a number of supply (or push) side considerations. These push factors included the growing number of women in the labour force, the non-transferable skills of some workers in some industries, high marginal rates of personal taxation, rising unemployment and a growing interest in work-life balance issues (Butcher, 2002). Self-employment, or part-time work, for example, were attractive options for some.

Precariousness is defined by the fact that employment can be terminated with little or no notice by an employer, that the hours and functions of employment can be changed at short notice, that earnings are uncertain and low, that there is no (or little) protection against unacceptable working practices and that there is limited opportunity to gain skills or access education (Tucker, 2002). The International Labour Organisation definition stresses the casual nature of the employment and the fact that the employment could be ended at short notice (quoted in Tucker, 2002, p.15). Precarious employment tends to be concentrated in certain areas of the labour market (WEB, 2004) which includes less skilled work in service employment such as care or cleaning or manual employment in all sectors. In New Zealand, this is apparent in seasonal employment as well as significant parts of the service economy where demand is variable and employment options parallel this demand. In addition, '...smaller firms are more likely to hire workers on casual or temporary contracts than are medium or large-sized firms' (WEB, 2004, p.8).

There is also an important subjective dimension to how employees experience precariousness:

> ...it is the experience of the form of work, in its whole work context and in the life of the employee, which leads to the feeling of being in precarious employment. There is thus a subjective, or *internal* indicator of precariousness (WEB, 2004, p.69; emphasis in original).

This is associated with employment dissatisfaction as insecurity leads to a 'deterioration in the psychological contract between employer and employee' (Burchell, Nolan and Wichert, quoted in Kaiser, 2002, p.7). Kaiser (2002, p.28) goes on to suggest non-standard employment such as fixed-term and part-time employment 'imply a job-satisfaction loss' and while 'different self-employment constellations are negatively correlated with...reported job security and with job satisfaction', there is not an inevitable correlation. To conclude, the insecurity or precariousness of employment occurs along three dimensions: as a property of jobs; as a property of the environment in which these jobs exist; and as a reflection of the subjective experience of workers (Heery and Salmon, quoted in Doogan, 2001, p.436).

Precariousness is an important dimension of non-standard work – but it is also something that standard workers are not immune from. But there is an important qualification. Some choose non-standard employment for a number of personal and work reasons. Perhaps the critical distinction is whether non-standard work is a desirable employment option – or not. In relation to the growth of part-time work, for example, the question is whether the work is voluntary or involuntary.

> The first group consists of those who have chosen to find employment that offers them part-time work for a variety of reasons ranging from child or elder care to being financially able to take on part-time work. The second group, the involuntary part-timers, are those who have taken part-time work because they were unable to find full-time work for reasons such as the work not

accommodating their needs or being in their field (McOrmond, 2004, p.27).

Across the spectrum of non-standard work, there will be those who chose to work in this way because it suits their personal circumstances while for others, it is a forced option.

The empirical research suggests that there are two divergent experiences of non-standard forms of work. Cohen and Mallon (1999) talk of participants (who worked as portfolio workers) as experiencing freedom in two ways: freedom from employers, departments and organisations and freedom to 'create, develop, manage'. But in further discussing these 'freedoms', they also noted that they saw their previous employment and organisations in a different light (not **as** restrictive as previously thought) and that there were 'definite constraints and limitations, including greater insecurity, irregular working patterns and a feeling of being tied to their work on an everyday, operational scale' (Scase and Goffee, quoted in Cohen and Mallon, 1999, p.340). In this sense, career was being redefined, especially given that there was a 'lack of wider social approval' (Cohen and Mallon, 1999, p.341). This suggests that there are different experiences and trajectories for those engaged in non-standard work. Simply, there are those for whom variants of non-standard work provide an opportunity to engage in ways of working which are satisfying and financially rewarding while for others, it represents a forced option with its precarious, low-waged nature and little future in terms of career advancement or improved pay. However, the literature on 'good' non-standard employment tends to focus on skilled professionals and various forms of self-employment and 'provides an extremely optimistic picture of the self-determined, self-actualised worker variously described as a 'symbolic analyst' (Reich), an 'intelligence' (Handy) and a 'knowledge worker' (Jones, quoted in Mckeown, 2003, p.2).

Mckeown (2003) goes on to suggest that there are three options rather than two, with some forms of non-standard work acting as traps with low earnings, others as a transitional option before gaining permanent employment and then as preferred career option for those able and ambitious. However, given that the restructuring of employment and the redundancies which have prompted many of these shifts, even skilled workers who move from standard to non-standard employment are experiencing downward mobility, income variability and greater levels of precariousness (Mckeown, 2003).

It is hard to escape the conclusion that the increase in non-standard work, driven as it has been by the goal of increasing labour flexibility, has produced significantly more 'bad' jobs, identified by their precariousness. There is evidence that supports Beck's argument about the temporal destandardisation of employment producing insecurity and individual stress.

New ways of working?

One key issue is the extent to which non-standard working is new at all. Certainly, the New Zealand experience (see below) is that there were many in the itinerant primary workforce who can be classified as non-standard workers, especially in relation to the labour market engagement of Maori until the post-war period. From the 1940s through to the 1970s, standard forms of employment predominated. With the economic restructuring of the 1970s and 1980s, non-standard work gained in importance again. As Tucker (2002, p.17) notes:

> It is widely argued that non-standard work forms are not new.... They were common until the 1940s, declined in importance during the economic growth years of the 1950s through to the mid-1970s, and re-emerged in the late 1970s. This was due in part of the expansion of part-time work and the beginnings of corporate downsizing in the 1970s and 1980s. Since then non-standard work forms have continued to gain in momentum.

This suggests that the period of mass employment underpinned by the protections of employment regulation and the welfare state might prove to be a period of exceptionalism, sandwiched by periods in which non-standard work is a predominant or widely experienced form of labour market engagement. To this extent, non-standard work is not new. But the nature of a contemporary globalised capitalism and the implications for labour engagement and flows is markedly different to the pre-1940s situation. The form non-standard work takes, who participates and contextual considerations are all very different. It is helpful to consider the experiences of particular groups.

Youth

The non-linear paths into employment of youth and their involvement in non-standard work has attracted a lot of attention. The question of whether entry into the labour market is now significantly different from the past and whether entry via non-standard employment produces subsequent scarring are important policy and research questions. The literature (see Leggatt-Cook, 2005; Osborne and Warren, 2006) highlights the variable paths to employment for youth, with extended education and training, shifts between various sorts of employment and education/training, either as self-chosen or as part of work schemes, and the precarious nature and low pay of youth labour markets. However, the question of how best to characterise the transition from school/tertiary institutions to work is still a matter of debate. Furlong et al (see Goodwin and O'Connor, 2005, p.206) has queried whether the assumed non-linearity and complexity is applicable to all contemporary transitions for youth. They point out that for some, there is still a linearity and smoothness of the transition. This gives rise to the issue of whether this linearity and smoothness existed more extensively in the past. Rather, there might have always been a mix of transitional options or paths (Goodwin and O'Connor, 2005). Vickerstaff (2003) compares the contemporary experience of apprenticeships with that of the past (mid-twentieth century), and argues that they are not so different. Essentially, she notes that those with few or poor educational qualifications currently move between employment, unemployment and various training options whereas those in the past tended to move from job to job. However, it is accepted that youth transitions have now become more extended, especially as there are greater numbers staying at school or attending some post-compulsory education or training. New Zealand research (Dupuis and McLaren, 2006; Leggatt-Cook, 2005) points to participation in post-compulsory education as a major reason for the engagement of youth in temporary, casual or part-time work. As youth shift between work and education or training, they experience 'serial short-life engagements' (Ferguson et al, 2000, p.283).

This extended – and more diverse – set of transitions means that youth are remaining financially dependent on families for longer periods (Goodwin and O'Connor, 2005). Individual trajectories might be best characterised as more diverse, involving a variety of work and non-work experiences or positions, including '...study, temporary employment, unemployment, training, self-employment, part-time or full-time employment, "fiddly jobs" in the black economy' (Bradley and Devadason, 2008, p.120). As Bradley and Devadason (2008, p.120) conclude, '[t]here is no simple linear route to adult employment and economic independence'.

There are important generational shifts in attitudes to work with an emphasis amongst Generation Y on a balance between work and non-work life aspects, a value placed on getting experience, and a reluctance to commit to a single company (see Leggatt-Cook, 2005). There is a question of whether new entrants to the labour market seek self-actualisation and autonomy by repeated job switching as part of a trial stage (see Mckeown, 2003). The decade of the 1990s and the period since 2008 suggests that the appeal of the 'logic of autonomy' (see Bogenhold and Staber, quoted in Mckeown, 2003, p.3) whereby young skilled professionals at least are looking to maximise personal autonomy might have been less important than the impacts of declining labour demand, much tighter labour markets and the redundancies associated with ongoing sector adjustments. But this does suggest new subjectivities as 'young people are able to normalize these experiences of serial short-life engagements with courses and jobs...' (Fergusson et al, 2000, p.283) producing a discourse of 'normalized dislocation' (Fergusson et al, 2000,p.289).

The variable experiences of education to employment transitions and of non-standard work for youth is apparent in New Zealand research. Local research on multiple job holding and young people found that many were ambivalent about why they held these jobs (Osborne and Warren, 2006). Some were certainly keen to work this way while others saw it as a transitional option before getting something more appropriate. The result is that there were multiple reasons and experiences, some positive and many negative, for multiple job holding amongst younger (18–34 years) New Zealanders.

> Individual reasons for multiple job holding related to young peoples' life cycle stage, desire to broaden work skills and experience, general disposition and expectations about work, and extra financial needs. Some saw multiple job holding as a transitional work arrangement while studying or waiting for the 'right job to come along' (Osborne and Warren, 2006, np).

There were sector-related reasons so those in the creative sector (as one example) looked elsewhere to obtain income that could support their ambitions.

Youth transitions to employment are now more diverse and non-linear than in the past, even if we accept that the past was not as linear and smooth as once assumed. Moreover, there is now evidence to indicate that there is a youth labour market which has particular characteristics (Pollock, 1997). Moreover, delayed entry due to extended periods of education and training, and the nature of the youth labour market has the effect of prolonged financial dependency on families and/or the state and greater levels of engagement in non-standard employment.

Gender

There are a number of considerations. One is that the growth in non-standard occupations has occurred in those that are female dominated. These include domestic services such as child or elder care and cleaning, or parts of the health and educational sectors. Almost half of the growth in non-standard employment in the EU involved females who were in fixed-term or temporary contracts (McOrmond, 2004, p.30) while two-thirds of those engaged in non-standard work were female (Kaiser, n.d., p.6). The second reason is that non-standard forms of employment are attractive to women who are entering or re-entering the workforce for a number of personal reasons. Domestic care responsibilities, which are still predominantly associated with females, make part-time employment an option for those wanting to combine these responsibilities with employment. These developments were also associated with major changes in the composition of households. In the 1940s and 1950s, less than 10% of married women were in paid employment with the rest engaged in domestic duties. By the 2001 census, only 8% of New Zealand adults lived in 'traditional breadwinner couple [household] where the man was in full-time work and the woman was not in the labour force at all' (McPherson, 2004, p.3). This has contributed to female labour force participation given the income requirements of households while females remain largely responsible for domestic care. In addition, the youth labour market is gendered. Employment for young men has declined while employment for young women has increased, although it is not a 'trade-off' because males have lost full-time employment while females have gained part-time and contract employment (Pollock, 1997).

The numbers of women engaged in the labour force in non-standard employment has been a major factor in the growth of such employment in the last three decades although 'as part-time and temporary work arrangements have spread, the proportion of men with such employment has risen, thus narrowing the difference between the sexes' (Krahn, 1995, p.41). The growth in non-standard work, especially forms such as part-time work, has been particularly associated with growing female labour market participation. But the deindustrialisation and downsizing of the 1990s and since has also impacted on men and produced greater participation in categories of non-standard work such as casual, contract and own account self-employed.

Ethnicity

The engagement of many Maori in standard work lasted for a relatively brief period, essentially from 1945 through to 1987. But Maori involvement in non-standard work did not cease in 1945, especially as Maori were disproportionately involved as seasonal labour in primary production. But rural-urban migration to provide semi and unskilled labour in the expanding urban manufacturing industries from the 1960s and the resulting employment was curtailed by the economic changes from the mid-1980s. The economic reforms of the 1984 Labour Government hit Maori particularly hard. A similar experience occurred with those Pacific peoples who migrated in the 1960s and 1970s. During the 1986–91 period, 28,347 (19.6%) of Maori workers lost their jobs, while the labour force participation rate for Pacific peoples dropped from 71% to 54%. The effect was that between 1986 and 2001, the numbers of Maori engaged in non-standard work grew considerably (e.g., Maori in part-time work, increased from 15% to 33.6%). As the 2008 economic crises unravelled, similar job losses and/or a shift from standard to non-standard work was apparent for Maori and Pacific peoples at rates much higher than for Pakeha.

The New Zealand experience of non-standard work

New Zealand experienced major transformations in the way that the labour market operated and was regulated in the late 1980s and 1990s. As Rasmussen, Lind and Visser (2004, p.640) comment: '[t]he combination of comprehensive reforms and economic stagnation led to widespread labour market adjustments and working time patterns'. The 'labour market reforms...transformed the country from one of the most highly regulated to one of the most deregulated countries in the OECD'.

With the help of James Newell, the Labour Market Dynamics Research Programme sought to track the resulting changes in the New Zealand labour market from the 1980s through to 2006, essentially to see if there were shifts from standard employment to non-standard employment. Using census material, standard work was defined as those who were employed full-time for a wage or salary in one job and who worked more than 30 hours and less than 50 hours per week. By definition, everyone else was involved in non-standard work. This included those working less than 30 hours per week or those on more than 50 hours, unpaid workers in a family business, and the self-employed. The discussion that follows draws on this material. However, in terms of non-standard work there are certain limitations in the available statistics. For example, there are no statistics available on important aspects of non-standard work such as casual or temporary employment, and as Baines and Newell (2005, p.2) note: 'the statistics on multiple job holding have not evolved beyond the point of recognising that the phenomenon exists'. The statistical information indicates that a person has more than one job but there is no record of how many jobs are involved.

In the period which spans the initial stage of labour market change there is evidence that there were substantial shifts in the nature of labour market engagement. Between 1981 and 1986, the proportion employed in standard work dropped by 22.8%, illustrating the impact of the Labour Government's 'reforms' as state sector employment declined, deindustrialisation became obvious and the levels of employment dropped or altered. Another more modest drop occurred in the 1991 and 1996 period when those in standard work declined by 9.2%. As the labour market experienced significant shortages in labour supply after 2000, there was a slight reversal of the trends from standard to non-standard employment; standard employment grew by 3.8%. The overall effect is that in 1981, 77.2% of New Zealanders were engaged in standard work but this had dropped to 45.2% by 2006.

Different dynamics are apparent in the various stages of these shifts. In the mid-1980s, the decrease in standard workers reflected a decrease in full-time work of 8.4% and a decline of 4.4% of salaried and waged workers as employment contracted in the newly privatised organisations or the numbers employed in particular industries declined. In the shift away from standard work in the 1990s, the major shifts occurred in those working full-time (those on less than 30 hours per week increased by 4.7% as part-time work replaced full-time work) and those working more than 50 hours per week increased (2.8%), placing New Zealand second only to Japan in terms of a long hours working culture.

In the 25 year period between 1981 and 2006, standard employment dropped from 77.2% to less than half (45.4%) while non-standard work involved about one worker in 5 (22.8%) at the beginning of the period but over half of all workers were non-standard by 2006 (54.6%; see Table 5.1). Some categories such as self-employed changed little, but the self-employed with no employees (own account self-employed) doubled (7.3% to 12.2%), unpaid workers in a family business quadrupled and part-time work went from 6.3% to 22.4%.

There were important age differences in these shifts. In 1981, more than 80% of 15 to 19 year olds were engaged in some form of standard work but this began to change through the 1990s and so by 2006, only 30% of this age group were engaged in such work. This reflects a number of factors, including the significant increases in those staying at school or going from compulsory education on to further education or training. But this voluntary withdrawal from the labour market was also accompanied by the increasingly poor labour market engagement of youth. In the 2009 recession, almost 20% of those under 20 years of age were unemployed and those under 24 years who were unemployed made up almost half of all unemployed. In general, those entering work for the first time were more likely to be non-standard workers, as they juggled further education and training with

Table 5.1   The Proportions Involved in Standard and Non-standard Work, 1981–2006

	1981	1991	2001	2006
Standard work[1]	77.2	50.2	41.6	45.4
Non-standard work	22.8	49.8	58.4	54.6
Part-time	6.3	17.7	22.9	22.4

1 Defined as wages/salaried, 30–50 hours per week, not multiple job holders

employment, or they gained their first experiences of employment through non-standard work options. Those exiting employment were also likely to experience non-standard employment.

Baines and Newell (2005) tend to emphasise the supply side decisions as an explanation for the growth of non-standard work in New Zealand, specifically as a 'pathway of entry to and exit from the labour force and as an adaptation to sustain livelihoods by applying certain types of specialist skills in diversifying circumstances' (Baines and Newell, 2005, p.64). But there were also important structural changes taking place. In the wake of the reforms in the mid-1980s, some industries were employing a lot fewer workers by 1991 than they had five years previously. The impacts were most obvious in those sectors which were either privatised or which no longer were protected. The primary sector lost 21,000 (12%) jobs, building and construction 18,000 (17%), transport, storage and communication 27,000 (24%) and manufacturing 83,400 (26%). The loss of these 150,000 jobs was compensated by the 50,000 additional people employed in financial services and community and social services. WEB (2004, p.9) argues that demand side factors provide a more likely explanation of these shifts, and especially the growth of casual and temporary employment, and they stress two particular aspects: cost minimisation and accommodating fluctuating demand. Furthermore, small firms have fewer options in terms of permanent employment and dismissal and will therefore have more workers on temporary and casual contracts (WEB, 2004, p.9).

By 2006, non-standard work arrangements involved more than half of all New Zealanders who were employed. How did those responsible for government research and policy (and others) respond to the emerging evidence of these developments? The Prime Ministerial Task Force on Employment (1994) was among the first to note that non-standard work was becoming more common although there was no indication of exactly how significant non-standard work was. As Butcher (2002) notes, the Task Force did express some concerns, including the fact that this involved less secure and lower-paid employment, with less access to employment benefits such as protection. The next major studies were from Brosnan and Walsh (1996) and Nick Carroll (1999). Brosnan and Walsh were interested in the way that labour market regulation and policy changes had impacted on labour market participation although they tended to discount the possibility that the Employment Contracts Act had contributed to the casualisation of the female work force (Butcher, 2002). They were also sceptical of any suggestion that non-standard work was growing in significance. Carroll, followed by Tucker (2002) reflected a growing, but still limited, interest from inside the government, in this case from the Department of Labour, in non-standard work. Both were engaged in the question of how non-standard work might be defined, the size of the non-standard workforce and who might be engaged in such work. Nick Carroll (1999) explored what the term might mean and the evidence for non-standard work as part of the labour market. This was followed by Deborah Tucker (2002) when she conducted an extensive review of the available literature. She surveyed 'the literature around 'non-standard' and 'precarious' employment and provided an introduction to the issues concerning the interface between some types of non-standard employment and 'precariousness' (Tucker, 2002, p.2). The hesitancy of what was to follow in the Tucker report was signalled by the use of quotation marks, although there is some excellent material provided. This hesitancy was also apparent in a reluctance to see non-standard work as a significant element of contemporary employment in New Zealand.

The majority of both the international and domestic literature is in agreement that non-standard employment has increased over the last 15 to 20 years. Views differ, however, as to the actual extent of the increase and the adequacy of national datasets, because of disagreement over definitional and measurement issues (Tucker, 2002). Moreover, there has been an ongoing reluctance locally to concede that non-standard work has now become a major feature of employment in New Zealand. In part, this reflects a certain orthodoxy since the late 1980s that flexible labour is critical to firm, industry and national economic competitiveness. It might also reflect the policy challenges in terms of providing options that address the very different circumstances of the various forms of non-standard work, especially if flexibility is not to be compromised. One of the issues that is disputed is whether non-standard work inevitably leads to 'bad' jobs. The enthusiasm of Carroll and Tucker to explore such issues was not shared more generally by other researchers and policy analysts, and not by the relevant ministers. One of the issues was that much of the policy framework was built around explicit or implicit assumptions of full-time paid employment, and accommodating non-standard work was a significant challenge.

Portfolio working: A case study

One area that has been researched in New Zealand is that of portfolio working, or as it tends to be called locally, multiple job holding. In a major research project, Taylor Baines and Associates provided some compelling examples of the impact of multiple job holding in New Zealand, with a particular focus on primary production. In 1981, 4.2% of New Zealanders had multiple jobs and this had increased to 10.1% by 2001. The authors of one report (Baines and Newell, 2005) argue that the growth had eased by 2000 and possibly plateaued. They noted that there are important gender differences. In 1981, men were slightly more likely than women to be involved in multiple job holding (4.4% versus 4%) but that 'women embraced multiple jobs more rapidly than men until 1996' (Baines and Newell, 2005, p.iv). By 2001, 10.7% of women were portfolio workers compared to 9.5% of men. In terms of ethnicity, Pakeha were the most likely to be multiple job holders (11.1% versus Maori as the next group at 7.2%, followed by Asians at 6.5% and Pacific peoples at 3.8%). In the 1980s, those aged 35–39 were most likely to be portfolio workers but this had changed significantly by 2001; 15–16 year olds and those 75 years and older now had rates of multiple job holding which saw them join the 40–44 age group as those having high rates. Baines and Newell have also looked at socio-economic status and multiple job holding. They conclude:

> It appears that throughout the 1980s, adoption of multiple job holding may have represented an economic adaptation by lower socio-economic status groups to increasingly stringent labour market circumstances (combining removal of agricultural subsidies from the struggling farm sector, restructuring of previously labour-intensive government departments, recession and the removal of protections in low-skill manufacturing industries). In the 1990s, the largest increases in MJH came at the top (SEI 7&8) and bottom (SEI 2) of [the] SEI scale... One set of drivers influenced higher income professionals – perhaps sharing specialist skills between different organisations, or maximising individual skills across a range of work opportunities, albeit over longer hours. The

other set of drivers influenced the low skill occupations – maximising income also through longer hours and splicing part-time jobs into a satisfactory livelihood (Baines and Newell, 2005, p.60).

A particular focus in this project concerned rural experiences of multiple job holding, giving it a very New Zealand feel but also a sense of how different parts of the economy, with their specific labour markets, were adjusting to the changes of recent decades. The political economy and the labour requirements of primary production had been changing for some time, although as elsewhere, the key years were 1986–88, the so-called 'rural downturn' (Robertson, Perkins and Taylor, 2007). Financial difficulties were reflected in stress levels and one strategy was to look at the diversification of employment and income. The research examined options that were now being more widely adopted, including off-farm employment, pluriactivity and multiple job holding (Robertson, Perkins and Taylor, 2007). In this assessment of the trends through the 1990s as neo-liberalism impacted on farm incomes and options, the researchers rejected the term 'pluriactivity' as failing to capture the more significant on and off farm employment, and opted instead for multiple employment to signal the fact that it encompassed those 'who choose to engage in more than one job at once, or over the year as the seasons dictate different work availability' as well as the fact that there was more than one job 'for more than one employer or family business or farm in the course of a week' (Robertson, Perkins and Taylor, 2007, p.5). This evidence of expanded multiple job holding in primary production was not confined to farm families but included those who were associated with primary production in a range of aspects.

This project explores a particular slice of non-standard work in New Zealand. Multiple job holding now occurs amongst 10% of those engaged in employment although the statistical details of the second or subsequent jobs is not collected and so the research offered by Taylor Baines is a major source of information on the reasons for multiple job holding, as well as the experiences of those involved.

The future trajectory of non-standard work: A footnote

In March 2009, *The Economist* (14 March 2009) headlined an issue with 'The Jobs Crises'. The crises, according to the contributing journalists, reflected the impact of the global economic downturn on employment in OECD countries. The flexibility of labour markets had resulted in significant job losses, both as a result of off-shoring to locations that offered cheaper options, including of the cost labour, as well as the collapse of companies and, in some cases, industries. Mass unemployment was the prospect. But what concerned the lead writer of *The Economist* was that this might jeopardise labour flexibility.

> Over the next couple of years, politicians will have to perform a difficult policy u-turn; for, in the long term, they need flexible labour markets... The bare truth is that the more easily jobs can be destroyed, the more easily new ones can be created (*The Economist*, 14 March 2009, p.11).

What *The Economist* signals is an ongoing debate about the desirability of flexible labour and the importance of the 2008 crises in contributing to the continuing shift to non-standard work. Recessions encourage a 'cost hunt', essentially 'by reducing, at least temporarily, variable costs, notably employment levels' (Grass and Hayter, 1989, p.241). This is accompanied by concerns with labour productivity, the intensification of workloads and subcontracting (vertical disintegration) to seek cost reductions (Grass and Hayter, 1989). The effects are obvious in New Zealand where the unemployment rate at the beginning (mid-2008) of the latest recession was 3.4% but had, by December 2008, risen to 4.8%, and then by July 2009 was at 6%. One widespread response has been to implement shortened working weeks or require periods of unpaid leave to be taken, thereby establishing a form of de facto part-time employment for permanent employees. The justification is labour hoarding or retaining existing human capital. While the impact on labour market engagement is widespread, some groups are particularly vulnerable. The share of adults aged 65 to 69 working has increased because of the lack of retirement income and declining property or investment values while the numbers of minority groups who have lost employment is much higher than for majority group men or women. Youth rates of unemployment are more than three times the national average. The economic downturn and adjustments after 2008 indicates that non-standard work remains an important option in ensuring flexibility.

Conclusion

A range of factors have contributed to the growth of non-standard work. Some are structural and reflect the shift from primary and secondary production towards service sector employment in the late twentieth century. Deindustrialisation, in particular, saw the downsizing of companies and off-shoring as Fordist production was uneconomic and uncompetitive in New Zealand. Those groups, notably Maori and Pacific peoples, who were disproportionately involved in this form of production experienced significant job loss, with 20% of Maori losing their jobs between 1987 and 1989 and experiencing further job losses from 2008 at two to four times that of Pakeha (depending on age and industry). This was underlined from the 1980s by the privatisation or corporatisation of government activities; jobs in the post-office, forestry or railways were no longer a guarantee of standard employment and careers. Even certain occupations that had long been seen as stable career options became increasingly non-standard; midwives became self-employed while accountants were often employed on casual contracts, both inside the state and in the private sector. The structural shifts and the changing nature of employment invited new considerations amongst employees and families. In order to maintain or maximise income, options such as portfolio working or part-time/ casual employment were an increasingly significant response. For some, it was to preserve minimal income levels while for the skilled and higher-income workers, the reasons might include personal and familial benefits from flexible employment options or push factors such as the downsizing associated with the move to flat management structures or declining profitability in sectors such as insurance or banking (Robertson, Perkins and Taylor, 2007).

Since the 1980s/early 1990s, employers in both the private and public sectors have attempted to increase flexibility and reduce costs by making greater use of part-time, temporary or contract labour. Some workers – students and young parents for example – may prefer the flexibility of part-time or temporary work; others, particularly professionals, may enjoy the greater autonomy of self-employment. However, faced with a difficult labour market, many take such jobs involuntarily or work at a second job to 'make ends meet' (Krahn, 1995, p.35). And by 2006, more than half of all those in paid employment in New Zealand were in non-standard jobs. There is every indication that the most recent economic crises will add to the existing pressures to enhance labour flexibility or to reduce labour costs. Non-standard work is a key feature of current and future labour markets. To this extent, the casualisation/precariousness of employment and its destandardisation marks an important characteristic of reflexive modernity.

Acknowledgements

The Labour Market Dynamics Research Programme was funded by the Foundation for Research, Science and Technology. I would like to acknowledge the contribution of the LMD research managers, Eva McLaren, Carina Meares and Bronwyn Watson, especially Bronwyn for help in locating material for this chapter.

References

Baines, J. and Newell, J. (2005) *Trends in the New Zealand Labour Market, Non-Standard Work and Multiple Job Holding, 1981–2001*, Working Paper No. 11, Taylor Baines and Associates.

Beck, U. (1992) *The Risk Society: Towards a New Modernity*, London: Sage.

Bradley, H. and Devadason, R. (2008) 'Fractured transitions: Young adults' pathways into contemporary labour markets', *Sociology*, 42(1): 119–136.

Brosnan, P. and Walsh, P. (1996) 'Plus ça change: The Employment Contracts Act and non-standard employment in New Zealand', *Labour, Employment and Work in New Zealand*, Proceedings of the Seventh Conference, Victoria University of Wellington.

Butcher, A. (2002) *A Review of the Literature on Non-Standard Work and the New Economy*, Working Paper, No. 9, Albany: Labour Market Dynamics Research Programme, Massey University.

Carroll, N. (1999) 'Non-standard employment: A note on the levels, trends, and some implications', *Labour Market Bulletin*, 101–121.

Castells, M. (1996) *The Rise of the Network Society*, Cambridge, Mass: Blackwell.

Cohen, L. and Mallon, M. (1999) 'The transition from organisational employment to portfolio working: Perceptions of "boundarylessness"', *Work, Employment and Society*, 13(2): 329–352.

Dekker, R. and Kaiser, L.C. (2000) 'Atypical or flexible? How to define non-standard employment patterns – The case of Germany, the Netherlands and the United Kingdom', Paper prepared for European Analysis Group, The Netherlands.

Doogan, K. (2001) 'Insecurity and long-term employment', *Work, Employment and Society*, 15(3): 419–441.

Dupuis, A. and McLaren, E. (2006) *Non-standard Work and Young(er) Workers*, Research Report 2006/7, Albany: Massey University Labour Market Dynamics Research Programme.

Fergusson, R., Pye, D., Esland, G.M., McLaughlin, J.E. and Muncie, J. (2000) 'Normalized dislocation and new subjectivities in post-16 markets for education and work', *Critical Social Policy*, 20(3): 283–305.

Goodwin, J. and O'Connor, H. (2005) 'Exploring complex transitions: Looking back at the "Golden Age" of from school to work', *Sociology*, 39(2): 201–220.

Gottfried, H. (2008) 'Pathways to economic security: Gender and non-standard employment in contemporary Japan', *Social Indicators Research*, 88, 179–196.

Grass, E. and Hayter, R. (1989) 'Employment change during recession: The experience of forest product manufacturing plants in British Columbia, 1981–1985', *Canadian Geographer*, 33(3): 240–252.

Kaiser, L. (n.d.) *Standard and Non-Standard Employment: Gender and Modernism in European Labour Markets*, mimeo.

Kaiser, L.C. (2002) *Job Satisfaction: A Comparison of Standard, Non-Standard and Self-Employment Patterns Across Europe with a Special Note to the Gender/ Job Satisfaction Paradox*, Berlin: German Institute for Economic Research Berlin.

Krahn, H. (1995) 'Non-standard work on the rise', *Perspectives*, Winter, 35–42.

Leggatt-Cook, C. (2005) *Contemporary School to Work Transitions: A Literature Review*, Research Report 2005/4, Albany: Massey University Labour Market Dynamics Research Programme.

Mckeown, T. (2003) *Non-Standard Employment – When Even the Elite are Precarious*, Working Paper 5/03, Melbourne: Department of Management, Monash University.

McOrmond, T. (2004) 'Changes in working trends over the past decade', *Labour Market Trends*, January, 25–35.

McPherson, M. (2004) *Paid Work and Personal Relationships*, Auckland: EEO Trust.

Osborne, R. and Warren, J. (2006) 'Multiple job holding – A working option for young people', Paper to Labour, Employment and Work Conference, Wellington.

Pollock, G. (1997) 'Uncertain futures: Young people in and out of employment since 1940', *Work, Employment and Society*, 11(4): 615–638.

Rasmussen, E., Lind, J. and Visser, J. (2004) 'Divergence in part-time work in New Zealand, the Netherlands and Denmark', *British Journal of Industrial Relations*, 42(4): 637–658.

Robertson, N., Perkins, H.C. and Taylor, N. (2007) 'Multiple job holding: Interpreting labour market change and economic diversification in rural communities', Paper to the Institute of Australian Geographers Conference, University of Melbourne, 1–6 July.

Spoonley, P. and Davidson, C. (2004) 'The changing world of work', in Spoonley, P., Dupuis, A. and de Bruin, A. (eds), *Work and Working in Twenty-First Century New Zealand*, Palmerston North: Dunmore Press.

The Economist (2009) 'The jobs crises', 14 March.

Tucker, D. (2002) *'Precarious' Non-Standard Employment – A Review of the Literature*, Wellington: Labour Market Policy Group.
Vickerstaff, S.A. (2003) 'Apprenticeship in the "golden age": Were youth transitions really smooth and unproblematic back then?', *Work, Employment and Society*, 17(2): 269–287.
WEB (2004) *Report of Exploratory Case Study Research into Precarious Employment*, Wellington: WEB Research.

Part II

Organisational Influences and Individual Effects

6
Recent Research on Workplace Learning and its Implications for National Skills Policies Across the OECD

Ewart Keep

Introduction – The policy backdrop

For at least the last decade there has existed a standard, Organisation for Economic Cooperation and Development (OECD)-wide policy discourse, derived from relatively uncomplicated readings of human capital theory. It asserts that skills, learning and knowledge are now key drivers of competitive advantage in an era of globalisation. This line of thinking has been widely absorbed, elaborated, embellished and reiterated within national strategies and policy statements in many developed countries. It has had a particularly strong impact in England, and played a major role in shaping the New Labour government's thinking on education and training (E&T) policy (see the Leitch Review, 2005, 2006; H M Government, 2009)

The upshot is that many governments have assumed that the primary aim of public policy should be to generate ever-larger investment in, and outputs and stockpiles of, certified units of human capital within the labour market in order to engender improved economic performance. In other words, more is deemed, in a very simple-minded fashion, to be better (Leitch Review, 2005, 2006). As Ashton observed:

> The analogy with physical investment encourages the view of training as a series of finite activities, the more one invests in education and training the greater the return in terms of earnings, productivity and economic growth. The necessity to provide a convenient measure of this investment leads academics to focus on formal

education and training provision, as these can readily be derived from government statistics (Ashton, 1998, p.61).

As a result, in much of the English-speaking world policy has concentrated on the expansion of post-compulsory education (not least higher education), subsidy to employers to support their training efforts, in some cases the marketisation of publicly-funded forms of skills provision, reform of vocational qualifications systems and curricula, and attempts to secure a higher level of accreditation of prior learning (APL) among the adult workforce. Levels of 'reform' and E&T policy churn have often been high.

Underlying this policy narrative and its resultant activity, there are large but oft-hidden problems. First, notions that human capital is the 'killer factor' in determining the outcome of international competition between individuals, organisations, sectors, regions and nation states may be only partially true (see Keep, Mayhew and Payne, 2006).

Second, the policy narrative generally tends to focus attention on discrete, formalised and certified types of learning (Ashton, 1998). This is problematic because we know from research that, for most of the adult working population, the vast bulk of learning is informal, uncertified and takes place on-the-job (Eraut and Hirsh, 2007; Felstead et al, 2004). Policy therefore tends to be addressing and impacting upon only a small sub-section of skill acquisition activity (see below for further details).

Third, in the English-speaking world the policy narrative has often had surprisingly little to say about how skill can be mobilised in order to confer a competitive edge – this is simply assumed to occur more or less automatically once the investment in E&T has been made. This belief is deeply problematic, as the evidence suggests that on its own the amassing of large stocks of certified human capital – in the shape of qualifications held by national workforces – has not necessarily led to tremendously impressive economic outcomes at the level of the nation state, in large measure because the economy has been unable to fully absorb and deploy this investment. Examples here would include New Zealand, Canada and Scotland (Business NZ et al, 2008; Keep, Mayhew and Payne, 2006; Scottish Government, 2007). Moreover, detailed research suggests that, skills, on their own, also appear to make little difference to performance at organisational level (Tamkin, Cowling and Hunt, 2008).

A growing realisation by policymakers in some countries that more skill is a necessary but of itself insufficient precondition to delivering the desired social and economic outcomes, is starting to shift attention towards issues of skill usage and to how government and other actors might attempt to boost the levels of underlying demand for skill in the economy (see the Scottish Skills Strategy (Scottish Government, 2007); the National Skills Policy Collaboration, Australia (2009), and the New Zealand Skills Strategy (Business NZ et al, 2008) for examples of this trend). These developments in policymakers' perceptions of the nature and causes of (and solutions to) the 'skills problem' have both been fed by much of the research that is discussed below, but also have consequent implications for the research agenda, and for the shape of future policy and practice.

A new research and policy agenda

This chapter will examine the findings from a selection of this emerging body of research on workplace learning and explore some of its main implications for both public policy and individual employers. In attempting this, the aim is not to try and provide a detailed analysis of what is now a large and complex body of research. There is simply not the space to assay such an approach. Instead, an outline of the main elements of the theoretical frameworks that have been developed and some key research findings are offered, in the hope that they will whet the reader's appetite to engage with the original source material. It will also share some issues with several other chapters in this volume, not least that by Buchanan (Chapter 3).

Research on workplace learning

Twenty years ago in the English-speaking world, research on workplace learning was relatively sparse, and often based around theoretical perspectives derived from psychological experiments rather than any significant volume of hard evidence on actual learning practices in real workplaces – for example, Kolb's learning cycle and notions of single and double-loop learning (Kolb, 1984). It also placed a great deal of stress on a normative model of learning and on discussing what ought to happen, rather than what evidence might reveal about practice in real life (Grugulis, 2007).

As Ashton (1998) noted, what was lacking was research that offered hard data on how people learned in and through their day-to-day jobs, how lower status (i.e., non-professional and non-managerial) workers learned through work, and what features of organisational design and routine aided or impeded learning on the job. In addition, there were few if any means to gauge on a systematic basis the extent or quality of individuals' involvement in less formalised types of learning, and no diagnostic tools that could be deployed to indicate the breadth and depth of informal learning opportunities within any individual workplace.

The last decade has witnessed a significant series of steps forward in terms of both the quantity and quality of research in this field (Unwin, 2008), not least as a result of investments made by the UK's Economic and Social Research Council (ESRC) through its Learning Society, Future of Work, and Teaching and Learning Research Programmes. All of the gaps identified above have been addressed to some extent, and a substantial body of data and analytical and diagnostic tools has emerged.

The growing acknowledgement and measurement of workplace learning

Despite the tendency noted above for much of public policy on skill to obsess about the provision of formalised, certified episodes of education and training, often conducted in the full-time E&T system or via off-the-job courses, there has been an increasing stress within the international research literature upon the importance of 'informal' learning on the job and therefore in the workplace (see, for Australian, Finnish, Japanese and American, examples, Billett, 2001; Engestrom, 2001; Koike, 1997; Lave and Wenger, 1991).

One of the reasons that informal learning has tended to remain more or less invisible to policymakers is the difficulty of quantifying it. However, this is an area where significant progress has been made and there are now tried and tested survey methodologies available (see Felstead et al, 2004, 2005; Felstead et al, 2007) that can be used to track the volume and intensity of a range of informal learning activities and opportunities within the workplace. Additionally, in contrast to traditional models of human capital, there is an increasing conceptualisation of forms of informally gained skills, knowledge and competence that are collectively held by particular work groups (Sandberg, 2000), elements of which can be captured through efforts to measure the existence and strength of 'communities of practice' (see Felstead et al, 2007).

Moreover, as Sparrow and Raghavan (2006) report, some organisations have started to develop their own internal methods of conceptualising and measuring non-certified forms of human capital, and of also quantifying their usage and impacts on organisational performance. At the same time, academic researchers have deployed case study methodologies that help draw out some of the linkages between informal workplace learning and various aspects of organisational performance (see Fuller et al, 2003; Stevens, Ashton and Kelleher, 2001).

Given the salience of measurement issues within public policy on E&T, the developments outlined above offer opportunities through which informal learning in the workplace can be charted and hence incorporated within policy objectives. In effect, the recently-emerged ability to gauge levels and trends in informal workplace learning help place it on the policymakers' map.

The workplace as a site of learning – The working as learning framework

Besides developing the means to quantify the intensity of informal learning, Felstead and colleagues (2009) have recently provided a new and comprehensive articulation of the different schema that have been advanced in relation to the means by which the workplace provides a frame or context for learning. This Working as Learning Framework (WLF) offers a general model for analysing the context provided by an organisation as a site of learning (and of skill usage) which embraces a multi-level approach to conceptualising the social relationships and processes that go to make up a particular workplace. The WLF model melds together three theoretical perspectives from different social science disciplines – the productive systems approach from economics, notions of discretion and trust from the sociology of work tradition, and from earlier workplace learning traditions the notion of learning environments (Felstead et al, 2009).

The productive system approach, developed by institutional economists, offers a systemic mapping and analysis of the networks within which economic activity (from production to consumption) is organised and conducted. It, 'traces the overall configuration of social relationships within economic systems, stretching from individuals and small work groups through to global financial and political systems' (Felstead et al, 2009, p.18). It is a perspective that has not hitherto been deployed within the workplace learning literature, and offers the promise of being able:

> To investigate where effective control over the whole productive process is located and how this impacts on learning within any particular workplace. It highlights the importance of establishing the locus of power within the productive system as a whole. It requires us to consider how the meaning, impact and outcomes of learning processes within workplaces are, in part, shaped by a wide range of relationships that exist beyond and outside the employing establishment or organization (Felstead et al, 2009, pp.18–19).

The various case studies that form the bedrock of Felstead and his colleagues' research demonstrate the deployment of this analytical frame, which rests upon two axes – vertical interconnections of scale which are termed 'structures of production' (ranging from international governance down to the local workplace), and horizontally through different 'stages of production' (from sourcing raw materials through to consumption) (see Felstead et al, 2009, pp.19–24).

The overall effect of this approach is that, in contrast to traditional neoclassical economics, rather than view the firm as an isolated, individual economic actor floating free within an atomised marketplace, the productive systems perspective firmly locates the organisation and its associated workplace(s) within the wider chains of economic, social and power relationships that structure the opportunities and options that the organisation's owners, managers and workers face. Thus, as Newsome, Thompson and Commander (2009) demonstrate, it is not possible to fully understand the competitive strategies, production regimes, work organisation or skill usage of UK food manufacturing firms without some appreciation of the nature of their relationships with their immensely powerful, monopsonistic customers – the giant multiple food retail chains. In essence, pressure for cost savings from the supermarkets tends to lead to 'low road' production strategies; intensified and Taylorised work organisation; and high surveillance, low trust and low discretion employee relations, all of which help ensure limited opportunities for dignity within work and very circumscribed opportunities for learning therein.

The second element of the WLF is a focus upon how work is organised, and the impact that choices about work processes and job design have upon the degrees of trust and discretion that can be vested in relationships between different parties. For example, as Billett (2000, p.141) argues, 'if permitted only discretion, workers are unlikely to be required to deploy a broad range of attributes associated with non-routine decision-making'. Thus trust and the discretion that it affords represents a critical dimension in determining the skill that a worker needs to acquire and can subsequently deploy within their job. One of the key values of underlining issues of trust and discretion is that by so doing Felstead et al (2009) help connect skills issues back to wider research and policy concerns about the design and conduct of employee relations.

The final and arguably key element of the WLF centres on the workplace as a learning environment, and it is to this that we now turn.

Learning environments – Analytical frameworks and diagnostics

The concept of learning environments is not new. Pettigrew et al noted as long ago as 1988 that what they termed receptive and non-receptive training contexts appeared to have a major impact on the strategies and means by which organisations sought to develop their employees. What was absent until recently however, was any coherent framework for defining the different dimensions of what made any given workplace more or less likely to need and support learning by employees. Such a framework, along with an associated diagnostic tool, has emerged as a result of research undertaken by Fuller and Unwin (2003 and 2004) on apprenticeships in the UK. Building on conceptual foundations laid by Lave and Wenger (1991), and Engestrom (2001), Fuller and Unwin have produced (2006) the concept of a continuum of learning environments, ranging from the expansive to the restrictive.

The approach rests on three central aspects of participation in workplace learning:

- engaging in multiple and overlapping communities of practice at and beyond the workplace;
- access to multidimensional approaches to the acquisition of expertise through the organisation of work and job design;
- opportunities to pursue knowledge-based courses and qualifications related to work.

Workplaces at the expansive end of the continuum, 'are defined as ones in which these aspects of participation are extensively and fully realized, whereas "restricted learning environments" limit these opportunities' (Felstead et al, 2009, p.27).

Examples of characteristics of expansive learning environments include access to learning fostered by cross-organisation experiences; gradual transition to full, rounded participation as a trained worker; workforce development used to align the goals of developing the individual and organisational capability; a wide distribution of skills across the workforce; and a multidimensional view of expertise. By contrast, in a restrictive learning environment, access to learning is narrow and restricted in terms of task, knowledge and location; transitions to qualified worker status are fast and undertaken as quickly as possible; workforce development is utilised to tailor individual capabilities to organisational need; the distribution of skills across the workforce is polarised; and there is a unidimensional, top-down view of expertise (see Fuller and Unwin, 2006, Figure 2.2, pp.40–41).

Alongside the development of the expansive – restrictive learning environment concept, research undertaken by Eraut et al (2000, 2005a, b) has explored how informal learning opportunities are embedded within work processes, both for initial and for mid-career workers. Such learning was, 'mainly triggered by consultation and collaboration within the working group, consultation outside the working group and the challenge of the work itself' (Eraut and Hirsh, 2007, p.25).

Eraut et al (2000) identified two critical sets of factors. The first, learning factors, were determined by the challenge and value of the work; the quality of feedback, support and levels of trust; and by the confidence, commitment, personal agency and motivation of the individual worker. The second, context factors, were set by the allocation and structuring of work; the nature of encounters and relationships with people at work; and by individual participation and workers' own expectations of their performance and progression (Eraut and Hirsh, 2007, p.31). A critical dimension to making learning successful was found to be balancing the different elements. For example, within the learning factors, the level of challenge needed to be matched with the worker/trainee's level of confidence. Too sudden an increase in challenge could lead to a loss of confidence and to poor learning. As Eraut and Hirsh observe:

> the allocation and structuring of work was central to our participants' progress, because it affected (1) the difficulty or challenge of the work, (2) the extent to which it was individual or collaborative, and (3) the opportunities for meeting, observing and working alongside people who had more or different expertise, and for forming relationships of mutual trust that might provide feedback and support (2007, p.32).

Besides illuminating the processes whereby learning is made integral to work processes, this body of research has also provided a range of diagnostic tools that make it possible to assess the range, quality and depth of learning that is potentially available within any particular workplace. As will be discussed below, this has profound implications for the development of training policy and practice.

Overview

The foregoing research is very different from the traditional human capital-based measures that have hitherto often formed the basis for policy formulation. Its importance rests on the fact that its findings imply that traditional public policy models of skill development centred on formalised training are, at best, just one part of a much wider menu of means by which the skills of the workforce can be created, maintained and enhanced. We now have clear evidence that the ways in which work is structured and managed can make a very significant difference to the volume, breadth, depth and quality of learning that occurs as a direct result of the undertaking of basic work processes – in other words, people learning on and through doing their jobs. That such learning has always existed is not a secret, though its importance has often been masked by the training function and policymakers' enthusiasm for more formalised types of learning provision. What recent research demonstrates is that the volume of such learning often exceeds that generated through more formal means, and also that the quality and quantity of informal learning in and through work can be encouraged, managed, directed and strengthened via conscious elements of design and intervention. Informal learning does not have to be haphazard, ill-directed or low quality, and its volume and quality can at least partially now be measured.

A second major element of recent advances in understanding is that they refocus attention on issues to do with employee relations, work organisation and job design. Perhaps the key finding to emerge from the research reviewed above is that the manner in which work is structured, organised and managed has a profound impact on both the range and level of skills that can be created in any given work setting, and also on the range and level of skills that can be productively deployed therein. In other words, skill creation and skill usage are intimately bound together within the workplace, and expansive environments are both more liable to be able to absorb additional skills created and/or funded externally (via publicly-funded programmes) and also to renew and supplement such skills through additional and supportive informal learning. Thus skill formation and mobilisation are inextricably inter-related with many core aspects of wider employee relations, work design and business strategy agendas. The policy implications of this overall conclusion are reviewed below.

The implications

Although at least some aspects of the above findings may seem relatively obvious to practitioners, or to anyone who has researched the link between skills and performance by any means other than staring at large datasets and running regressions upon them, the point to note here is that the importance of the workplace as a site of learning, and the role that its configuration and management plays in both skill acquisition and usage, has hitherto tended to remain at least partially hidden from policymakers in the English-speaking world. By contrast, countries that have relatively strong traditions of apprenticeship as a key source of initial skill formation (often linked to extensive licence-to-practice forms of labour market regulation), and industrial relations traditions that embrace co-determination and/or strong collective bargaining over skills, are likely to be more aware of, and place greater importance upon some of the issues flagged up above.

Within the Anglo-Saxon tradition, an expansion of tertiary educational provision rather than apprenticeships has been the preferred route to upgrading initial vocational education and training. At the same time, particularly in the UK, the tendency has been to treat the firm as 'black box' into which skills are injected from an external E&T system (Keep, 2002, 2006).

The other problem that policymakers often face is their own desire for simplicity and for analytical frames that create uncomplicated, single category phenomena that can be addressed via equally basic, one-size-fits-all policy interventions or schemes. Unfortunately, one of the key realities revealed by research is that workplaces are exceedingly varied environments with widely differing skill requirements (Smith and Sadler-Smith, 2006), ranging from high end, knowledge-intensive teamworking among professional staff managed via sophisticated forms of human resource management (HRM); to workplaces that are characterised by monotonous, low-end drudgery that revolves around the repetition of simple Taylorised tasks using very limited skills and performed for low wages and managed via relatively repressive command and control systems (see Felstead et al, 2009 for examples of both ends of this spectrum). Such research evidence as we have suggests that it is at least possible that the gap between the leading and the trailing edge of practice in workplace management may be widening (Coats, 2009). Acceptance of a complex ecology of workplace practice and of organisational environments leaves policy facing the need to think in terms of interventions that encompass a mixture of common minimum standards (for example, on minimum wages) and highly tailor-made interventions and programmes of developmental support on the other.

Plainly the research reviewed in this chapter raises a host of issues for both public policy and for organisations and their development. What follows below focuses on three particularly pressing challenges.

The challenge of the impoverished workplace

Although there has been much talk about transitions to a knowledge driven economy (see Thompson, 2005 for a robust rebuttal of the concept as a universal model), the realities of work and workplaces across the developed world remain highly complex, with a spectrum of experiences of work and how it is ordered and managed that range from good to appalling and all points in between. Moreover, as Coats (2009) notes, survey evidence, especially from within the EU (see Fitzner et al, 2007), suggests that overall national levels of job quality (as measured, for example, by the perceived monotony of the work) vary significantly. Coats argues that, 'the quality of employment available to workers is shaped (if not determined) by national policy choices and institutions' (2009, p.32).

The problem is that in large parts of the English-speaking world, job quality is often limited, and at the same time there has been an absence of strong public policy interest in quality of working life issues. In the space available here it is not possible to chart the nature and cause of this in any detail. The main elements that underpin the persistence of poor jobs, which vary in relevance and force from country to country, include:

- The decline in the power and influence of trade unions, which has aided the emergence of unilateral and relatively untrammelled and unchallenged managerial dominance in the workplace.
- A reliance (in some instances) on a platform of individual legal rights for workers as a means of safeguarding against outright exploitation within the employment relationship.
- A lack of legitimacy for, and therefore any great force behind, public policy interventions within the workplace, particularly any that might pertain to how labour is deployed and managed. The model, as noted above, has been one wherein the firm is treated as a 'black box', where as long as workers are treated legally, the state and its agencies have no cause to take any interest in what happens.
- The failure of the sophisticated HRM model to take hold in many workplaces and to produce the promised results in terms of the emergence of a relatively benign, individualised model of high performance, high involvement, high trust employee relations regime (Coats, 2009). Some organisations have gone down this road, but it has remained a minority and there are good reasons for thinking that this may well remain the case (Godard, 2004).

The overall result has been the persistence of a significant number of workplaces characterised by low paid, dead-end, often relatively lowly skilled employment, where roles are heavily Taylorised, job content impoverished, skill acquisition and usage very tightly circumscribed by the design and management of the productive process, and where work intensification, managerial surveillance and exploitation remain prevalent (see for example the workplaces surveyed in Coats, 2009; Hopkins, 2009; Lloyd, Mason and Mayhew, 2008; Mulholland, 2009; Newsome et al, 2009). In many of these jobs, work neither generates much in the way of meaningful learning opportunities, nor significant opportunities for the job holder to deploy their existing range of technical and social skills and knowledge to productive effect. For example, Hopkins describes factory work where deskilling meant that the ability to understand the native language (in this case English) was no longer a prerequisite for employment, 'as workers can be physically shown their job rather than having it verbally explained to them' (2009, p.130). In essence, people are employed to undertake extremely simple, repetitive tasks, and to do what they are instructed by their managers. High levels of skill, autonomy or any capacity for innovation or independent thought are entirely superfluous – indeed in some cases they are to be actively discouraged as they might countermand or hinder management's designs for how the tasks are to be performed (see Mulholland, 2009).

Such workplaces represent a range of problems for public policy, not least in terms of offering work that is unlikely to allow those who undertake it much opportunity for dignity or creativity (Newsome, Thompson and Commander, 2009), and which evidence suggests may have adverse impacts on health, life expectancy and opportunity (Marmot, 2004). From the perspective of skills, without an increase in 'better jobs' it will be hard to create higher skills within many workplaces, and harder still for externally generated upskilling to be put to much (if any) productive use therein. As Unwin (2008) notes in discussing the work of Ashton and Sung (2006), if progress is to be made 'employers need to consider how to organise work so that it enables people to contribute and use their expertise whilst, at the same time, ensuring that their employees have the necessary skills and knowledge to perform well' (2008, p.3).

This link between notions of decent work and skill formation and usage is not new. Green (2006) has argued that higher levels of skill across the workforce mean that public policy attention needs to focus on job quality in order to ensure better utilisation. At the same time, a central tenet of the Australian skill ecosystems approach to skill policy formation that development of the workforce needs to go hand in hand with development of the workplaces within which skill is created and used (see Buchanan, 2006), and that skill formation and deployment is inextricably linked to wider employment relations policies (Alcorso and Windsor, 2008). In the UK skills and employment relations policies exist in entirely separate boxes, and the means by which the challenge of bad jobs has been 'solved' by government has been to conclude that such work is residual in nature and that employment as a whole is on a road to a universal knowledge driven economy which once reached will allow all workers ample opportunity to gain and deploy high levels of skill, secure rewarding work and higher wages, and offer significant opportunities for autonomy and creativity (Keep, 2008a, 2009).

Unfortunately, there is very strong evidence that the more extreme versions of the knowledge driven economy are wrong – low paid work in circumscribed, relatively lowly-skilled jobs is not vanishing (Abrams, 2002; Ehrenreich, 2001; Lawton, 2009; Lloyd, Mason and Mayhew, 2008; Toynbee, 2003). As a result, there are major challenges ahead for governments. The global recession is liable to not only reduce overall levels of employment, but also to fuel an increase in low end employment and to produce slower rates of growth in the number of good jobs within national economies. The range of policy responses that might be made is limited (see Lloyd, Mason and Mayhew, 2008 for a review), and most are not easily constructed within a neo-liberal paradigm.

The challenge of re-thinking publicly-funded E&T interventions

As noted above, there has evolved a strong tradition in public policy on skills across much of the OECD that centres on ramping up the volume of publicly-funded E&T at every level. England forms an extreme, but illuminating example of such tendencies, with the state offering national learning entitlements to bring the entire adult workforce up to a qualification threshold that it is believed will help ensure 'employability' and provide a platform for subsequent skill enhancement, as well as increasing levels of subsidy to a widening range of employers' formalised training activities, via policy levers such as the Train to Gain scheme (see Keep, 2008b), and Sector Skills Compacts. Besides subsidy, the state has also centred attention on providing employers with a skills 'brokerage' service, whereby state-funded intermediaries act to help companies diagnose their training needs and then point employers towards a range of external learning providers (public and private) who can satisfy their requirements.

Leaving aside the problem of high levels of deadweight within such arrangements (i.e., the state paying for much that would have happened anyway) (Abramovski et al, 2005; Keep, 2008b) and their potentially limited impact on companies' long-term interest in and commitment to training (Keep, 2008b; Ofsted, 2008); it is important to note that the central focus of policy has been on formalised, certified types of training activity, largely sourced from external providers rather than being generated within the employing organ-isation. The implicit model is one where, much as with cleaning and catering, training is seen as an activity best outsourced, with training expertise and the skills it produces being injected into the workplace.

The result is the potential for a major disjuncture between busi-ness need and training provided, and between skill formation and its potential usage in particular work settings (Felstead et al, 2009; Ofsted, 2008; Wolf et al, 2006). By contrast, there has hitherto been limited public policy interest in trying to help organisations to help themselves by boosting the inherent internal capacity of the organ-isation to plan, structure and deliver learning opportunities from within (see below), or to contemplate work re-organisation or job re-design as a precursor to enhanced deployment of skill. This may now be starting to change. As a result of its skills strategy (Scottish Government, 2007) Scotland has embarked upon a major initiative aimed at trying to explore how skill utilisation can be improved.

A policy focus on the utilisation of skill obviously requires some means to assess both current levels and also identify any trends. In the UK the series of Skills Surveys has, among other issues, asked indi-vidual workers about the skills and qualifications needed to both obtain and undertake their current jobs (Ashton et al, 1999; Felstead et al, 2007). However, it is also perfectly possible to ask employers about the topic, and one example is the Australian Survey of Employer Use and Views of the VET System (SUEV), which is run by the National Centre for Vocational Education Research (NCVER) (for details of SUEV, see Watson, 2008). For example, employers were asked to rate the skill levels of their employees relative to their organisational need, with respondents being asked to rate the skills of their employees as being above, adequate for, or below what was required (Watson, 2008, p.9). The somewhat startling finding in 2005 was that only 5% of employers thought the skills of their workforce were generally below what was required, 58% thought that they were adequate, and no less than 37% believed that their employees had skills at levels above what was required (Watson, 2008, p.9).

Traditional conceptualisations of innovation are another area that, in some countries at least, will need to be re-thought. In the UK, innovation has generally tended to be viewed as centred on forms of high-level, university-driven, science-based R&D and associated knowledge transfer and exploitation activity undertaken between higher education, specialist R&D organisations and high technology industry. To characterise it crudely, it has been about people in white coats, test tubes and patents – a top-down, hard science model of innovation (see, for instance, Anderson, 2009; Brown, 2009; and Rees, 2009).

The idea that the bulk of innovation might be about incremental refinements in both the productive process and the products generated by lower level workers employed outside the R&D department has not found much purchase in UK policy, yet research in Scandinavian economies that are noted for their relatively effective innovation systems suggests that the top-down approach is not always either applicable or effective and that other models that embrace shopfloor innovation and the input of a wide cross-section of the workforce can also be critical to success (see Karnoe, Kristensen and Anderson, 1999; and Maskell et al, 1998). If we accept that much innovation and productivity enhancement in fact comes from informal learning and a bottom-up model of product and process enhancement (see Felstead et al, 2009; Fuller et al, 2003; Stevens, Ashton and Kelleher, 2001) then the focus of public policy interventions to support innovation is liable to undergo at least a partial shift.

The internal training capacity of organisations

Because public policy has tended to obsess about the external provision of skills, with employers cast as either welfare (subsidy) recipients or as customers/purchasers of services from outside training providers both public and private, in the English-speaking world we sometimes appear to know remarkably little about the current state of training function within organisations – how it is staffed, by whom, and what its capabilities are. If we are going to bring about a step change in employer's training efforts – formal or informal – then a robust, well-staffed, expert and highly competent training/human resource development (HRD) function with a sophisticated approach to blending formal and informal learning methods seems to be a prerequisite (Smith and Sadler-Smith, 2006). Such a function could be 'in-house', but equally well be a resource shared among a group of firms within a locality or a sectoral 'cluster' (for example, via a Group Training Association).

This area offers one potentially significant focus for future national skills policies. Rather than obsess about the volume of learner number throughput and resultant qualification achievement being generated through formalised learning, policymakers could choose to refocus some of their attention and resources upon building up the training capacity (individual and collective) of organisations within the economy.

A second foundation for strengthening the internal organisational capacity for supporting learning is line management staff with appropriate skills, attitudes and priorities. Managers are critical to establishing an expansive learning environment (Hirsh et al, 2004), but in many instances the current state of management is far from ideal and there is a major job to be done in equipping line managers with the understanding to assess learning needs, to embed learning opportunities in work routines, and to encourage and nurture a learning culture (Eraut and Hirsh, 2007; Fuller and Unwin, 2004; Hirsh et al, 2004). As Eraut and Hirsh note, 'managers have not been selected in the past for their interest in either learning or supporting the learning of others. Nor is the support of learning their only challenge' (2007, p.85).

What the foregoing suggests is that, as an essential prerequisite for future skills policy formulation, a 'state of the training function and organisational training capacity' assessment should be a research priority. This would need to include the ability and willingness of line management to deliver aspects of training and development.

Final thoughts

A key conclusion from skills policy research over the last few years has been the need to connect strategies on skills with those on economic development, business improvement and work organisation and job design (Keep, Mayhew and Payne, 2006). What the research on workplace learning reviewed in this chapter suggests is that, in addition, skills policies need to reconnect with employee relations policies and to start to be based upon a conception of work that embraces job quality, discretion and learning as inter-linked elements in what makes for success. Without more 'good jobs' there is limited utility in providing more skilled workers. An holistic approach to workforce capabilities and to the management and deployment and motivation of labour seems liable to generate better results than ill-connected initiatives targeted at some, isolated elements of this agenda. Such an approach is demanding – for policymakers, managers and other actors – but it is liable to be the one that has the potential to generate the next set of major gains.

References

Abramovski, L., Battistin, E., Fitzsimons, E., Goodman, A. and Simpson, H. (2005) 'The impact of the employer training pilots on the take-up of training among employers and employees', *DfES Research Report* RR694, Nottingham: Department for Education and Skills.

Abrams, F. (2002) *Living Below the Breadline: Living Below the Minimum Wage*, London: Profile Books.

Alcorso, C. and Windsor, K. (2008) *Skills in Context: A Guide to the Skill Ecosystem Approach to Workforce Development*, Sydney: NSW Department of Education and Training.

Anderson, R. (2009) 'A chance for universities to step up to the plate', *The Guardian (Education Guardian)*, 10 March, p.10.

Ashton, D. (1998) 'Skill formation: Re-directing the research agenda', in Coffield, F. (ed.), *Learning at Work*, Bristol: Policy Press, pp.61–69.

Ashton, D., Davies, B., Felstead, A. and Green, F. (1999) 'Work skills in Britain', *SKOPE Monograph* No. 1, Coventry: University of Warwick, SKOPE.

Ashton, D. and Sung, J. (2006) 'How competitive strategy matters? Understanding the drivers of training, learning and performance at the firm level', *SKOPE Research Paper* No. 66, Oxford: Oxford University, SKOPE.

Billett, S. (2000) 'Performance at work: Identifying smart work practice', in Gerber, R. and Lankshear, C. (eds), *Training for a Smart Workforce*, London: Routledge, pp.123–150.

Billett, S. (2001) *Learning in the Workplace: Strategies for Effective Practice*, Crows Nest NSW: Allen & Unwin.

Brown, G. (2009) 'Romanes Lecture', 27 February, http://www.number10.gov.uk/Page18472 (accessed 16/03/2009).

Buchanan, J. (2006) *From 'Skill Shortages' to Decent Work: The Role of Better Skill Ecosystems*, Sydney: New South Wales Board of Vocational Education and Training.

Business NZ/CTU/NZ Industrial Training Federation/NZ Government (2008) *New Zealand Skills Strategy – A Discussion Document*, Wellington: Department of Labour.

Coats, D. (2009) 'The sunlit uplands or bleak house? Just how good are today's workplaces?', in Bolton, S.C. and Houlihan, M. (eds), *Work Matters – Critical Reflections on Contemporary Work*, Basingstoke: Palgrave Macmillan, pp.21–37.

Ehrenreich, B. (2001) *Nickel and Dimed: Undercover in Low-Wage USA*, London: Granta Books.

Engestrom, Y. (2001) 'Expansive learning at work: Towards an activity-theoretical reconceptualization', *Journal of Education and Work*, 14, 133–156.

Eraut, M., Alderton, J., Cole, G. and Senker, P. (2000) 'Development of knowledge and skills at work', in Coffield, F. (ed.), *Differing Visions of a Learning Society, Vol 1*, Bristol: Policy Press, pp. 231–262.

Eraut, M., Maillardet, F., Miller, C., Steadman, S., Ali, A., Blackman, C. and Furner, J. (2005a) 'What is learned in the workplace and how? Typologies and results from a cross-professional longitudinal study', EARLI Biannual Conference, Nicosia.

Eraut, M., Maillardet, F., Miller, C., Steadman, S., Ali, A., Blackman, C. and Furner, J. (2005b) 'An analytical tool for characterising and comparing professional workplace learning environments', paper for BERA Annual Conference.

Eraut, M. and Hirsh, W. (2007) 'The significance of workplace learning for individuals, groups and organisations', *SKOPE Monograph*, Cardiff: Cardiff University, SKOPE.

Evans, K., Hodkinson, P., Rainbird, H. and Unwin, L. (eds) (2006) *Improving Workplace Learning*, TLRP's Improving Learning Series, London: Routledge.

Felstead, A., Gallie, D., Green, F. and Zhou, Y. (2007) *Skills at Work 1986–2006*, Oxford: University of Oxford, SKOPE.

Felstead, A., Fuller, A., Unwin, L., Ashton, D., Butler, P., Lee, T. and Walters, S. (2004) 'Applying the survey method to learning at work: A recent UK experience', *Learning as Work Research Paper* No. 3, Leicester: University of Leicester, Centre for Labour Market Studies.

Felstead, A., Fuller, A., Unwin, L., Ashton, D., Butler, P. and Lee, T. (2005) 'Surveying the scene: Learning metaphors, survey design and the workplace context', *Journal of Education and Work*, 18, 359–383.

Felstead, A., Fuller, A., Jewson, N., Unwin, L. and Kakavelakis, K. (2007) *Learning, Communities and Performance: Evidence from the 2007 Communities of Practice Survey*, Leicester: National Institute of Adult Continuing Education.

Felstead, A., Fuller, A., Jewson, N. and Unwin, L. (2009) *Improving Working as Learning*, TLRP's Improving Learning Series, London: Routledge.

Fitzner, G., Williams, N. and Grainger, H. (2007) *Job Quality in Europe and the UK: Results from the 2005 European Working Conditions Survey*, London: Department of Trade and Industry.

Fuller, A., Ashton, D., Felstead, A., Unwin, L., Walters, S. and Quinn, M. (2003) *The Impact of Informal Learning at Work on Business Productivity*, London: Department of Trade and Industry.

Fuller, A. and Unwin, L. (2003) 'Learning as apprentices in the contemporary UK workplace: Creating and managing expansive and restrictive learning environments', *Journal of Education and Work*, 16(4): 407–426.

Fuller, A. and Unwin, L. (2004) 'Expansive learning environments: Integrating personal and organizational development', in Rainbird, H., Fuller, A. and Munro, A. (eds), *Workplace Learning in Context*, London: Routledge.

Fuller, A. and Unwin, L. (2006) 'Expansive and restrictive learning environments', in Evans, K., Hodkinson, P., Rainbird, H. and Unwin, L. (eds), *Improving Workplace Learning*, London: Routledge, pp.27–48.

Godard, J. (2004) 'A critical assessment of the high-performance paradigm', *British Journal of Industrial Relations*, 42(2): 349–378.

Goodison Group (2008) Note of a Goodison Group Seminar on Skills, Scottish Parliament, 6 October, Edinburgh: Goodison Group (mimeo).

Green, F. (2006) 'Skills and job quality', in Porter, S. and Campbell, M. (eds), *Skills and Economic Performance*, London: Caspian Publishing.

Grugulis, I. (2007) *Skills, Training and Human Resource Development: A Critical text*, London: Palgrave Macmillan.

Hirsh, W., Silverman, M., Tampkin, P. and Jackson, C. (2004) 'Managers as developers of others', *IES Report* 407, Brighton: Institute of Employment Studies.

H M Government (2009) *New Opportunities, Fair Chances for the Future*, Cm 7533, London: The Stationery Office.

Hopkins, B. (2009) 'Inequality street? Working life in a British chocolate factory', in Bolton, S.C. and Houlihan, M. (eds), *Work Matters – Critical Reflections on Contemporary Work*, Basingstoke: Palgrave Macmillan, pp.129–144.

Karnoe, P., Kristensen, P.H. and Anderson, P.H. (eds) (1999) *Mobilizing Resources and Generating Competencies*, Copenhagen: Copenhagen Business School.

Keep, E. (2002) 'The English vocational education and training debate – fragile "technologies" or opening the "black box": Two competing visions of where we go next', *Journal of Education and Work*, 15(4): 457–479.

Keep, E. (2006) 'State control of the English education and training system – Playing with the biggest train set in the world', *Journal of Vocational Education and Training*, 58(1): 47–64.

Keep, E. (2008a) 'From competence and competition to the Leitch Review – The utility of comparative analyses of skills and performance', *IES Working Paper* No. 17, Brighton: Institute of Employment Studies.

Keep, E. (2008b) 'A comparison of the Welsh workforce development programme and England's train to gain', *SKOPE Research Paper* No. 79, Cardiff: Cardiff University, SKOPE.

Keep, E. (2009) 'The limits of the possible: Shaping the learning and skills landscape through a shared policy narrative', *SKOPE Research Paper* No. 86, Cardiff: Cardiff University, SKOPE.

Keep, E., Mayhew, K. and Payne, J. (2006) 'From skills revolution to productivity miracle – Not as easy as it sounds?', *Oxford Review of Economic Policy*, 22(4): 539–559.

Koike, K. (1997) *Human Resource Development*, Japanese Institute of Labour, Tokyo.

Kolb, D. (1984) *Experiential Learning: Experience as the Source of Learning and Development*, New York: Prentice Hall.

Lave, J., and Wenger, E. (1991) *Situated Learning*, Cambridge: Cambridge University Press.

Lawton, K. (2009) *Nice Work if You Can Get It*, London: Institute of Public Policy Research.

Leitch Review of Skills (2005) *Skills in the UK: The Long-Term Challenge*, London: H M Treasury.

Leitch Review of Skills (2006) *Prosperity for All in the Global Economy – World Class Skills*, London: H M Treasury.

Lloyd, C., Mason, G. and Mayhew, K. (2008) *Low-Wage Work in the United Kingdom*, New York: Russell Sage Foundation.

Marmot, M. (2004) *Status Syndrome*, London: Bloomsbury.

Maskell, P., Esklinen, H., Hannibalsonn, I., Malmberg, A. and Vatne, E. (1998) *Competitiveness, Localised Learning and Regional Development*, London: Routledge.

Mulholland, K. (2009) 'Life on the supermarket floor: Replenishment assistants and just-in-time systems', in Bolton, S.C. and Houlihan, M. (eds), *Work Matters – Critical Reflections on Contemporary Work*, Basingstoke: Palgrave Macmillan, pp.162–179.

National Skills Policy Collaboration (2009) *Investing Wisely*, Sydney: Australian Industry Group, Australian Confederation of Trade Unions, Australian Education Union, Dusseldorp Skills Forum, and Group Training Australia.

Newsome, K., Thompson, P. and Commander, J. (2009) 'The forgotten factories: Supermarket suppliers and dignity at work in the contemporary economy', in Bolton, S.C. and Houlihan, M. (eds), *Work Matters – Critical Reflections on Contemporary Work*, Basingstoke: Palgrave Macmillan, pp.145–161.

Ofsted (2008) *The Impact of Train to Gain on Skills in Employment*, Ref. 070250, London: The Office for Standards in Education, Children's Services and Skills.

Pettigrew, A., Hendry, C. and Sparrow, P. (1988) *The Role of Vocational Education and Training in Employers' Skill Supply Strategies*, Sheffield: Training Agency.

Rees, M. (2009) 'The stimulus of science', *The Guardian*, 16 April, p.31.

Sandberg, J. (2000) 'Competence – The basis for a smart workforce', in Gerber, R. and Lankshear, C. (eds), *Training for a Smart Workforce*, London: Routledge, pp.47–72.

Scottish Government (2007) *Skills for Scotland – A Lifelong Skills Strategy*, Edinburgh: Scottish Government.

Smith, P.J. and Sadler-Smith, E. (2006) *Learning in Organizations – Complexities and Diversities*, London: Routledge.

Sparrow, P. and Raghavan, R. (2006) 'Incentivising employer investment: How do strategic actors answer the question: "How do people add value to our organisation?"', paper prepared for Sector Skills Development Agency Expert Panel, Manchester: Manchester Business School (mimeo).

Stevens, J., Ashton, D. and Kelleher, M. (2001) 'The developing contribution of workplace learning to organisational performance', in SKOPE, *Workplace

Learning in Europe, Oxford: Oxford University, European Consortium of Learning Organisations/ETDF-FEFD/SKOPE/CIPD.

Tamkin, P., Cowling, M. and Hunt, W. (2008) *People and the Bottom Line*, Brighton: Institute of Employment Studies.

Thompson, P. (2005) *Skating on Thin Ice – The Knowledge Economy Myth*, Glasgow: Strathclyde University.

Toynbee, P. (2003) *Hard Work: Life in Low Wage Britain*, London: Bloomsbury.

Unwin, L. (2008) 'State-of-science review: SR-A2 – Learning at work: Opportunities and barriers', Foresight Project on Mental Capital and Wellbeing, London: Government Office for Science.

Watson, I. (2008) *Skills in Use – Labour Market and Workplace Trends in Skills Usage in Australia*, Sydney: New South Wales Department of Education and Training.

Wolf, A., Jenkins, A. and Vignoles, A. (2006) 'Certifying the workforce: Economic imperative or failed social policy?', *Journal of Education Policy*, 21(5): 535–565.

7
High-Performance Work Systems and Employee Well-being in New Zealand

Peter Boxall and Keith Macky

There is a long tradition of interest in how to enhance worker motivation and raise organisational productivity through improving the design of work. The human relations movement, and such concepts as socio-technical work systems, industrial democracy, and job enrichment, have all had their day in the sun. The notion of 'high-performance work systems' (HPWSs) is the most recent manifestation of this concern. The term largely originated in the USA, where it arose in the policy and academic debate over the decline of US manufacturing competitiveness in the face of challenges from other advanced manufacturing societies, most notably Japan, and more recently, from a variety of low-cost developing countries. A landmark report in 1990, *America's Choice: High Skills or Low Wages!*, issued by the Commission on the Skills of the American Workforce, expressed strong criticism of the Fordist/Taylorist models of work design prevalent in US mass-production industries, where core production jobs were often low in responsibility, discretion and skill (Cordery and Parker, 2007). It argued for substantial investment in 'high-performance work organisation' and in greater workforce skills (Cappelli and Neumark, 2001). This message was reinforced by Appelbaum and Batt (1994) in *The New American Workplace* and by Appelbaum et al (2000) in *Manufacturing Advantage*. These were both influential books which argued that new technology alone could not save domestic American manufacturing: reforms to work systems, which achieved higher performance through increased employee involvement, higher skills and better performance incentives, would also be needed.

High-performance work systems are thus closely connected to issues of human capability in the workplace. Advocates of HPWSs argue that they unlock and expand human capabilities and make work more satisfying (see Chapter 2). They depend for their effectiveness, in fact, on the responses of workers. In this chapter, we critically examine the notion of HPWSs and describe the results of a study of worker responses to HPWSs in New Zealand workplaces. Over the last few years, our research interest has focused on what workers experience in the workplace, including their responses to management practices and to trade unions, and how this connects to their well-being. Well-being in the workplace is a broad concept, including a range of variables such as job satisfaction, stress, fatigue, and work-life balance.

We believe that the most useful definition of HPWSs is one which is based around high-involvement work processes. We begin by unpacking the elements of HPWSs and flesh out the high-involvement model, setting up our preferred conceptual framework and reviewing research on the outcomes, both positive and negative, for workers and firms. This leads into a summary of the findings of our recent study in New Zealand of worker responses to HPWSs, drawing on two major empirical papers (Macky and Boxall, 2008a, b). We conclude with some wider observations on the potential for HPWSs in the New Zealand workplace. While our research suggests that a supervisory style which fosters empowerment is widespread in New Zealand, and that this suits both parties, more extensive systems of high involvement are expensive and are only likely to grow if they clearly benefit both firms and workers.

HPWSs: The international context

While American sources still dominate, the notion of HPWSs is not restricted to the US context. It is now popular in any advanced industrial society, whether large (like the US, France or the UK) or small (like Australia and New Zealand), where people have concerns about productivity and connect these concerns to the way in which workers are managed. A key stimulant of this concern was the rise of Japanese high-quality production systems in the 1970s and 80s, including such techniques as quality circles, just-in-time inventory, and flexible, team-based production (Boxall and Macky, 2007; Boxall and Purcell, 2008). Faced with competitors who were simultaneously raising product quality, reducing production costs and improving rates of innovation, some elements of Western manufacturing (like the British motorcycle industry) simply disappeared while others soon learnt they had to fundamentally change their production systems and grow their reputation for quality and value. A long overdue focus on the internal operations of companies began to take hold after many years in which operations or production management had been taken for granted. In the automobile manufacturing industry, struggling Western firms made major efforts to reform their production systems by adopting Japanese 'lean production' principles (Womack, Jones and Roos, 1990). This meant moving away from the low-discretion, control-focused work systems associated with Fordist operations management towards work systems which increased the involvement of production workers in problem-solving and decision-making and invested in the sort of employment practices that raised their skills and their performance incentives (MacDuffie, 1995).

Along with the Japanese quality challenge, another stimulant of change in work systems in manufacturing over the last 20 years has been the advent of advanced manufacturing technology (AMT) (Boxall and Purcell, 2008). This includes such technologies as robotics, computer-aided design (CAD), computer numerical control (CNC) machine tools, and electronic data interchange (EDI) systems. Research on AMT, including work conducted among Australian and New Zealand manufacturers (Challis, Samson and Lawson, 2005), shows that such technologies reach more of their potential when production workers' jobs are redesigned and their skills improved to enable them to enhance the operating performance of these technologies. Studies by Wall et al (1990, 1992), for example, show how work redesign and training that enables production operators to solve technical problems as they occur, reduces reliance on the need to call in specialist technicians for problem-solving and thereby enhances productivity. The productivity benefits come from quicker response to these problems and thus lower machine downtime. In the longer run, productivity improvements also come from more effective use of the capacity of operators for learning: employees who enjoy greater empowerment learn more about the reasons why faults occur in the first place and find ways to reduce their incidence.

The converse of this argument, however, is that empowerment and up-skilling is less relevant in low-technology, labour-intensive contexts, such as toy manufacture, clothing production, and white-ware assembly (fridges, freezers and laundry equipment) (Boxall and Macky, 2007; Boxall and Purcell, 2008). Companies in countries in which the costs of this kind of production process are too high tend to favour offshoring to low-cost environments over investment in HPWSs (as, for example, in the case of Fisher and Paykel Appliances, which has moved much of its whiteware production from New Zealand and Australia to Thailand and Mexico) (Macky, 2008).

While the initial focus was on the way production workers are managed in manufacturing, the topic of HPWSs is now part of a larger agenda concerned with competitive performance in both manufacturing and services. Not only is there concern about the ability of advanced, high-wage industrialised countries to sustain their domestic manufacturing capabilities (e.g., Konzelmann, Forrant and Wilkinson, 2004), but there is growing angst over the location of services in a globalised production environment. At the Brookings Institution Trade Forum in 2005 on the off-shoring of white collar work, Jensen and Kletzer (2005) reported that over the period from 2001 to 2003, 70% of the US workers displaced by global competition worked in services, not manufacturing.

How service firms might use HPWSs as a competitive asset in different industries, and across market segments within industries, is therefore a growing interest (e.g., Batt, 2002; Boxall, 2003). High-skill, high-involvement systems of managing people are naturally necessary in knowledge-intensive services because workers capable of providing such services need to be paid well and developed continuously but they are also of interest in those service industries which are able to segment customer needs and charge a premium for higher quality. In the hotel industry, for example, luxury hotel operators can improve revenue and customer retention through HR systems that empower front-line employees to personalise service (Haynes and Fryer, 2000). They therefore have an interest in investing in the employee development and management practices that will support a high-quality competitive strategy in this industry. Such investments in employees, however, are unlikely to be economic at the low-price end of the hotel industry where customers want a cheap bed 'without frills' (Boxall, 2003).

We now find ourselves in the midst of a lively debate over the impacts of HPWSs on firms and workers. Are HPWSs really the kind of 'high-road' to workplace reform in which both firms and workers benefit? At this stage, some scholars see benefits for both in HPWSs (e.g., Appelbaum et al, 2000) while others question the gains for firms (e.g., Cappelli and Neumark, 2001; Way, 2002) or for workers (e.g., White et al, 2003) and some, quite rightly, question the value for both parties (e.g., Godard, 2004). In order to reach any sort of conclusion on likely benefits, we need to tease out more fully what we mean by HPWSs, a concept which remains poorly defined and contentious.

High-performance work systems: Unpacking the concept

At its most basic level, the notion of HPWS constitutes a claim that there exists a system of work practices that leads in some way to superior organisational performance. There are three concepts explicitly embedded in this proposition: performance, managerial work and employment practices, and systemic effects (Boxall and Macky, 2009). To understand what is meant by an HPWS, we need to examine each of these concepts in turn.

Let us begin with the last of these elements: systemic effects. The systemic notion has been readily identified in a number of HPWS literature reviews (e.g., Becker and Gerhart, 1996; Delery and Shaw, 2001; Dyer and Reeves, 1995). In MacDuffie's (1995, p.200) terms, 'bundling' of work practices is critical in HPWSs: 'it is the combination of practices into a bundle, rather than individual practices, which shapes the pattern of interactions between and among managers and employees'. On any reading, the idea that there are systemic or synergistic effects in the cluster of chosen HR practices is a key part of the HPWS proposition. What tends to vary in the literature, however, is the extent to which this systemic notion reaches out to companion elements of a business: its technology or proprietary knowledge, product- or service-mix, financing, supply chain, and governance, for example. Narrowly conceived, bundling is an issue of design within the components of an HR system: making training consistent with a change to self-directed teams, for example. More broadly conceived, it entails complementarity between changes in HR systems and other strategic changes in the workplace: for example, moving to a high-involvement HR model because management is making a major investment in advanced technology in the workplace which will not realise its potential unless operating workers are more highly engaged in technical problem-solving (Wall, Jackson and Davids, 1992). Given the embeddedness of work systems within wider production or operational strategies (MacDuffie, 1995; Purcell, 1999), we consider the narrow conception of synergy as far too limiting. We think that complementarity needs to be understood not only within the sphere of HRM but within the broader management system of the workplace or business unit. Thinking about HPWSs in this way is likely to be much closer to the way that senior managers think about their businesses.

Organisational performance, the dependent variable in HPWSs, is an omnibus term, like 'organisational effectiveness'. It is something that can be conceived in a variety of ways, incorporating short- and long-run economic outcomes and wider notions of social legitimacy or corporate social responsibility (Boxall and Purcell, 2008; Edwards and Wright, 2001; Paauwe, 2004). In terms of HPWSs, however, most researchers have focused on economic performance criteria, as Godard's (2004) evaluation of HPWS studies indicates. This means that HPWSs, to be deemed successful, need primarily to enhance cost-effectiveness. If the financial benefits do not exceed the costs, HPWSs are not economically rational for firms.

We say this while acknowledging that the measurement of cost-effectiveness is far from straightforward. We agree with those who see profit as too distal a performance indicator and favour approaches in which the costs and benefits of HPWSs are examined as closely as possible to the work outcomes that the specific group of employees concerned can materially influence, as in the studies of MacDuffie (1995) in automobile manufacturing, of Ichniowski et al (1997) and Ichniowski and Shaw (1999) in steel making, and of Appelbaum et al (2000) in steel making, clothing manufacturing and medical electronics manufacturing. These studies were all conducted at the plant level on a well-defined group of production workers using performance metrics deemed relevant by plant managers in terms of the specific production processes concerned.

However, the question of performance does not rest there. A key premise that runs through the literature is that HPWSs depend on positive responses from employees (e.g., Delbridge, 2007; Godard, 2004; Macky and Boxall, 2007). Workplace performance is influenced by team performance and, prior to that, individual job performance, which in turn is a function of interactions between employee ability, discretionary effort, and performance opportunities. The question becomes: do the benefits to workers (e.g., in perceived autonomy, skill development and wage increases) exceed their costs (e.g., in work stress and work-life imbalance), and thereby motivate individual employees to up-skill themselves and seek to apply additional performance effort when opportunities exist for them to do so? Research on worker responses and outcomes is therefore essential in any comprehensive evaluation of the performance of HPWSs.

While the dependent variable in HPWSs is complicated, there is even greater difficulty with the independent variable. The managerial practices that are deemed to constitute an HPWS are subject to a confusing array of definitions and assertions, as Wood's (1999) review indicates. Becker and Gerhart (1996) illustrate the diversity in a table of five leading HPWS studies, all conducted within the US. These studies list as many as eleven and as few as four practices. There is no one practice common to these five studies and there is sometimes disagreement as to whether a practice, such as variable pay, has positive or negative effects on performance.

On top of this kind of theoretical dispute, there is the fact that the further one moves from a focus on the American context, the more socio-cultural variations in HPWS practices have to be accommodated. For example, a practice such as an employee grievance procedure, which Huselid (1995) considers a high-performance indicator in the US, is simply a legal requirement in countries like the UK and New Zealand, and therefore hardly something that differentiates superior performers. Some practices considered high performing in the US are wired into the institutional requirements elsewhere: they are 'table stakes' in these contexts, not a source of high performance (Boselie, Paauwe and Jansen, 2001; Boxall and Purcell, 2008). Legal differences are the more straightforward aspects of socio-cultural variation. Underpinning cultural assumptions are much more challenging: some practices which may work well in the Anglo-American world are understood quite differently, and much less positively, in less individualist cultures (Trompenaars and Hampden-Turner, 1997).

Approaches to constructing the independent variable in HPWSs in which researchers aggregate their perceptions of 'best practices', without regard to a specific context, are therefore fundamentally contentious (Boxall and Macky, 2009). Work systems and employment practices vary significantly across occupational, hierarchical, work-place, industry, and societal contexts (e.g., Appelyard and Brown, 2001; Kalleberg et al, 2006; Lorenz and Valeyre, 2005). Any assertion in the literature that there is some kind of general consensus around systems of best practices is patently false and arguments that a particular set of practices is self-evidently highly performing are not defensible (Bryson, Forth and Kirby, 2005; Marchington and Grugulis, 2000; Wood, 1999).

It is our contention, therefore, that attempts to define HPWSs *solely* through identifying a set of practices are fundamentally flawed (Boxall and Macky, 2009). Even if a set of context-delineated practices could be agreed upon, there is the problem that data which does not account for variations in *how* the same practice is implemented can never be totally trustworthy (Purcell, 1999). How such practices as appraisal and merit pay are actually implemented varies enormously, leading to very different impacts on employee trust, satisfaction, commitment, and performance. A firm may notionally have a practice in place but in a very demoralised or dysfunctional condition. To make genuine theoretical progress, researchers must therefore go beyond the construction of lists of practices and seek to identify the processes and mediating variables which a set of practices is supposed to influence (Becker and Gerhart, 1996). This is where the language of HPWSs simply fails us: there is nothing in the term itself that signifies the paths that are envisaged to lead to superior individual, team or organisational performance and we must accept that there is diversity in the paths that organisations follow (Bryson et al, 2005; Orlitzky and Frenkel, 2005). What alternatives do we have that are more descriptive of the pathways that might characterise an HPWS? In the following section, we explain the options and the pathway we think most appropriate.

Focusing on high-involvement work processes

We come closer to describing HR systems in meaningful terms when we identify the principal themes that underpin them: in other words, when we describe the major philosophies that management is trying to pursue. An adjective will never be found that describes completely all that management is trying to do in managing a group of workers but it helps if we get closer to the dominant themes (Lepak and Snell, 1999; Lepak et al, 2006).

It is useful to start from the observation that any HR system encompasses the management of some work domain and the management of the people who do the work in question. Thus, HR systems involve two broad types of practice: work practices and employment practices (Godard, 2004; Whitfield and Poole, 1997). Work practices are to do with the way the work itself is organised, including its normal structure (e.g., Taylorised jobs, supervised group work, self-managing teams, highly autonomous professional jobs) and any associated opportunities to engage in problem-solving and change-management regarding work processes (such as quality circles and team meetings). Employment practices include all the practices used to recruit, deploy, motivate, consult, negotiate with, develop and retain employees, and to terminate the employment relationship.

Together, the work and employment practices embedded in an HR system affect performance on multiple levels (Boxall and Purcell, 2008; Lepak et al, 2006). On one level, they influence the abilities (A), motivations (M), and opportunities (O) to perform of individual employees (the 'AMO' model of individual performance) (e.g., Blumberg and Pringle, 1982; Campbell et al, 1993; Huselid, 1995). In other words, every HR system works through its impacts on the skills and knowledge of individual employees, their willingness to exert effort, and their opportunities to express their talents in their work. However, HR systems also affect a range of variables on a more collective level, helping to build organisational capabilities, and influencing the organisational culture, and social and psychological climate in which individuals are embedded (e.g., Evans and Davis, 2005; Snell, 1999). The individual and collective levels are inextricably linked because the performance opportunities of individuals and their motivations are influenced by the quality of resources, collaboration and trust in their working environment.

Bearing in mind that HR systems have these multi-level impacts, we can try to describe the main thrust of management's approach to work organisation in respect of a particular work domain and the main thrust of its approach to employing the people concerned. The main variations on the HPWS terminology – high-involvement work systems (HIWSs) and high-commitment management (HCM) – are, in fact, focused on one or the other of these two categories. We have a school of thought, tracing back to Lawler (1986), concerned with high-involvement *work* practices and we have a school of thought, tracing back to Walton (1985), concerned with high-commitment *employment* practices (Wood, 1999; Wood and Wall, 2007).

Both of these are more descriptive terms for HR systems because they signal to us the dominant theme informing a stream of managerial action. It is descriptively helpful to draw a contrast between work processes in which managers try to control decisions and those that seek to make workers more responsible and involve them more fully in decision-making (e.g., Godard, 2004; Ramsay, Scholarios and Harley, 2000). Similarly, it is descriptively helpful to contrast employment practices which seek little enduring employee commitment from those that seek a much longer, more motivated attachment to the organisation. High-involvement and high-commitment management are also less loaded terms than the notion of high-performance work systems: they do not *assume* that 'the particular configuration of management practices is necessarily performance-enhancing' (Bryson et al, 2005, p.460). This has to be demonstrated in specific contexts, not simply asserted in a generalised way.

We consider that the most logical line of analysis in advanced economies is one which focuses on the reform of work through higher employee involvement. At the heart of high-involvement work reforms are practices that attempt to reverse the Taylorist process of centralising decision-making and problem-solving in the hands of management (Edwards and Wright, 2001). This is obviously relevant to those contexts where Taylorism has had a major impact but is now part of a system of management which is under-performing or at risk of complete failure. Researchers are *not* talking about professional and technical occupations which have always enjoyed a high level of autonomy but have in mind waged production workers in Fordist/ Taylorist production environments. In these contexts, movement towards a high-involvement goal implies making better use of employee capacities for self-management, personal development and problem-solving. However, research across the European Union suggests that such work reforms remain subject to demanding production targets and rarely go as far as the levels of autonomy and learning opportunities enjoyed by those in managerial, professional or technical occupations (Lorenz and Valeyre, 2005).

The specific practices that are intended to reform a Taylorist heritage can be expected to vary across industry circumstances (Boxall and Macky, 2007, 2009). While allowing for industry differences, one would nonetheless expect there to be observable change away from heavily Taylorised or very narrowly conceived jobs if a firm is now pursuing an HIWS with a group of workers historically subject to high managerial control (Wood and Wall, 2007). The acid test of high involvement is not whether a particular practice, such as teamwork, is being implemented but whether employees in this occupational category experience a positive shift in their responsibilities and decision-making powers relative to their historical norm. As MacDuffie's (1995) analysis shows in the automobile industry, a movement to more highly involving work processes (either on-line or off-line or both) will also call for the kind of hiring and development practices that foster greater skill and the kind of performance incentives that motivate workers to exercise their greater discretion and skill (see also Appelbaum et al, 2000, pp.41–42). Using the AMO framework, a choice to improve employee involvement opportunities in the work process will logically lead to companion improvements in the ability and motivation dimensions ('O' leads to 'A' and 'M') (Appelbaum et al, 2000, pp.39–44). The governance of such a change clearly depends on management seeing the value in all this and having the focus, funding and stamina required, including a commitment to enhance the skills of first-line supervisors (Boxall and Macky, 2007). In unionised workplaces, a more trusting and cooperative relationship with the relevant unions is also clearly desirable. This is now sometimes advanced under the aegis of a workplace 'partnership'.

High-involvement work processes: Conceptual model and existing research

In terms of studying the high-involvement model, we find the work of Vandenberg et al (1999), which draws on Lawler's writings (e.g., 1986), particularly useful. Vandenberg et al (1999) specify a conceptual model (Figure 7.1) in which business or employer practices are linked to involvement processes and thence to worker psychological states and measures of organisational effectiveness. They posit two paths: a cognitive path in which high-involvement processes take 'greater advantage of the skills and abilities' employees possess and a motivational path in which involvement processes increase 'workers' satisfaction and other affective reactions' (Vandenberg et al, 1999, p.304).

The Vandenberg et al (1999) framework uses Lawler's (1986) 'PIRK' rubric: high-involvement processes encompass workplace power (P),

Figure 7.1   Conceptual Model of High-Involvement Work Processes

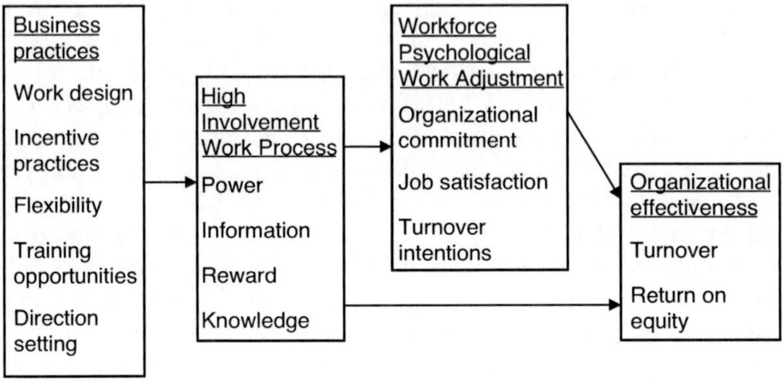

Source: Vandenberg et al (1999, p.307)

information (I), rewards (R) and knowledge (K). These four variables are seen as mutually reinforcing. In other words, high-involvement work processes empower workers to make more decisions, enhance the information and knowledge they need to do so, and reward them for doing so. In effect, this parallels the set of lenses in the AMO framework: for the high-involvement model to work, it must positively affect employee abilities, motivations, and opportunities to contribute. Improvements in knowledge enhance ability while empowerment and information enhance the opportunity to contribute. Rewards are a direct attempt to enhance motivation, which may also be improved through empowerment (enjoying more autonomous work), information (feeling better informed), and knowledge (enjoying a growth in skills).

The kind of framework shown in Figure 7.1 takes us in a simple but important way beyond the counting of HR practices. It means that we are not restricted to understanding high-involvement work systems only through certain specific practices. Our ability to discern shifts in the extent of involvement across diverse occupational and industry contexts is thus considerably enhanced. Vandenberg et al (1999) measure each process dimension in the PIRK framework through employee responses to multi-item scales. They find in a study of 49 North American life insurance companies that high-involvement processes do act positively through both (indirect) motivational and (direct) cognitive paths. Company performance is higher (measured by higher ROE and lower employee turnover), as is employee morale. It would be better if less distal measures of performance were inserted into the model, such as measures of operating performance, but the model does ensure that processes *as experienced by employees* are measured in the space between management practices and organisational outcomes.

Positive associations with worker well-being are also found in other surveys of worker responses to higher involvement using the PIRK model. In a study of 573 full-time workers in a US health care site, Mackie, Holahan and Gottlieb (2001) show benefits for employee mental health – lower levels of depression – from greater exposure to employee involvement processes. Similarly, Bauer's (2004) analysis of the *European Survey on Working Conditions 2000* shows that workers particularly value improvements in autonomy and communication rather than practices such as teamwork and job rotation *per se*.

On the other hand, Godard (2001), in his nationally represent-ative telephone survey of 508 Canadian workers, is the most com-parable study in a stream of work that is skeptical about the beneficial impacts for workers (see also Ramsay et al, 2000; White et al, 2003). Godard (2001) does not test the PIRK model but does measure some psycho-social variables (belongingness, task involvement and empowerment). His key finding is that while modest levels of 'high-performance' work practices may benefit employees, high levels become stressful. These findings stand in contrast to those of Appelbaum et al (2000, p.229) who argue from their evidence that greater employee involvement is not associated with 'intensification or speed-up'.

Overall, then, we need to exercise caution and need a fuller picture of the potential impacts on employees of managerial attempts at HIWSs (Boxall and Macky, 2009). This is depicted in Figure 7.2. Proponents of HIWSs, such as Appelbaum et al (2000), clearly envisage a shift from quadrant 4, the historical home of Taylorised mass-production industries, to quadrant 1. Critics, such as Godard (2004), however, envisage the possibility that the involvement processes pur-sued by managers may incorporate higher levels of work intensifi-cation which actually lead into quadrant 2. Yet other critics, within the labour-process tradition, argue that some attempts at involvement are fakes that increase demands on workers without increasing their

Figure 7.2   Four Configurations of Involvement and Intensification

		Low Intensification	High Intensification
Involvement	High	1. Ideal HIWS model: higher involvement without increased stress	2. Highly empowered but highly pressured HR model
	Low	3. Unrationalised low-skill work	4. Traditional Taylorism and fake attempts at involvement

Source: Boxall and Macky (2009)

sense of empowerment (Delbridge, 2007). This would leave quadrant 4 workers exactly where they are despite a managerial rhetoric of high involvement.

What about the employer side of the story? A sustainable HIWS pattern must also benefit firms or economically-rational managers will shut down operations or relocate production. As argued earlier, the value to firms is best demonstrated by studies which measure the benefits and costs at the point of production (i.e., studies that observe the operational outcomes of an actual production process or, next best, a plant or establishment). The studies of MacDuffie (1995) in automobile manufacturing and of Appelbaum et al (2000) in steel making, clothing manufacturing and medical electronics manufacturing, which were all conducted at the plant level using productivity indices relevant to the production processes concerned, are supportive of associations between high-involvement practices and operating performance in these industries. In the case of apparel manufacturing, however, Appelbaum et al (2000) note that the modular (team-based) work systems they studied, while valuable for through-put time and, thus, a fast-response manufacturing capability, did not, on average, improve cost performance. A stiffer test of the company benefits would consider only longitudinal, not cross-sectional data, in which we see a positive change in performance *after* the work reforms are implemented and controlling for other sources of performance variation (Cappelli and Neumark, 2001; Ichniowski et al, 1997). It is very hard to meet these exacting standards. Many studies so far have, in effect, measured the relationship between *current* HR practices and *historical* business performance (Way, 2002; Wright et al, 2005).

We know of no longitudinal studies of economic performance specifically measuring involvement processes through the PIRK model. There are, however, longitudinal studies in the steel industry that operationalise high-involvement work practices and which get close to the point of production. Ichniowski et al (1997) find positive impacts on productivity of high-involvement HR systems in a sample of US steel-finishing lines. This finding is reinforced by a subsequent study by Ichniowski and Shaw (1999) which compares the operating performance of US and Japanese steel finishing lines. This study finds that Japanese plants – all characterised by participative work practices – and US plants using high-involvement processes have equivalent productivity levels and outperform US plants with traditional (Fordist) or partially reformed work systems. The finding is also supported by Appelbaum et al (2000) whose three-industry data set includes some longitudinal data on steel manufacturing (see pp.130–137).

On the other hand, cross-industry studies sound a different note. Cappelli and Neumark (2001), using a national probability sample of US manufacturing establishments and examining work practices and outcomes in firms in 1977 and then again some 20 years later, conclude that high-involvement work reforms raise labor costs and that this implies that employees benefit through above-average remuneration rises, a picture reinforced by Osterman's (2006) study of the wage impacts of high-performance work organisation in US manufacturers. However, the statistical case for productivity benefits is weaker and the effects on profitability are unclear. British studies mirror these findings with analysis of the WERS 1998 survey indicating that 'high-involvement management' is associated with a wage premium (Forth and Millward, 2004). While also associated with a productivity benefit in unionised firms, no association is shown with financial performance in either unionised or non-unionised contexts (Bryson et al, 2005). A study of some 3,000 small US firms (less than 100 employees) by Sean Way (2002) also calls for caution, indicating that the benefits may not outweigh the costs in small organisations. As with the research on worker outcomes, we therefore need to exercise caution with the research on benefits to employers. The diffusion of full-blown HPWSs is actually much more limited than its advocates imagine and this should remind us that employers are unlikely to make such investments when they consider that the costs will outweigh the benefits (Blasi and Kruse, 2006).

HIWSs and worker outcomes: The New Zealand evidence

There have been few large-scale surveys in New Zealand on worker responses to changes in the management of work. One important exception, however, is the *New Zealand Worker Representation and Participation Survey* (NZWRPS) (Haynes et al, 2005), which found that employees exercise a relatively high level of influence in their day-to-day jobs in the New Zealand workplace. Haynes et al (2005, p.245) observed that New Zealand workers both experienced and desired higher levels of influence than their counterparts in the USA and the UK. That survey was conducted in 2003, after the Labour-led government's legislative reforms encouraging union and employee voice and at a time when growth in jobs and low unemployment were naturally supportive of worker influence in decision-making. We wished to use more extensive measures than those available in NZWRPS and wanted to assess more fully the response of New Zealand workers to high-involvement work processes. We were guided by Lawler's PIRK framework, described above, but also wished to include variables on work intensification, given the concern in the literature that HPWSs might force harder rather than smarter working (Figure 7.2). In our first paper (Macky and Boxall, 2008a), we therefore tested dual hypotheses: one positing benefits to workers from high-involvement processes and the other positing negative outcomes. These hypotheses were as follows:

Hypothesis 1: Perceptions of greater exposure to practices associated with high employee involvement will predict positive employee outcomes in the form of higher job satisfaction, lower stress and fatigue, and better work-life balance.

Hypothesis 2: Perceptions of greater exposure to practices associated with high employee involvement will predict negative employee outcomes in the form of lower job satisfaction, higher stress and fatigue, and poorer work-life balance.

Our research framework is shown in Figure 7.3. The survey constructed from it incorporated all these variables plus a range of other variables drawn from the broad literature on HPWSs, enabling us to examine job quality in New Zealand in a very comprehensive way. The data was collected in late 2005 and is based on computer-assisted tele-phone interviews (CATI) of 1,004 randomly selected New Zealand employees. The interviews took, on average, 30 minutes to complete. To be included in the study, participants needed to be employees aged 18 and over, have worked for their employer for at least six months, in a firm with a minimum of ten employees. Of those contacted who met these criteria, the response rate for the survey was 34.2%. Respondents with more than one employer (7.2%) were asked to respond to the survey questions for the job in which they currently worked the most hours.

Of the participants, the vast majority were permanent (93.5%) rather than temporary employees, worked an average of 39.12 hours a week (SD = 12.94) with a range from three to 95 hours, had a median weekly take home pay of NZ$600 (range: $40 to $2,500), and had worked for their main employer for a median of 4.5 years (range: six months to 40 years). The respondents were more likely

Figure 7.3   New Zealand Study of HIWSs: Research Framework

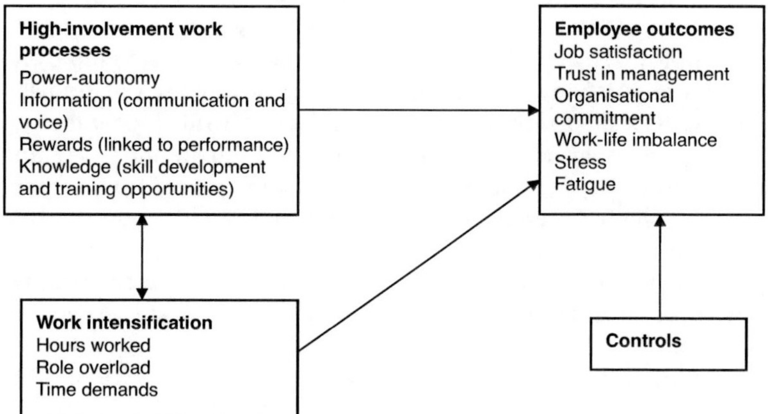

to be female (60.8%) than male, and were aged between 18 and 89 years at their last birthday (mean = 43.60 years; SD = 11.65). In terms of firm size, the median number of employees was 120 (range: 10 to 21,000) and 64.2% of the respondents had a union at their place of work that they could join if they wished (54.3% of whom were members of that union).

The main limitations in the sample are that women are over-represented relative to their proportion in the national workforce (a common problem with telephone surveys). Nor do we report the views of any workers in micro-firms with less than ten employees. However, the analyses show that gender does not appear to be related in any systematic way with the reported experience of high-involvement work processes.

What, then, are the results? The descriptive results show that employee empowerment levels are high in New Zealand (4.11 out of 5 on a Likert scale anchored from 1 = strongly disagree to 5 = strongly agree) with the other high-involvement variables still at the positive end of the scale but less so (information = 3.54; rewards = 3.19; knowledge = 3.56). Most NZ workers, therefore, agree that they are empowered in the workplace while being less enamoured of the extent to which they are rewarded, informed and trained. The multi-variate analyses add strength to the idea that there are likely to be gains for workers in an involvement-oriented model of HPWSs (Hypothesis 1 rather than 2) (Macky and Boxall, 2008a). In particu-lar, our study finds a clear relationship between high-involvement work processes and employee job satisfaction. When employees' experience of knowledge, information, rewards and power increases, the employment relationship moves in a direction that employees find more satisfying. We also find that a greater sense of empower-ment is associated with lower fatigue and stress, while higher rewards are associated with better work-life balance. Furthermore, we find no evidence that employees who experience greater involvement are more likely to report increased stress or fatigue or poorer work-life balance.

In respect of HIWSs, our results are consistent with the positive findings of Vandenberg et al (1999) and Mackie et al (2001) men-tioned above. This is interesting in that all three studies draw their definition of high-involvement processes from Lawler's (1986) PIRK model and all three studies adopt an approach which hinges on measuring employee experiences and attitudes. Our findings therefore throw light on employee reactions to the implementation of particular kinds of managerial policy. As Purcell (1999) reminds us, so much of what accounts for differences in the climate of employee relations relates to *how* policies are actually carried out. The fact that our study more effectively measures employees' experience of high-involvement processes may account for why we find a positive picture rather than the sort of negative outcomes reported by British researchers such as White et al (2003) and Green (2004), whose measures of high-performance practices rely on the items available in existing surveys (*Working in Britain* and *WERS*). These surveys were designed for other purposes, and the practices they measure map less well onto an involvement model of HPWSs.

On the basis of this New Zealand evidence, then, high-involvement work processes offer a distinct possibility of a managerial 'high-road' to organisational success that also benefits employees. Enhanced autonomy and rewards, implemented with greater information-sharing and employee development and without greater pressure, are indeed attractive to NZ workers. There is also in the data, however, a 'low-road', consistent with much of the evidence elsewhere regarding the intensification of work. We do find a relationship between work intensification and the negative outcomes of job dissatisfaction, fatigue, job stress and imbalance between work and non-work life. Perceived overload in an employee's work role and perceptions of pressure from managers to take work home, work overtime or otherwise exceed one's contracted hours appear to be more important than actual working hours for job (dis)satisfaction and fatigue, although all three intensification variables are associated with work-life imbalance and stress.

Our study does not rule out the possibility that managers may simultaneously pursue strategies aimed at encouraging involvement while also intensifying work. This is quite likely, for example, when downsizing occurs but management still wants to make better use of the skills and initiative of the employees who remain (e.g., Bacon and Blyton, 2001). In this kind of situation, however, our findings suggest the benefits for employees will be less than optimal.

These results are expressed in terms of the overall picture across the New Zealand workforce. People are often interested in whether there are nuances within this picture. In our second paper (Macky and Boxall, 2008b), we used the fuller range of measures available in our survey to analyse job quality in New Zealand across a range of sectoral, occupational, organisational and employee variables. The analyses did show some interesting variations. While the general picture is that New Zealand workers feel relatively empowered, there are some nuances in the picture associated with employment sector and occupation.

Employees in the private sector feel better rewarded for their performance, though not as much as we might expect. Since the state sector reforms of the 1980s, public sector pay practices may well have converged towards private sector ones in terms of performance appraisal, 'merit pay' and bonus practices. At the same time, perceptions of a strong internal labour market may have diminished in the public sector. Private-sector workers perceive themselves as having better chances of promotion from within than those in the public sector. The statutory requirement on public sector agencies to openly advertise vacancies at all levels may well have contributed to the view that internal candidates are not particularly advantaged. The other contrast is that professionals, technicians, and associate professionals in the private sector clearly feel much better informed than their public sector counterparts. Thus, to some extent, our data confirm the problems that others, such as Bach and Kessler (2007), see with the management of professionals in the public sector.

While the control variables used in this study were not central to its purpose, there is an interesting story in respect of organisational size and unionisation. Employees in larger firms see themselves as having a better internal labour market, as one would expect, but they do not, in any other respect, see themselves as experiencing more HPWS processes or practices than those in small firms. While lack of internal career opportunities is a serious problem for small firms trying to retain talented workers (Boxall et al, 2003), there is much that small firms can do to work with HPWS processes to enhance worker well-being. Although small size often imposes career constraints, smallness actually offers advantages in terms of flexible work design. We also find that older workers feel more empowered and better informed and that those with longer tenure feel more empowered. As in the UK (Green, 2008), greater employee loyalty is associated with greater autonomy. We also find that the better paid are better informed and feel better rewarded in terms of their performance.

The story in respect of unions is that employee feelings of empowerment, information and reward are not any higher in unionised firms. However, employees in unionised organisations do perceive better opportunities for training and development. This suggests some broadening of the impact of New Zealand unions and an important one because skill formation is critical to productivity growth. That said, the challenge for unions lies in making a more distinct impact on the organisation of work. A union role in fostering high-involvement work practices is not yet evident in the perceptions of New Zealand employees. Furthermore, given that the participants for this research worked in many firms of varying types, our findings do not provide any support for the notion that the implementation of HPWSs is linked to whether or not a firm is unionised. If managers have implemented HPWSs as a way to reduce or avoid unionisation, we find no evidence that it has had any effect.

In summary, we find that people feel relatively empowered right across the New Zealand workforce. At the same time, there are some statistically significant differences between employee experiences in the private and public sectors, across occupational groups, and across variables such as employee age, tenure, pay levels, organisational size and unionisation.

Conclusions

This chapter has set the current interest in HPWSs within its international context and argued that the most useful definition of the notion is one which lays emphasis on high-involvement work processes. High levels of employee involvement in problem-solving and decision-making are important in those manufacturing and service industries in which firms are seeking to exploit advanced technology or compete through esoteric expertise or high quality. Such systems bring both benefits and costs and there is a substantial debate around whether they deliver net gains for companies and workers. Using the PIRK (power-information-rewards-knowledge) model derived from Lawler (e.g., 1986) and Vandenberg et al (1999), we discuss the results of our survey of New Zealand workers' responses to high-involvement work processes.

The big picture in our data is that New Zealand workers – across sectors and occupations – perceive themselves to be relatively empowered. As a general rule, New Zealanders at work can participate in solving problems and shaping their jobs to a relatively high degree. Their level of empowerment grows as they become more experienced and the longer they stay with an employer. This confirms the picture of high levels of employee influence found in the *New Zealand Worker Representation and Participation Survey* (NZWRPS) (Haynes et al, 2005). It seems likely that most employers like to work with a relatively empowering supervisory style. In New Zealand's small, informal workplaces, this is only logical. It makes use of workers' on-the-job experience, enhances operating flexibility, and reduces the costs of supervision.

However, it is useful to make a distinction between an informal model of empowerment, which is widely enacted by supervisors and appreciated by workers, and a full-blown model of a high-involvement work system in which there are major companion investments in such areas as training, communication, promotion, remuneration, and employee relations. Our data suggest that the associations between empowerment and the other three variables in the PIRK model of high-involvement are not as strong as they could be if firms are seeking a high level of complementary reinforcement in a high-performance work system. Employee motivation and loyalty would likely be improved if the quality of information, rewards and training more closely matched the level of empowerment we find in New Zealand.

Here we may be seeing something of a trade-off for companies on economic grounds. While high-tech developments in New Zealand industry will require high-involvement work systems to reach their profit potential, as the research on implementing advanced manufacturing technology shows, and the same is true of moves to higher quality services, there is likely to be an economic limit to such investments in labour-intensive manufacturing and in less skilled services. It is not therefore surprising that empowerment is more widespread in the New Zealand workplace than are more extensive systems of high involvement. There is little doubt that empowerment sits well with New Zealand workers. It is strongly connected to their satisfaction with work and undoubtedly helps to express their capabilities, whatever their level of education and skill. In terms of its direct, informal expression in the workplace, it is also clearly valuable to employers. However, what needs further consideration is how New Zealand can encourage more widespread use of high-involvement work systems in which investments in employee development and reward structures are higher. Such systems are not easily diffused because of their costs. They are more likely to flourish where there are major companion investments in advanced technology or where there is a concentration of knowledge-intensive services. Such developments exist in all advanced economies, and New Zealand is no exception, but widespread expansion in these directions in a way that would significantly enhance productivity is a major challenge for a small, remote country lacking economies of scale.

References

Appelbaum, E. and Batt, R. (1994) *The New American Workplace*, Ithaca: ILR Press.

Appelbaum, E., Bailey, T., Berg, P. and Kalleberg, A. (2000) *Manufacturing Advantage: Why High-Performance Work Systems Pay Off*, Ithaca: ILR Press.

Appelyard, M. and Brown, C. (2001) 'Employment practices and semiconductor manufacturing performance', *Industrial Relations*, 40(3): 436–471.

Bach, S. and Kessler, I. (2007) 'Human resource management and the new public management', in Boxall, P., Purcell, J. and Wright, P. (eds), *The Oxford Handbook of Human Resource Management*, Oxford: Oxford University Press.

Bacon, N. and Blyton, P. (2001) 'High involvement work systems and job insecurity in the international iron and steel industry', *Canadian Journal of Administrative Sciences*, 18(1): 5–16.

Batt, R. (2002) 'Managing customer services: Human resource practices, quit rates, and sales growth', *Academy of Management Journal*, 45, 587–597.

Bauer, T. (2004) 'High performance workplace practices and job satisfaction: Evidence from Europe'. Discussion Paper No. 1265, Institute for the Study of Labor (IZA).

Becker, B. and Gerhart, B. (1996) 'The impact of human resource management on organizational performance: Progress and prospects', *Academy of Management Journal*, 39(4): 779–801.

Blasi, J. and Kruse, D. (2006) 'US high-performance work practices at century's end', *Industrial Relations*, 45(4): 547–578.

Blumberg, M. and Pringle, C. (1982) 'The missing opportunity in organizational research: Some implications for a theory of work performance', *Academy of Management Review*, 7(4): 560–569.

Boselie, P., Paauwe, J. and Jansen, P. (2001) 'Human resource management and performance: Lessons from the Netherlands', *International Journal of Human Resource Management*, 12(7): 1107–1125.

Boxall, P. (2003) 'HR strategy and competitive advantage in the service sector', *Human Resource Management Journal*, 13(3): 5–20.

Boxall, P., Macky, K. and Rasmussen, E. (2003) 'Labour turnover and retention in New Zealand: The causes and consequences of leaving and staying with employers', *Asia Pacific Journal of Human Resources*, 41, 195–214.

Boxall, P. and Macky, K. (2007) 'High-performance work systems and organisational performance: Bridging theory and practice', *Asia Pacific Journal of Human Resources*, 45(3): 261–270.

Boxall, P. and Macky, K. (2009) 'Research and theory on high-performance work systems: Progressing the high-involvement stream', *Human Resource Management Journal*, 19(1): 3–23.

Boxall, P. and Purcell, J. (2008) *Strategy and Human Resource Management*, Second Edition, Basingstoke and New York: Palgrave Macmillan.

Bryson, A., Forth, J. and Kirby, S. (2005) 'High-involvement management practices, trade union representation and workplace performance in Britain', *Scottish Journal of Political Economy*, 52(3): 451–491.

Campbell, J.P., McCloy, R., Oppler, S. and Sager, C. (1993) 'A theory of performance', in Schmitt, N. and Borman, W. (eds), *Personnel Selection in Organizations*, San Francisco: Jossey-Bass.

Cappelli, P. and Neumark, D. (2001) 'Do "high performance" work practices improve establishment level outcomes?', *Industrial and Labor Relations Review*, 54, 737–776.

Challis, D., Samson, D. and Lawson, B. (2005) 'Impact of technological, organizational and human resource investments on employee and manufacturing performance: Australian and New Zealand evidence', *International Journal of Production Research*, 43(1): 81–107.

Commission on the Skills of the American Workforce (1990) *America's Choice: High Skills or Low Wages!*, Rochester, NY: National Center on Education and the Economy.

Cordery, J. and Parker, S. (2007) 'Work organization', in Boxall, P., Purcell, J. and Wright, P. (eds), *The Oxford Handbook of Human Resource Management*, Oxford: Oxford University Press.

Delbridge, R. (2007). 'HRM and contemporary manufacturing', in Boxall, P., Purcell, J. and Wright, P. (eds), *The Oxford Handbook of Human Resource Management*, Oxford: Oxford University Press.

Delery, J. and Shaw, J. (2001) 'The strategic management of people in work organizations: Review, synthesis, and extension', *Research in Personnel and Human Resources Management*, 20, 165–197.

Dyer, L. and Reeves, T. (1995) 'Human resource strategies and firm performance: What do we know and where do we need to go?', *International Journal of Human Resource Management*, 6(3): 656–670.

Edwards, P. and Wright, M. (2001) 'High-involvement work systems and performance outcomes: The strength of variable, contingent and context-bound relationships', *International Journal of Human Resource Management*, 12(4): 568–585.

Evans, R. and Davis, W. (2005) 'High-performance work systems and organizational performance: The mediating role of internal social structure', *Journal of Management*, 31(5): 758–775.

Forth, J. and Millward, N. (2004) 'High-involvement management and pay in Britain', *Industrial Relations*, 43(1): 98–119.

Godard, J. (2001) 'High performance and the transformation of work? The implications of alternative work practices for the experience and outcomes of work', *Industrial and Labor Relations Review*, 54(4): 776–805.

Godard, J. (2004) 'A critical assessment of the high-performance paradigm', *British Journal of Industrial Relations*, 42(2): 349–378.

Green, F. (2004) 'Why has work effort become more intense?', *Industrial Relations*, 43(4): 709–741.

Green, F. (2008) 'Leeway for the loyal: A model of employee discretion', *British Journal of Industrial Relations*, 46(1): 1–32.

Haynes, P. and Fryer, G. (2000) 'Human resources, service quality and performance: A case study', *International Journal of Contemporary Hospitality Management*, 12(4): 240–248.

Haynes, P., Boxall, P. and Macky, K. (2005) 'Non-union voice and the effectiveness of joint consultation in New Zealand', *Economic and Industrial Democracy*, 26(2): 229–256.

Huselid, M.A. (1995) 'The impact of human resource management practices on turnover, productivity, and corporate financial performance', *Academy of Management Journal*, 38(3): 635–672.

Ichniowski, C., Shaw, K. and Prennush, G. (1997) 'The effects of human resource management practices on productivity: A study of steel finishing lines', *American Economic Review*, 87(3): 291–313.

Ichniowski, C. and Shaw, K. (1999) 'The effects of human resource management systems on economic performance: An international comparison of US and Japanese plants', *Management Science*, 45(5): 704–721.

Jensen, J.B. and Kletzer, L. (2005) 'Tradable services: Understanding the scope and impact of services offshoring', http://www.brookings.edu/es/commentary/journals/tradeforum/agenda2005.htm

Kalleberg, A., Marsden, P., Reynolds, J. and Knoke, D. (2006) 'Beyond profit? Sectoral differences in high-performance work practices', *Work and Occupations*, 33(3): 271–302.

Konzelmann, S., Forrant, R. and Wilkinson, F. (2004) 'Work systems, corporate strategy and global markets: Creative shop floors or "a barge mentality"?', *Industrial Relations Journal*, 35(3): 216–232.

Lawler, E. (1986) *High-involvement Management*, San Francisco: Jossey-Bass.

Lepak, D. and Snell, S. (1999) 'The strategic management of human capital: Determinants and implications of different relationships', *Academy of Management Review*, 24(1): 1–18.

Lepak, D., Liao, H., Chung, Y. and Harden, E. (2006) 'A conceptual review of human resource management systems in strategic human resource management research', *Research in Personnel and Human Resources Management*, 25, 217–271.

Lorenz, E. and Valeyre, A. (2005) 'Organisational innovation, human resource management and labour market structure: A comparison of the EU-15', *Journal of Industrial Relations*, 47(4): 424–442.

MacDuffie, J.P. (1995) 'Human resource bundles and manufacturing performance: Organizational logic and flexible production systems in the world auto industry', *Industrial and Labor Relations Review*, 48(2): 197–221.

Mackie, K.S., Holahan, C.K. and Gottlieb, N.H. (2001) 'Employee involvement management practices, work stress, and depression in employees of a human services residential care facility', *Human Relations*, 54(8): 1065–1092.

Macky, K. (2008) 'Fisher & Paykel appliances: A Thailand adventure', in Hill, C., Cronk, T. and Wickramasekera, R., *Global Business Today: An Asia-Pacific Perspective*, Sydney: McGraw-Hill Irwin, pp.537–539.

Macky, K. and Boxall, P. (2007) 'The relationship between high-performance work practices and employee attitudes: An investigation of additive and interaction effects', *International Journal of Human Resource Management*, 18(4): 537–567.

Macky, K. and Boxall, P. (2008a) 'High-involvement work processes, work intensification and employee well-being: A study of New Zealand worker experiences', *Asia Pacific Journal of Human Resources*, 46(1): 38–55.

Macky, K. and Boxall, P. (2008b) 'Employee experiences of high-performance work systems: An analysis of sectoral, occupational, organisational and employee variables', *New Zealand Journal of Employment Relations*, 33(1): 1–18.

Marchington, M. and Grugulis, I. (2000) '"Best practice" human resource management: Perfect opportunity or dangerous illusion?', *International Journal of Human Resource Management*, 11(6): 1104–1124.

Orlitzky, M. and Frenkel, S. (2005) 'Alternative pathways to high-performance workplaces', *International Journal of Human Resource Management*, 16(8): 1325–1348.

Osterman, P. (2006) 'The wage effects of high performance work organization in manufacturing', *Industrial and Labor Relations Review*, 59(2): 187–204.

Paauwe, J. (2004) *HRM and Performance: Achieving Long-Term Viability*, Oxford: Oxford University Press.

Purcell, J. (1999) 'The search for "best practice" and "best fit": Chimera or cul-de-sac?', *Human Resource Management Journal*, 9(3): 26–41.

Ramsay, H., Scholarios, D. and Harley, B. (2000) 'Employees and high-performance work systems: Testing inside the black box', *British Journal of Industrial Relations*, 38(4): 501–531.

Snell, S. (1999) 'Social capital and strategic HRM: It's who you know', *Human Resource Planning*, 22(1): 62–65.

Trompenaars, F. and Hampden-Turner, C. (1997) *Riding the Waves of Culture: Understanding Cultural Diversity in Business*, London: Nicholas Brealey Publishing.

Vandenberg, R.J., Richardson, H.A. and Eastman, L.J. (1999) 'The impact of high involvement work processes on organizational effectiveness: A second-order latent variable approach', *Group & Organization Management*, 24(3): 300–339.

Wall, T., Corbett, M., Martin, R., Clegg, C. and Jackson, P. (1990) 'Advanced manufacturing technology, work design and performance: A change study', *Journal of Applied Psychology*, 75(6): 691–697.

Wall, T., Jackson, P. and Davids, K. (1992) 'Operator work design and robotics system performance', *Journal of Applied Psychology*, 77(3): 353–362.

Walton, R. (1985) 'From control to commitment in the workplace', *Harvard Business Review*, 63(2): 77–84.

Way, S. (2002) 'High performance work systems and intermediate indicators of firm performance within the US small business sector', *Journal of Management*, 28(6): 765–785.

White, M., Hill, S., McGovern, P., Mills, C. and Smeaton, D. (2003) 'High-performance management practices, working hours and work-life balance', *British Journal of Industrial Relations*, 41(2): 175–195.

Whitfield, K. and Poole, M. (1997) 'Organizing employment for high performance: Theories, evidence and policy', *Organization Studies*, 18(5): 745–764.

Womack, J., Jones, D. and Roos, D. (1990) *The Machine that Changed the World: The Triumph of Lean Production*, New York: Rawson Macmillan.

Wood, S. (1999) 'Human resource management and performance', *International Journal of Management Reviews*, 1(4): 367–413.

Wood, S. and Wall, T. (2007) 'Work enrichment and employee voice in human resource management-performance studies', *International Journal of Human Resource Management*, 18(7): 1335–1372.

Wright, P.M., Gardner, T.M., Moynihan, L.M. and Allen, M.R. (2005) 'The relationship between HR practices and firm performance: Examining causal order', *Personnel Psychology*, 58(2): 409–446.

8
Developing the Next Generation: Employer-Led Channels for Education Employment Linkages

Paul Dalziel

Introduction

Recent research in New Zealand has identified that young New Zealanders in education are experiencing problems as they prepare for employment. The New Zealand Council for Educational Research *Pathways and Prospects* study, for example, is following over 100 young people in their first four years after leaving school (Vaughan, 2005; Vaughan et al, 2006). It reports that many young people in the first months of choosing a post-school pathway feel they have not received enough good guidance at school to make their decisions. A year later, many remain confused about how to get help. The Marsden Fund project, *In Transition*, identified similar concerns among another group of over 100 young people as they left school (Higgins and Nairn, 2006). Apart from a minority who had made an early career choice, these young people did not find the career information provided to them helpful in their choice-making. The majority found it confusing to be faced with so much information and so many apparent choices; few were able to make judgements about the quality of the material they encountered. A PhD thesis at the University of Canterbury highlighted the particular difficulties young Maori students experience after leaving school (Phillips, 2003). Her research is consistent with the call made at the Hui Taumata (2005, p.13 and p.14) for Maori and educationalists to take responsibility for factors that are currently holding back young people, with 'improving career advice to support lifelong employment and employability' identified as a key component.

The Labour Market Dynamics Research Programme led by Professor Paul Spoonley at Massey University has reported that 43% of people aged 15–34, and 46% of Maori in this group, feel their current job is not very closely related or not related at all to their educational qualifications (Cunningham et al, 2005; Dupuis et al, 2005). These figures imply a high social cost, since international studies reveal that successful education employment matching raises individual earnings for many years. A British study of graduates reported an earnings premium of between 8% and 20% six years after graduation (Battu et al, 1999). An Israeli study of vocational education found that successful matching can increase annual earnings by up to 10% (Neuman and Ziderman, 1990). A more recent Australian study reported returns to required education, if correctly matched to employment, of 18.2% for men and 14.9% for women (Voon and Miller, 2005).

The OECD has completed a comprehensive summary of youth transitions in New Zealand, which concluded that 'the recent performance of the youth labour market in New Zealand is very good compared with many other OECD countries' (OECD, 2008, p.9). Nevertheless, it highlighted some weaknesses too: a hard-core of youth at risk of poor labour market outcomes and social exclusion; not enough people pursuing vocational studies despite excellent labour market prospects in many trade professions; some tertiary institutions not providing youth with the right skills; and difficulties in reaching young people who disengage from school at an early age.

New Zealand policymakers are well aware of the importance of issues such as these, and the government invests heavily in helping young people make education employment choices during their transition years. Schools, for example, must 'provide appropriate career education and guidance for all students in year 7 and above' (NAG, 2006, No. 1, item vi). Policy initiatives include the www.in-transit.govt.nz website, the Gateway programme, Designing Careers, the Secondary-Tertiary Alignment Resource (STAR), Youth Transitions Services, He Ara Rangatahi, a $12.7 million boost to Career Services in the 2006 Budget, and the CPaBL programme. In 2008, the government published a policy document inviting public feedback on *Schools Plus*, a major development involving eleven Ministers (Ministry of Education, 2008). The vision for *Schools Plus* was very broad: 'transforming secondary schooling to encourage young people to stay and compete qualifications, and strengthening partnerships between schools, tertiary education organisations, employers, industry training organisations and non-government organisations to extend the learning opportunities available to students, and to connect young people to their next steps beyond school' (Ministry of Education, 2008, p.1).

Despite the number of agencies involved, despite the scale of public investment in these policies, and despite the policies' strategic importance for both individual well-being and New Zealand's national goals, there hasn't previously been a research programme specifically devoted to understanding and improving education employment linkages by young New Zealanders. The education employment linkages (EEL) research programme is a five-year research programme on successful education employment linkages for youth in New Zealand, funded by the Foundation for Research, Science and Technology (see www.eel.org.nz). It brings together research strengths in the Agribusiness and Economics Research Unit (AERU) at Lincoln University, the New Zealand Council for Educational Research and He Pārekereke at Victoria University of Wellington to fill this gap.

This chapter has three purposes. The first is to introduce the overall EEL research programme. This is achieved in the following section which sets out the programme's research aims and objectives, and describes the methods by which the research will be carried out over its five years. The second purpose is to explain a recent development in the economics literature on education employment linkages that will be an important guiding principle for the research team. Thus two sections of the chapter describe the standard model of human capital investment that has been at the core of economic research in this area, and then more recent papers that have adopted dynamic choice modelling techniques to understand youth transition. The third purpose is to describe the research that will be devoted to understanding employer-led channels in the overall system of helping young people make good education employment linkages. This is undertaken in the chapter's last section before a brief conclusion.

The EEL research programme

The aim of the research programme is to answer the question: How can formal support systems best help young New Zealanders make good education employment linkages to benefit themselves, their communities, and the national economy? To achieve this aim, the programme has four core objectives, each headed by an objective leader (see Dalziel et al, 2007):

1. To research and deliver new knowledge about effective systems in school communities for helping young New Zealanders make good education employment linkages (Karen Vaughan).
2. To research and deliver new knowledge about effective systems in regional communities for helping young New Zealanders make good education employment linkages (Jane Higgins).
3. To research and deliver new knowledge about effective systems in Maori and Pacific communities for helping young New Zealanders make good education employment linkages (Hazel Phillips).
4. To research and deliver new knowledge about systems for conveying the needs of employers to young New Zealanders, in order to improve education employment linkages (Paul Dalziel).

The research programme is built on the 'individual career management' paradigm that has emerged as the new standard of international best practice in this field (Bezanson, 2005; ISCDPP, 2006; Jarvis, 2003, 2006; OECD, 2004a, 2004b, 2006). This places the individual choice-maker at the centre of career management systems, based on strong international evidence that education employment matching is helped by good career development education (Bimrose, 2006; Bowes et al, 2005; Bysshe et al, 2002; Department for Education and Skills, 2006; DEST, 2005; Hughes et al, 2002; Smith et al, 2005). The young individual choice-maker does not make choices in isolation, of course, but encounters systems of support outside his or her immediate family. This is recognised in the four objectives of the research programme, which focus respectively on secondary school communities, on regional communities, on Maori and Pacific communities, and on employer-led channels.

The programme is comprised of five phases that are integrated across the four objectives. The objective leaders have begun in Phase 1 by working together on a cross-disciplinary literature review to place the research in its international context (Higgins et al, 2008). This phase 1 has adopted the 'systematic literature review' method (Hughes et al, 2005; Smith et al, 2005) to determine what is already known internationally about youth education employment linkages. Conceptual frameworks identified in that review will inform analysis in each subsequent stage. Phases 2 and 3 will include content analysis of documents, population and sample surveys, semi-structured interviews, and focus groups to understand current systems for helping young people make good education employment linkages. Phase 4 will involve three case studies in each objective, using intensive qualitative research tools to explore how positive outcomes are being achieved. In the final stage of the programme, Phase 5, the research team will choose two diverse sites where key stakeholders in local secondary school communities, in the wider local community, in local Maori and Pacific communities, and in local employer organisations, are willing to trial improved systems for better education employment linkages by young people. These pilots will integrate, apply and disseminate the new knowledge produced in the programme, thus meeting the overall research aim.

As noted above, the key research question is: How can formal support systems best help young New Zealanders make good education employment linkages to benefit themselves, their communities, and the national economy? These support systems are conceptualised as 'human activity systems' (Checkland, 1981) with four primary sites of engagement: school communities; regional communities; Maori and Pacific communities; and employer-led channels. The design of research methods has paid attention to two dimensions that the team thinks are particularly important for social scientists embarking on a new programme of policy-oriented research:

1. *Cross-disciplinary collaboration.* Each phase of the research is designed to move beyond cooperation (working together for individual ends) to achieving genuine cross-disciplinary collaboration among the key researchers (working together for a common end). Jeffrey (2003) notes that collaboration requires explicit planning and resources, and identifies four tools for collaboration: the development of a common vocabulary, the use of metaphor as an aid to understanding, the contribution of each discipline to the creation of common narratives within the project, and awareness of the forms of dialogue being utilised within the team. The budget provides for four meetings of the research team each year. Integration of disciplinary perspectives will be achieved at these

meetings, using tools such as those listed above, to achieve what Jeffrey calls the products of collaboration: process, understanding, utility, and knowledge integration. This reflective process will culminate in year 5 with an article analysing how the team's education, sociology, indigenous studies and economics perspectives were integrated in the programme's cross-disciplinary collaboration.

2. *Research validity.* The programme approaches research validity in terms of Cresswell and Miller's (2000) lens of the researcher, lens of the research participants, and lens of people external to the research. Each lens represents a viewpoint from which validity may be established. Different lenses of validity can be relevant at different stages of the research. In Phase 2, for example, the research will produce system maps to which no individual currently has access, and so the lens of the researcher is appropriate to identify when the maps are adequately drawn. In this case, validity will be achieved by using population surveys and expert informant interviews. A combination of researcher and participant lenses will be used in later phases, adding the tools of member checking (taking data and its interpretation back to research participants), prolonged engagement in the field by the researchers (particularly in the case study and pilot stages) and collaboration in the analysis of data with participants. Validity of the overall project will be addressed through the lens of people external to the study, made possible by the research team's collaboration with an external reference group of policy end-users and through the programme's links with four international experts.

The traditional economics model of human capital choices

Economics is based on the study of choices. Following the foundational contributions of Theodore Shultz (1961) and Gary Becker (1962, 1964), education choices have been typically modelled by economists as investment decisions, in which individuals make economic sacrifices in order to invest in acquiring 'human capital'. Recent reviews of this literature include Harmon et al (2003), Sianesi and Van Reenen (2003) and Tobias and Li (2004). In this model, an individual considers their potential net income (that is, after paying taxes and study costs) over their working life under two scenarios. Scenario 1 assumes that the individual chooses not to enrol in any further study. In scenario 2, there is an initial period of negative values for net income, during which the individual is engaged in full-time study. During this period, the person is not earning a wage and is paying tuition and other costs of study. Once the person graduates, however, he or she will expect to earn a higher income than someone who has not studied.

Thus there are two costs of investment in education: the fees and other costs of study, and the opportunity cost of foregone income during the period of education. A necessary condition for a person to choose education as a good investment is that the net present value of the benefits is not less than the net present value of the costs (net present value is a standard technique used by economists to compare costs and benefits that occur at different times).

It is not a sufficient condition, however, since there may be other constraints that prevent an individual from making their preferred choice. People who choose education must endure a period when their net income after study costs is negative. If young people have no access to credit or savings, they may be constrained in their choices to those paths in which net income is always positive, and so will not be able to enrol in study even if the net present value of the benefits is greater than the net present value of the costs. This analysis provides part of the economic case in favour of government-sponsored student loans schemes for post-compulsory education, although it must be said that the United States evidence suggests that credit constraints do *not* affect the choice to enrol in post-compulsory education (Cameron and Taber, 2004; Keane and Wolpin, 2001).

Another potential constraint is access to information, perhaps mediated through family influences and neighbourhood networks that often reinforce each other. Gaviria (2002, p.331) captures the flavour of the literature on family background as follows: 'If one were to summarize the main message of the massive scientific literature dealing with family influences, a single line would suffice: it pays to choose one's parents.' Ludwig (1999, p.17) summarises his own research project on this topic as follows:

> All adolescents seem to implicitly underestimate the educational
> requirements of their occupational goals, and teens (particularly

males) in high-poverty urban areas have less accurate information than those in other neighborhoods. Information varies across neighborhoods in part because of the effects of family socio-economic status on information, including the education and employment experiences of parents.

A characteristic of this theoretical approach is that it models a *single* choice being made at a *single* key moment in the young person's transition into the labour market. The model can allow for the choice taking some time to be settled, but the essence of its approach is that at some moment the choice-maker calculates the benefits and costs of further investment in education and on the basis of that calculation makes a rational choice (recognising multiple family and social influences on the individual's underlying preferences) about whether or not to study further.

Such a model has important implications for career guidance in secondary schools. If our understanding is that sometime before the age of 18 (say) most young people will have made their career and related education choices, then it is sensible for career advisors in schools to focus on providing students with as much information as possible to help them make that choice. Borghans et al (1996, p.71) summarise the problem well when they observe in a Dutch setting: 'On the one hand, the labour market is very complex, while on the other hand students who have to make their educational choice are rather inexperienced, and make such choices only a few times during their career.' The authors recommended from their study that better labour market information should be provided to students, including professional forecasts of the future labour market situation of different vocational specialisations.

The New Zealand Council for Educational Research has published a report on careers education in secondary schools (Vaughan and Gardiner, 2007). Among other things, the project asked careers staff in schools to indicate how important they considered a series of different careers activities. Nearly every activity was rated as important or very important/vital, but the three activities that rated the highest (scoring 75% or higher in the top category) were: students get advice on subject options related to careers; students gather or are given information about tertiary study and employment; and students are interviewed or counselled one-to-one about careers

(Vaughan and Gardiner, 2007, p.39). These results are consistent with the model just described, and fit in with its implication that advisors should help students make good choices by providing them with good information and advice.

As noted earlier in this chapter, there has been a paradigm shift in the international literature on careers guidance. This shift is reflected in a move towards a new name for people working in careers guidance from 'careers advisors' to 'careers educators'. This new paradigm puts less emphasis on providing information and advice *to* students in favour of teaching students *how* to access information for themselves and to develop their own career planning skills. This paradigm shift in the careers guidance field parallels an interesting and important shift in the economics approach to modelling education employment choices, which is the subject of the next section.

The new economics model of human capital choices

A feature of the traditional economics model is that the decision to invest in human capital is considered as a single choice made at a moment in time. More recent models have begun to treat human capital decisions as sequential choices, repeated year after year. These models recognise that people do not make a unique choice to undertake a certain level of life-time investment in education, but every year weigh up their options about education and employment.

A major breakthrough in this line of enquiry came with the stochastic dynamic programming model of Keane and Wolpin (1997), which Belzil (2007, p.1076) has described as 'most probably the most important contribution to the empirical schooling literature since Willis and Rosen (1979)'. In the model, each individual makes a choice every year beginning at age 16, with five alternatives: (1) participating in education; (2) working in a white-collar occupation; (3) working in a blue-collar occupation; (4) working in the military; or (5) engaging in home production. The model allows for a number of contributing factors such as: skill depreciation; experience in the first year of a new occupation; age effects; high school and college graduation effects; additional costs from changing occupations; non-pecuniary rewards in different occupations; consumption value of being at school, which varies with age; costs of returning to school after dropping out; age effects on the benefits from remaining at home; extra psychic benefits from completing a high school or college diploma; and an additional costs of leaving the military prematurely. The authors report that this extended model does a good job of fitting data gathered in the United States from the youth cohort of the National Longitudinal Surveys of Labor Market Experience (NLSY).

The mathematics and econometrics required to solve and estimate the model are very advanced. Nobody presumes that early school leavers can solve the necessary complex equations used by researchers, but the mathematics expresses the underlying assumption that different students make different choices year by year because of the different sets of constraints and opportunities open to them at any point in time. In a related paper, for example, Eckstein and Wolpin (1999) investigated factors influencing the decisions of young people to drop out of school, including the potential impact of part-time employment while at school. Their main result was that 'youths who drop out of high school have different traits from those who graduate – they have lower school ability and/or motivation, they have lower expectations about the rewards from graduation, they have a comparative advantage at jobs that are done by non-graduates, and they place a higher value on leisure and have a lower consumption value of school attendance' (Eckstein and Wolpin, 1999, p.1335).

A separate branch of the economics literature models sequential choices based on two or three periods (rather than the yearly analysis achieved in the above papers), but adds the key idea that one of the main functions of education is to enable students to discover more about their individual interests and abilities. An early expression of this idea was made by Manski (1989, p.305):

> Now consider a student contemplating enrollment. At this point, the student does not know whether he has the ability to complete the program under consideration. Nor does he know whether he will find it worthwhile to do so. The only way the student can definitively determine whether schooling is for him is by enrolling. Thus, the decision to enroll is a decision to initiate an experiment.

Two early models to incorporate this key idea were by Altonji (1993) and Weiler (1994). Both models allowed for two sequential decisions.

In the first decision, individuals choose whether to go on to higher education. During their undergraduate studies, they discover more about their abilities, their interest in study relative to work, and the costs and benefits of further study. These discoveries inform their second decision, which is whether to continue with their initial study plans.

More recently, Arcidiacono (2004) created and tested a more sophisticated model of post-compulsory education choices that is comprised of three periods. In the first period, individuals choose either to enter the labour force or go to college. If they choose to go to college, they choose the quality of the college (measured by the average SAT scores of its students) and one of four aggregate majors: natural sciences; business; education; and social science/humanities/other. At the end of the first period, the students get feedback on their abilities through grades on their studies. In the second period, individuals at college decide whether to drop out and enter the labour force or to continue their education for one more period. If they choose the latter, they again choose their college and major (this may be changed or not from their previous decision). In the third period, the individuals enter the labour force and earn income dependent on their qualifications and abilities.

Individual abilities are modelled as having measured and unmeasured components. The measured components are the math and verbal scores for the SAT Reasoning Test used by colleges as part of the admissions process in the United States. The unmeasured abilities include generic abilities to undertake college study and specific abilities to study for particular majors. Individuals (and ultimately employers) learn about these abilities by looking at the grades received in college study. The model assumes that the individual's enjoyment of education is related to the difference of the individual's ability compared to the average ability of classmates. The relationship is assumed to be quadratic, so that it is more costly for a low ability individual to go to a high quality college than for a high ability individual to go to a low quality college. This assumption produces an equilibrium in which high ability students tend to go to high quality colleges and low ability students tend to go to low quality colleges.

In the model, the expected earnings of an individual depend on the quality of college chosen, the major chosen, the individual's measured math and verbal abilities, the individual's expected grades depending on which school and which major are chosen, and other relevant individual characteristics such as gender. As well as expected earnings, the individual also enjoys some types of work more than others depending on their relative abilities and other individual characteristics. This flows over to their preferences for particular majors, again conditioned by relative abilities and individual characteristics. Thus a person who has a low math SAT score may not want to enrol in a math-intensive major, nor work in a math-intensive job, beyond the fact that it would be harder to succeed in the major or job given their poor math skills.

The mathematics and econometrics in the paper are again very sophisticated, but the basic point has been made. Individuals are assumed to be endowed with abilities (measured and unmeasured) relative to their peers and these abilities frame their education and employment choices, directly through their preferences for particular types of work and indirectly through expected earnings from different choices. As they learn more about their unmeasured abilities, the individuals may choose to change their education choices.

This is an exciting area of research, which incorporates into the human capital model insights from two branches of the economic literature. First, it draws on the signalling model introduced by Spence (1973, 1974) which develops the idea that qualifications allow highly skilled individuals to signal their ability to potential employers. This is because high ability individuals find education easier, and so choose more education, than low ability individuals. The signalling model suggests there should be an income premium to people who complete a qualification. This is due to the signalling effect of the completed qualification which is greater than for education which is incomplete. There is empirical evidence in support of this so-called 'sheepskin effect' (including for New Zealand; see Gibson, 2000). In his review of the signalling model, Riley (2001, p.460) explains that this interpretation is challenged if education does provide human capital:

> In the human capital model, the productivity of a college graduate is a function of what he has learned at college. This is positively related to his grades and the quality of the college that he attends. Presumably, those who drop out do so because they find the going tough and their grades are low. Thus, the productivity of the

dropouts is lower than that of a representative individual from the class. When income is regressed against years of college education plus a "sheepskin" dummy, the latter picks up the difference in the rate of capital accumulation among dropouts and the rest of the class.

Second, the sequential choice model draws on the occupational choice theory initiated by Roy (1951) which reflects the idea that people have different skills which lead them to different occupation choices on the assumption that they are motivated to maximise earnings. Earnings adjust in response to supply and demand, and so a general equilibrium emerges in which people choose the occupation where they have a comparative advantage based on their skills. Heckman and Honoré (1990) is a recent example of Roy's approach which adopts more general assumptions and modern econometric techniques to estimate the model empirically.

What are some of the implications of this new line of economics modelling, especially in contrast to the implications of the previous 'single choice' model? At this stage four have been recognised as particularly relevant for the education employment linkages research programme.

1. *Failure in education need not be a bad outcome.* This was the main point of Manski's (1989) original article. In an entrepreneurial culture, people should try new things and explore their potential interests and abilities. If they learn in the process that they do not have an ability to do well in a particular course of study, then this is important new information in their personal development.
2. *Persistence in failure is not likely to be a good outcome.* Generally students who discover they do not have an ability to do well in a particular course of study should not be advised to persist in their original plans. The new information about their abilities should be reflected in new career plans that build on their comparative advantage in skills. Policies that provide incentives to education institutions to encourage enrolled students to complete programmes may be counter-productive.
3. *Obtaining a qualification without genuine ability may not be a good outcome.* The review by Harmon et al (2003) draws on work by Chevalier (2003) to suggest that much of what appears to be

over-qualification in the United Kingdom labour force is explained by people having chosen to invest in qualifications that are above their genuine abilities (see also Hartog, 2000). Once employers discover their true potential, these workers are passed over for on-the-job training or promotion, and end up with a considerable discount on their life-time earnings.

4. *Matching qualifications to the right job is the best outcome.* There is strong evidence that 'the effects of finding employment related to one's field of study are substantial' (Grubb, 2002, p.318; see also Grubb, 1997). This differs depending on how much the skills involved in a field of study are occupation-specific. Robst (2007, pp.45–46), for example, reports from United States data that individuals who major in business management, engineering, the health professions, computer science, or law face more than a 20% wage penalty for working outside their field of study, but the wage effects are small or insignificant in liberal arts, English, the social sciences and education.

The last two points emphasise the importance of education employment linkages. Robst (2007, p.406) specifically comments that 'before choosing a major that focuses on occupation specific skills, students should be advised to make sure it is what they wish to pursue in their career [since] the cost to changing careers after getting the degree can be high'. Similarly, Grubb (1997, p.239) reflects wryly that 'it seems likely that many students are poorly informed about their choices and are mistakenly entering programs where the economic returns are insubstantial'.

Employer-led channels

The economics literature surveyed in the previous section suggests that successful formation of skills for work opportunities requires effective matching in three dimensions. The relationships are drawn in Figure 8.1. The individual has innate abilities that are not fully known to the individual, let alone to potential employers. Investment in education allows the individual to explore his or her potential abilities, and to build on them through acquiring increased human capital. To obtain the best return to that investment, the individual then needs to find an employment opportunity that makes use of his or her

Figure 8.1 Formation of Skills for Work

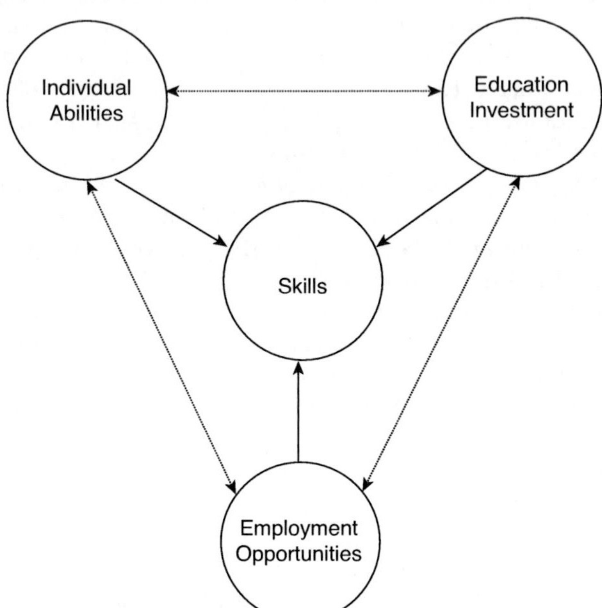

enhanced abilities. The combination of individual abilities, education investment and employment opportunities creates valuable skills, represented by the three solid lines in Figure 8.1. To be successful, there needs to be matching between individual abilities and education investment, between the individual abilities and employment opportunities, and between the education investment and the employment opportunities (each represented by the dashed line in the figure).

It is important to emphasise that current economics models treat these relationships as dynamic and uncertain. Employment opportunities are constantly changing as new technologies transform production systems and whole industries. There are a wide range of education institutions offering qualifications with a large variance in learning quality and relevance for employment. Individuals can discover their full potential abilities only by exploring different possibilities. This is a life-long process, far removed from the old assumption that most young people will have made their career and related education choices before the age of 18.

It is also apparent from Figure 8.1 that people wanting to form valuable skills for work need information about employment opportunities. How is this information obtained? In particular, how do young people still at secondary school obtain knowledge about employment opportunities and the associated requirements for investment in further education? This is a focus of the education employment linkages research programme, with one of its objectives devoted to understanding employer-led channels.

A stylised framework to begin this research objective is presented in Figure 8.2. It is 'stylised' because simple linear transition pathways such as those depicted in the figure are not as common for the modern generation as they once were. Nevertheless, the figure captures the concept that there are three important channels for information from employers to young people in secondary school (and their family, advisors and peers). There is a direct channel; there is an indirect channel through institutions offering further 'education' (leading to degree qualifications); and there is a second indirect channel through institutions offering further 'training' (leading to a vocational qualification). As well as tracing out the architecture of the system in Figure 8.2, the EEL research programme aims to test five hypotheses about the relative strengths of the linkages between different parts of the system:

1. *Linkages between employers and training institutions are strong.* The Industry Training Federation has a statutory obligation to provide leadership in the formation of skills for work, and it is hypothesised that this has created relatively strong linkages between employers and training institutions. The Skills New

Figure 8.2   Employer-Led Channels of Information

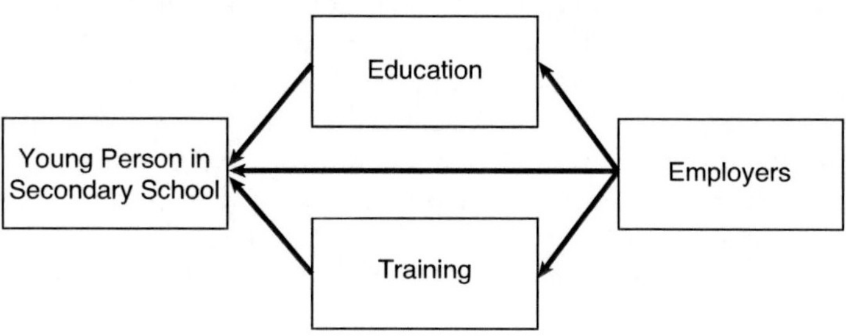

Zealand Tripartite Forum, for example, brings together government Ministers and officials, Business New Zealand, the New Zealand Council of Trade Unions and the Industry Training Federation to develop and implement a skills strategy for New Zealand (see its website at www.skillsstrategy.govt.nz). The involvement of Institutes of Technology and Polytechnics in leading the regional facilitation programme of the Tertiary Education Commission is likely to have reinforced these linkages.

2. *Linkages between employers and education institutions are not strong.* Over the last decade, there has been a marked increase in the engagement of New Zealand universities with regional and national industries. Nevertheless, there is an often-repeated view that universities do not have links with local employers that are as strong as their counterparts in the training sector. In part, this situation may reflect the distinctive contribution universities make to New Zealand's tertiary education system, which includes wider roles such as contributing to international research excellence and acting as critic and conscience of society.

3. *Linkages between education institutions and young people in secondary schools are strong.* Universities devote substantial resources to liaison with secondary schools. They provide career guidance offices of schools with large amounts of promotional material, organise functions and seminars for school teachers, host campus visits for school pupils, and arrange school visits from university academic and support staff. One of the research questions that the education employment linkages programme would like to explore is how much of this material is quality assured (particularly with respect to any claims made in it of employment opportunities arising from gaining the provider's qualifications).

4. *Linkages between training institutions and young people in secondary schools are not strong.* The OECD (2008) New Zealand country report on *Jobs for Youth* reported that 'not enough young people pursue vocational studies despite excellent labour market prospects offered by many trade professions' (p.9). A factor that might contribute to this observation is if training organisations do not have the same resources for communicating with young people in secondary schools as the education institutions.

5. *Linkages between employers and young people in secondary schools are weak.* If the hypotheses in (3) and (4) turn out to be supported by the evidence, then it is possible that the dominance of education

and training institutions in supplying schools with promotional material may mean that direct linkages between employers and young people in secondary schools are relatively weak. It is also possible, however, that web-based resources being created by Career Services (see www.careerservices.govt.nz) are having the opposite effect, making it easier for young people to access reliable information about post-education employment opportunities.

Conclusion

This chapter has introduced the education employment linkages research programme, selected for funding by the Foundation for Research, Science and Technology in 2007 under its *Building an Inclusive Society* portfolio. The aim of the research is to answer the question: How can formal support systems best help young New Zealanders make good education-employment linkages to benefit themselves, their communities, and the national economy? One of the four objectives in this research programme focuses specifically on employer-led channels for conveying information about employment opportunities to young people in secondary schools. The importance of these channels is based on a view that it is the successful combination of individual abilities, education investment and employment opportunities that creates valuable skills, as shown in Figure 8.1 (see also Stasz, 2001, for an insightful discussion on what is meant by the term 'skills for work' that compares the 'individualistic attributes' approach of economists and the 'interactive systems or social settings' approach of sociologists). The research team have drawn up five hypotheses about the strength of linkages between young people in secondary schools, training institutions, education institutions and employers, which taken together would suggest that employer-led channels of information to young people are weak in New Zealand. The direct channel may be the weakest of all current sources of information, while the other channels are weakened because either the linkages between employers and education institutions are not strong or the linkages between training institutions and young people in schools are not strong.

References

Altonji, J.G. (1993) 'The demand for and return to education when education outcomes are uncertain', *Journal of Labor Economics*, 11, 48–83.

Arcidiacono, P. (2004) 'Ability sorting and the returns to college major', *Journal of Econometrics*, 121, 343–375.

Battu, H., Belfield, C.R. and Sloane, P.J. (1999) 'Overeducation among graduates: A cohort view', *Education Economics*, 7, 21–38.

Becker, G. (1962) 'Investment in human capital: A theoretical analysis', *Journal of Political Economy*, 70, 9–49.

Becker, G. (1964) *Human Capital: A Theoretical and Empirical Analysis, with Special Reference to Education*, New York: Columbia University Press.

Belzil, C. (2007) 'The return to schooling in structural dynamic models: A survey', *European Economic Review*, 51, 1059–1105.

Bezanson, L. (2005) 'Career development: A time for transformation', Seventh annual lecture, Centre for Guidance Studies, University of Derby.

Bimrose, J. (2006) 'The changing context of career practice: Guidance, counselling or coaching?', Centre for Guidance Studies, University of Derby.

Borghans, L., de Grip, A. and Heijke, H. (1996) 'Labor market information and the choice of vocational specialization', *Economics of Education Review*, 15, 59–74.

Bowes, L., Smith, D. and Morgan, S. (2005) 'Reviewing the evidence base for careers work in schools,' Centre for Guidance Studies, University of Derby.

Bysshe, S., Hughes, D. and Bowes, L. (2002) 'The economic benefits of career guidance: A review of current evidence', Centre for Guidance Studies, University of Derby.

Cameron, S.V. and Taber, C. (2004) 'Estimation of educational borrowing constraints using returns to schooling', *Journal of Political Economy*, 112, 132–182.

Checkland, P. (1981) *Systems Thinking, Systems Practice*, Chichester: John Wiley.

Chevalier, A. (2003) 'Measuring over-education', *Economica*, 70, 509–531.

Cresswell, J.W. and Miller, D.L. (2000) 'Determining validity in qualitative inquiry', *Theory into Practice*, 39, 124–128.

Cunningham, C., Fitzgerald, E. and Stevenson, B. (2005) 'Pathways to employment: An analysis of young Maori workers', Massey University, Labour Market Dynamics Research Programme, research report No. 3/2005.

Dalziel, P., Higgins, J., Vaughan, K. and Phillips, H. (2007) 'Education employment linkages: An introduction to the research programme', EEL research report No. 1, AERU, Lincoln University, available from www.eel.org.nz.

Department for Education and Skills (2006) *Youth Matters: Next Steps*, London: HM Government, United Kingdom.

DEST (2005) 'The Australian network of industry careers advisers directions paper', Canberra, Department of Education, Science and Training.

Dupuis, A., Inkson, K. and McLaren, E. (2005) 'Pathways to employment: A study of the employment-related behaviour of young people in New Zealand', Massey University, Labour Market Dynamics Research Programme, research report No. 1/2005.

Eckstein, Z. and Wolpin, K.I. (1999) 'Why youths drop out of high school: The impact of preferences, opportunities, and abilities', *Econometrica*, 67, 1295–1339.

Gaviria, A. (2002) 'Intergenerational mobility, sibling inequality and borrowing constraints', *Economics of Education Review*, 21, 331–340.

Gibson, J. (2000) 'Sheepskin effects and the returns to education in New Zealand: Do they differ by ethnic groups?', *New Zealand Economic Papers*, 34, 201–220.

Grubb, W.N. (1997) 'The returns to education in the sub-baccalaureate labor market, 1984–1990', *Economics of Education Review*, 16, 231–245.

Grubb, W.N. (2002) 'Learning and earning in the middle, part I: National studies of pre-baccalaureate education', *Economics of Education Review*, 21, 299–321.

Harmon, C., Oosterbeek, H. and Walker, I. (2003) 'The returns to education: Microeconomics', *Journal of Economic Surveys*, 17, 115–155.

Hartog, J. (2000) 'Over-education and earnings: Where are we, where should we go?', *Economics of Education Review*, 19, 131–147.

Heckman, J.J. and Honoré, B.E. (1990) 'The empirical content of the Roy model', *Econometrica*, 58, 1121–1149.

Higgins, J. and Nairn, K. (2006) 'Choice and the children of New Zealand's economic reforms', *British Journal of Sociology of Education*, 27, 207–220.

Higgins, J., Vaughan, K., Phillips, H. and Dalziel, P. (2008) 'Education employment linkages: International literature review', EEL research report no. 2, AERU, Lincoln University, available from www.eel.org.nz.

Hughes, D., Bimrose, J., Barnes, S.-A., Bowes, L. and Orton, M. (2005) 'A systematic literature review of research into career development interventions for workforce development', Centre for Guidance Studies, University of Derby.

Hughes, D., Bosley, S., Bowes, L. and Bysshe, S. (2002) 'The economic benefits of guidance', Centre for Guidance Studies, University of Derby.

Hui Taumata (2005) *Hui Taumata 2005: Summary Report*, downloaded 9 June 2008 from http://www.huitaumata.maori.nz/pdf/summary-report.pdf.

ISCDPP (2006) 'Shaping the future: Connecting career development and workforce development', vision statement for the Third International Symposium on Career Development and Public Policy, Sydney, 21–24 April, 2006; downloaded 9 June 2008 from: http://careers.qut.edu.au/is2006/.

Jarvis, P.S. (2003) 'Career management paradigm shift: Prosperity for citizens, windfall for governments', discussion paper, National Life/Work Centre, Ottawa.

Jarvis, P.S. (2006) 'The changing face of career development', presentation to NATCON 2006 (National Consultation on Career Development), Ottawa Congress Centre, Ontario, 23–25 January.

Jeffrey, P. (2003) 'Smoothing the waters: Observations on the process of cross-disciplinary research collaboration', *Social Studies of Science*, 33, 539–562.

Keane, M.P. and Wolpin, K.I. (1997) 'The career decisions of young men', *Journal of Political Economy*, 105, 473–522.

Keane, M.P. and Wolpin, K.I. (2001) 'The effect of parental transfers and borrowing constraints on educational attainment', *International Economic Review*, 42, 1051–1103.

Ludwig, J. (1999) 'Information and inner city educational attainment', *Economics of Education Review*, 18, 17–30.

Manski, C.F. (1989) 'Schooling as experimentation: A reappraisal of the post-secondary dropout phenomenon', *Economics of Education Review*, 8, 305–312.

Ministry of Education (2008) *Schools Plus*, discussion document published by the Ministry of Education, Wellington.

NAG (2006) *National Administration Guidelines*, downloaded 9 June 2008 from: www.minedu.govt.nz/index.cfm?layout=document&documentid=8187&data=l.

Neuman, S. and Ziderman, A. (1990) 'Vocational schooling, occupational matching and labor market earnings in Israel', *Journal of Human Resources*, 26, 256–282.

OECD (2004a) *Career Guidance: A Guide for Policy Makers*, Paris: OECD.

OECD (2004b) *Career Guidance and Public Policy: Bridging the Gap*, Paris: OECD.

OECD (2006) 'The OECD thematic review on policies to facilitate school-to-work transition and improve youth employment', Paris: OECD.

OECD (2008) *Jobs for Youth: New Zealand*, country report prepared by Glenda Quintini, Paris: OECD.

Phillips, H. (2003) *Te reo karanga o ngā tauria Māori – Māori students: Their voices, their stories at the University of Canterbury, 1996–1998*, unpublished PhD thesis, University of Canterbury.

Riley, J. (2001) 'Silver signals: Twenty-five years of screening and signalling', *Journal of Economic Literature*, 34, 432–478.

Robst, J. (2007) 'Education and college match: The relatedness of college major and work', *Economics of Education Review*, 26, 397–407.

Roy, A. (1951) 'Some thoughts on the distribution of earnings', *Oxford Economic Papers*, 3(2): 135–146.

Shultz, T.W. (1961) 'Investment in human capital', *American Economic Review*, 51, 1–17.

Sianesi, B. and Van Reenen, J. (2003) 'The returns to education: Macro-economics', *Journal of Economic Surveys*, 17, 157–200.

Smith D., Lilley, R., Marris, L. and Krechowiecka, I. (2005) 'A systematic review of research (1988–2004) into the impact of career education and guidance during key stage 4 on young people's transitions into Post-16 opportunities', in Research Evidence in Education Library, London: EPPI-Centre, Social Science Research Unit, Institute of Education.

Spence, A.M. (1973) 'Job market signaling', *Quarterly Journal of Economics*, 87, 355–374.

Spence, A.M. (1974) *Market Signaling: Informational Transfer in Hiring and Related Screening Processes*, Cambridge: Harvard University Press.

Stasz, C. (2001) 'Assessing skills for work: Two perspectives', *Oxford Economic Papers*, 53, 385–405.

Tobias, J.L. and Li, M. (2004) 'Returns to schooling and Bayesian model averaging: A union of two literatures', *Journal of Economic Surveys*, 18, 153–180.

Vaughan, K. (2005) 'The pathways framework meets consumer culture: Young people, careers and commitment', *Journal of Youth Studies*, 8, 173–186.

Vaughan, K., Roberts, J. and Gardiner, B. (2006) *Young People Producing Careers and Identities*, Wellington: New Zealand Council for Educational Research.

Vaughan, K. and Gardiner, B. (2007) *Careers Education in New Zealand Schools*, Wellington: New Zealand Council for Educational Research.
Voon, D. and Miller, P. (2005) 'Undereducation and overeducation in the Australian labour market', *Economic Record*, 81, S22–S33.
Weiler, W.C. (1994) 'Expectations, undergraduate debt and the decision to attend graduate school: A simultaneous model of student choice', *Economics of Education Review*, 13, 29–41.
Willis, R. and Rosen, S. (1979) 'Education and self-selection', *Journal of Political Economy*, 87, S7–S35.

9
Unions, Workers and Developing Human Capability: A Social Psychological Perspective

Leda Blackwood

The concerns of human capability development have ostensibly been claimed by human resource management (HRM) discourse and practice that depoliticises (and individualises) the employment relationship, providing top-down approaches where the focus is on policies and practices that are aimed at the agentic and motivated worker, but designed in the interests of the employer (Cornelissen et al, 2007). The psychologically informed research that evaluates these practices for the most part also depoliticises and individualises the employment relationship. This may reflect what Zickar (2004) describes as the historical indifference of industrial and organisational psychology to unions and to the power dynamics between employers and workers. Investigation of workers' responses to HRM practice is limited to evidence of commitment and satisfaction (and their opposite) and to individual-level psychological explanations that atomise workers (Ellemers, DeGilder and Haslam, 2004). Although the existence of competing sets of values and interests that are shared by groups of workers is acknowledged, the emphasis is on intra-organisational solutions that can manage any ensuing tensions. The political achievement of linking the development of capable workers to productivity, and not to social justice outcomes, has consequences both for practice and for research. What is conspicuously absent is the notion of workers' organising to transform the organisation; and the role of outside actors (e.g., unions) in the development of this collective capability.

In this chapter, I take a social psychological perspective and argue that the dynamic interactions between individuals, organisations, and the institutions that structure the employment relationship give rise to our aspirational goals and so to the requisite capabilities. My principal interest is in how we might open up a space for thinking about the role of unions in the development of human capability in the workplace and in society more broadly. There are three parts to this chapter. The first provides the broad context of union agendas and debates around skills development and the organisation of workplaces and its contribution to productivity and union renewal. The second is more theoretical, exploring the psychological motivations and processes through which workers come to understand and seek to transform their experience of work. I then return to unions and report on work by the Industrial Relations Centre (Victoria University of Wellington, New Zealand) that tracks the development of provisions within collective bargaining. These capture the normative changes in what is expected within the employment relationship. Finally, I conclude with some thoughts about the challenge the human capability framework presents for unions and workers.

Union context and debates

In response to global capitalism, countries such as Australia, New Zealand (NZ) and the United Kingdom have been pursuing high-road approaches to economic growth that fit with notions of human capability development, a term that encompasses attributes of the individual and the organisation that can produce capable workers (see 'Australia 2020', Australian Government 2008; 'Workforce 2010', Department of Labour, New Zealand 2001; Realising Britain's Potential, HM Government 2008). In adherence to third-way precepts workers and employers are positioned as sharing the same interests, and it is assumed that capability development leads to increased productivity which leads to higher wages and organisational sustainability. As a bonus, it is often presented as productive of important psychological benefits where workers derive pride and respect from the meaningfulness of their work and from their social relations in the workplace. Under Labour governments in these countries, union movement leaders have championed the above arguments, often more so than employers (Heery, 2002; Kelly, 2004), and have been instrumental in the development of initiatives such as industry partnerships, quality circles, employee voice mechanisms, and workplace learning representatives.

Unions' mobilisation of a discourse that links capability development initiatives with an end goal of industry development and economic growth in part reflects one view that to secure their survival
under modern capitalism unions must demonstrate their legitimacy
on the basis of (a) workers' contribution to productivity; and (b) the
contribution of unions to the management of employment-related
conflict (Baccaro et al, 2003; Kochan and Osterman, 1994). This finds
expression for instance, in the NZ Council of Trade Union's 'Organising Plus' strategy for rebuilding the NZ union movement and in
particular, the industry partnerships approach. Although the objectives of building unity across the labour movement and increasing
union density and member activism are articulated within the strategy, these are presented as a means towards largely extrinsic ends.
The goal of a stronger, more dynamic union movement is to achieve
a highly skilled, highly productive, high wage economy where unions
are granted the right to exist as 'natural social partners'.

The accommodation of unions to the edicts of global capitalism
do not of course go unchallenged. For instance, interviews with NZ's
union leadership in 2006 and 2007 showed some reservations about
the Council of Trade Union's strategy – particularly around the underlying premise in respect of tying union legitimacy to productivity, and
more specifically the industry partnerships approach, where this
was seen by some as 'getting into bed with the bosses' (Blackwood,
2008). This fits with broader concerns within the industrial relations
(IR) literature that the acceptance of a neo-liberal agenda provides
the institutional conditions that are contributory of union disaffection
(Levesque et al, 2005; McCallum, 2002; Peetz, 2002). Internationally,
there is mounting criticism within labour movements (Baccaro
et al, 2003; Frege and Kelly, 2003, 2004; Hyman, 1999; Milkman and
Voss, 2004) of third-way social partnership arrangements and the
articulation of new (or renewed) forms of union organising that include
union democratisation processes that recognise and build from a
diversity of interests; building community alliances (associational
campaigning); and mobilising around shared community values. A
number of NZ union leaders showed a keen awareness of the need to
democratise their unions, providing more opportunities for member
input into and engagement with the work of the union and refocusing
organisers on providing leadership and 'lifting the sights of members'
in terms of what unions are about. For some, this was couched as

concern that the acceptance of unions' role as bargaining agents and not political organisations had endorsed a neo-liberal view of the world where 'union members start(ed) to think of themselves as consumers of union services, not as members of the union movement' (Blackwood, 2008). In this vein, some spoke of their current efforts to change their approach to organising and the structures supporting this through increased investment in education and training for delegates and the creation of bottom-up decision-making processes. In recent years some unions too, have had considerable success mobilising both workers and the public around social justice concerns for vulnerable workers (e.g., UNITE, SFWU) as well as around the kinds of higher order values that organisations typically include in their mission statements and corporate people promises (e.g., we are committed to quality service; Finsec, PSA).

A social psychological perspective

Within the competing discourses that frame the above debates there is a capable worker who has both agency and motivation directed towards the achievement of collective (or group) goals, whether this is the achievement of greater productivity or of challenging social and economic arrangements. The sense of what's required is also the same: (a) the development of leadership and a shared vision to achieve agreement over the collective goals and the behaviour required to achieve those goals; and (b) the development of social arrangements through team building and involvement in decision-making structures, often seen in instrumental terms (i.e., contribution to coordination and 'good' decisions), but critical to the formation of social bonds and motivation for group effort (see the NZ Department of Labour productivity agenda).

In so far as capability development has been linked to productivity and not to social justice outcomes, this can be seen as a political victory for its proponents with important consequences both for practice and for research. From a social psychological perspective, what is being mobilised (and contested) through these practices is the understanding and motivational aspects of social (or group) identity. Specifically it impacts on workers: (a) sense of a shared fate; (b) shared (normative) beliefs about values, goals, and behaviours (e.g., shared vision); and (c) social and emotional aspects (e.g., belonging, respect, and pride) that contribute to coordination and motivation, to people wanting to go the extra mile. The importance of this mobilisation of identity is underscored by a large body of research cited by Haslam and colleagues (2003a), where the social and emotional dimensions of organisational identity predict a range of organisational outcomes, including 'loyalty, productivity, organizational citizenship, desire to comply with organizational rules, reactions to organizational change, and willingness to communicate' (p.361). In the collective action literature too, including research looking at unions, strength of social and emotional attachment with the social movement or union has been found to outperform personally held union-related beliefs in the prediction of behaviour (Kelly and Breinlinger, 1996). Moreover, there is considerable evidence in both organisational and union-related research of individual-level interests and goals being sacrificed for the advancement of collective goals by those who strongly identify with the group (e.g., taking the blame for the group's poor performance: Taylor and Doria, 1981; or participating in prolonged strike action despite anticipated failure: Winterton and Winterton, 1989).

An understanding of the group-based psychological processes that underpin people's behaviour when group-based identities are activated has in recent years led to a re-examination of the often conflicting findings in organisational research on what contributes to the formation of organisational identity and commitment; of what can strengthen or undermine this; and of the material consequences for organisational behaviour; as well as in the social movement research on the conditions for collective action and the processes by which identities are politicised. This research is largely informed by the social identity perspective, comprising both social identity theory (Tajfel and Turner, 1979) and self-categorisation theory (Turner et al, 1987), which provides an account of behaviour that stands in stark contrast to traditional views of atomistic individuals guided by personal-level values and cost-benefit calculations. Importantly, this research has shown group-based identification as a psychological reality, something which when contextually salient has very real consequences for how people experience themselves and their world, and for how people act.

The discussion below focuses on the implications of this theory and body of research for thinking about the understanding, agency and motivation functions of identity, achieved through the implementation of practices associated with the high performance workplace but equally consistent with any identity project. What I am most interested in are those features that relate to: (a) leadership and the creation of shared vision; (b) the social-psychological factors that contribute to and are emergent of work-related group identification(s); and (c) the range of strategies that organisations (within the HR/IR organisational literature) or groups of workers (within the social movement literature) can adopt in the formation and pursuit of the things they value.

Leadership and the creation of agency through shared vision

Critical to the success of any political project is the achievement of a shared understanding of our world and the unity of purpose this provides to those who share a social identity (Reicher, Haslam and Hopkins, 2005; Turner, 2005). This unity produces the social power through which people can create a social world that celebrates the things they value and aspire to. It is perhaps the most fundamental capability of all and is what successful leaders, whether they are in work organisations or unions, seek to harness through what has been described as the 'entrepreneurship of identity': the creation of a shared vision of 'who we are' and 'what we want to be' (Reicher and Hopkins, 2001, cited in Haslam et al, 2003b). But, contrary to our more individualistic theories, leadership is viewed here as a group phenomenon – as involving both leaders and followers in the negotiation of meaning and intent. While in keeping with notions of the charismatic leader, successful leaders are those who can transform followers' identities, it is argued that this remains contingent on their not violating followers' understandings of either their identity or of their social reality (Reicher, Haslam and Hopkins, 2005).

This understanding of leadership as a more dynamic group process is underlined by research pointing to differential responses to leaders based on worker identification with the group and the perception of a leader's prototypicality of the group (van Knippenberg et al, 2005). For instance, for those who do not strongly identify with the group, research has found that evaluation of the group leader will be more influenced by whether they have the stereotypical traits of leadership and that loyalty and cooperation will derive from individual-level concerns (e.g., fairness and the exchange value of the relationship, Platow and van Knippenberg, 2001). On the other hand, for those who are strongly identified, negative and counter-stereotypical qualities of the leader will more readily be forgiven or attributed to external factors (Bruins, Ellemers and de Gilder, 1999) and what has been shown to be of greater importance is whether the leader is seen as a positive embodiment of the normative values and behaviours of the group (Duck and Fielding, 1999; Ellemers, de Gilder and Haslam, 2004; Hogg, Hains and Mason, 1998). Moreover, the more the leader is seen as this positive embodiment of the 'ingroup', the more their exercise of power will lead to greater willingness on the part of their followers to cooperate in the future. By contrast, an 'outgroup' leader's exercise of power will be seen as more illegitimate, punitive, and unreasonable (Haslam et al, 2001) and will result in less willingness to cooperate in the future (Ellemers et al, 1997). This understanding of leadership fits with the renewal of interest in the 'transformative' and 'charismatic' leader and in an emerging interest in leader 'authenticity' (Avolio and Gardner, 2005). However, because it locates the dynamic relationship between leader and follower within the group, it turns our attention to qualities of the group (e.g., normative values) and group processes (e.g., mutual social influence).

An ethnographic study conducted by Plankey Videla (2006) in a Mexican garment factory demonstrates the group dynamics involved in how this 'entrepreneurship of identity' is negotiated and achieved. Management through a discourse of loyalty and sacrifice constructed what she terms, a 'community of fate' ideology, with workers and management united in their commitment to the firm's new 'lean production' regime. For almost five years this produced workers who were willing to 'extend their physical, intellectual and emotional labour to the firm' (p.2099) and make substantial sacrifices. However, over time, management was observed to be failing to reciprocate workers' loyalty and share in the sacrifice, they were failing to embody the normative values of the group. This was experienced as a betrayal of trust and culminated in strike action. In a context of conflict with management, the union was able to form solidarity around a new 'community of fate', one defined by the workers' struggle against their employer. As one unionist calling for strike action declared, '...we are in this dance together' (p.2113).

Because the 'entrepreneurship of identity' around a shared vision is a negotiated act between leaders and followers, it presupposes that there is a shared basis for understanding the world. In this respect, according to Reicher and colleagues (2005; Reicher, 2004) this process does involve looking back to structure, to a social, political, and economic reality that positions us and may constrain the choices we are able to make. But as the above example demonstrates, this is an active process of (re)defining the political context that is also very much future-oriented. Both management and union leaders are engaged in a contest over what the boundaries of categories are [i.e., who is included (and excluded) from the group], and over the content of categories (i.e., how to make sense of who 'we' are, our values and goals and what is required to realise these).

In thinking about organisations' and unions' identity projects, the modern conundrum is that within the world of work there is a multiplicity of nested work-based and social identities as well as personal identities that may by in conflict with the broader or superordinate identities that they are seeking to create. When thinking about the strategic mobilisation of work-related categories, for instance, it is not simply the category but the relationships within which the category is nested that has behavioural consequences. Who we compare ourselves with in a given context has implications for how we understand ourselves, how we're positioned and the attributes we use to define ourselves (Haslam et al, 1992). Although in the context of competition with an outside organisation, management and workers may indeed feel united in the pursuit of shared goals there are also times when our identity as managers versus workers, as members of a team, or of an occupational grouping for instance, may be more salient.

It is for the above reasons that social psychologists who take a social identity perspective to questions of managing intergroup differences in work organisations recommend against top-down approaches where identity is imposed on workers in favour of a bottom-up process that builds a collective identity upon the recognition of distinct lower level (sub-group) identities. The most elaborated approach is Haslam and colleagues' (Haslam, Eggins and Reynolds, 2003) ASPIRe model, which describes a process for producing organisational identity around shared superordinate values that can (a) accommodate diversity or difference amongst sub-groups of employees and (b) ensure that any conflict that does arise is 'managed' so as to protect the organisation. Haslam et al sound a word of caution, however. Whilst all groups are motivated to shape what is valued and the interests of the superordinate identity, higher status groups have a greater capacity to do so. Within these projects, those sub-groups that are more powerful (e.g., managers and high-skill workers) may not be motivated to allow for the 'creative' conflict processes proposed.

Although designed with work organisations in mind, the model also resonates for superordinate identity projects such as those framed by the NZ productivity agenda or the Council of Trade Union's 'Organising Plus' agenda. The reality for New Zealand, as for our main comparators – Australia and the UK, is that union membership is predominantly located in the public service (53%). Within the private sector, membership continues to hold in traditional union strongholds (e.g., manufacturing 20%; and transport, storage and communication, 11%), that tend to be in business decline. But not in growth areas such as retail, restaurants and hotels (5%) (Feinberg-Danieli, Lafferty and Kiely, 2007). The vast majority of union members are part of the high-skill labour market and by virtue of their greater levels of security and their capacity to organise may feel greater value and confidence in entering into arrangements that are part of the productivity agenda. Indeed, unions such as the Public Service Association were already doing this in the 1990s. This was seen as feasible because in areas such as the public service and health: (a) there had been long-standing relationships with employers who respected the potential contribution of public sector unions and their largely high-skilled, professional members; and (b) the union itself was strong with a membership whose professional identity contained a strong ethic of public service and commitment to contributing to decision-making around service quality. The great bulk of workers however, do not enjoy this capability to define and pursue their values and interests, neither in their work, nor in the shaping of what the union movement is about, that broader superordinate identity required for a unified movement. Thus, the imbalance in power that is present between groups of workers has implications not just within our workplaces but within civil society too.

Social-psychological factors contributing to agency and motivation for group effort

The emphasis on democratisation and worker involvement in workplaces and unions is often explained in terms of the contribution workers can make to decision-making. In light of the research on leadership and the importance of leaders understanding and respecting their followers' own understandings of social reality, these processes are also thought to be crucial at a more fundamental level. By providing the conditions for achieving shared understanding, values, and goals these processes may contribute to workers' ability to organise, a key factor in agency. Moreover, by contributing to feelings of trust and respect, these processes should pay important dividends in terms of motivation and effort. Empirical support has been found for a range of organisational practices, such as participative decision-making (Yukl, 1989) and participative group goal-setting (Wegge, 2000), predicting organisational identity, commitment, and effort. There is also, however, a growing body of research (Haslam, Powell and Turner, 2000) to suggest that these same practices can set employees up for the feelings of disillusionment and powerlessness reported in the stress and job burnout literature. This has been found, for instance, where despite their best efforts employees can not live up to those shared values and goals because of inadequate resources or conflicting demands. Indeed, job burnout, which is defined as exhaustion, cynicism (or loss of ideal-ism and passion for the job), and a sense of personal inefficacy (see Schaufeli and Enzmann, 1998), has been most closely associated with high-skill occupations in human service organisations (Maslach, 2003), those very high performance work practice organisations that have typically been leaders in skill development including through the implementation of high involvement management practices.

Research that links the reduction of group effort associated with stress and job-burnout to people's sense of incongruency between work-related values and behaviours is part of a recent shift in focus to motivational aspects of identity (e.g., Simon, Lucken and Sturmer, 2006; Smith and Kessler, 2004; Sturmer, Simon and Loewy, 2008). A central tenet of social identity theory is that we derive self-esteem from our group memberships and so are motivated to emphasise similarities on favoured dimensions of the group as well as differ-ences with comparable outgroups (Tajfel and Turner, 1979). It is this that leads us to assimilate to group norms (we expect to be in agree-ment about values and behaviours) and to exert effort in the coor-dinated pursuit of group goals. According to Tyler and Blader's (2000) model of cooperation, because our group memberships are so impor-tant to our sense of self-esteem, it is our pride in and respect from the groups we belong to that has most impact on our psychological attachment and motivation to cooperate not just with the leader but with the group. Thus feeling organisational level pride and respect are more than an added benefit, cooperation with the organisation will be maintained to the extent that the organisation contributes to self-worth. Boezeman and Ellemers (2007) have found support for this and for the path proposed by Tyler and Blader (2000). Feeling respected by the organisation strengthens identity because it signals to us our standing in the group, it is an indicator of our success or failure in the eyes of valued others (Leary and Baumeister, 2000; Leary, 2005). There is indirect evidence to support this explanation with research (Simon, Luken and Sturmer, 2006) showing the effects of respectful treatment as more important for those members of an organisation who had fewer rights and opportunities to participate (i.e., those with low standing in the group). Once these group members felt respected as valued members of the group, personal-level concerns ceased to matter, what became more important were organisational-level concerns.

The importance of respectful treatment has received considerable attention, evident in research and initiatives around procedural justice, high involvement management, and employee voice (both union and non-union). There has been less attention to the group-based pride (or shame and cynicism) that derives from one's group's achievements and from how it is evaluated by outside actors. Consistent with the research on leadership cited above, Meyer and Allen (1997) and Mael and Ashforth (1992) have demonstrated increased employee turnover in response to a deteriorating public image of the organisation. Moreover, experimental research by Leach and colleagues (Leach, Ellemers and Barreto, 2007) suggests that in some contexts what matters more to our sense of group pride can be the perceived morality of our group (i.e., virtuosity, authenticity, and honesty) and not, as more functionalist accounts suggest, competence or achievement. Although this is an area requiring further research, it supports our understanding of the importance of congruency between an employer or union's articulated identity and workers' experience; and between the group identity as presented to outside audiences and the group's public reputation (Borgerson, Escudero-Magnusson and Magnusson, 2006; Hatch and Schultz, 2002).

Although there has been some research on the role of emotions in social movement participation (e.g., Drury and Reicher, 2005; van Zomeren et al, 2004), there is little if any union-related research on the emotional impact of union strategies on employee's union-related and work-related identities and behaviours. Two examples of union action, taken from very different organisations, are however, illustrative. In the first, with the assistance of their union, UNITE (a NZ union representing non-standard workers in fast-foods, cinemas, and casinos), young workers in a McDonalds forced management to adopt a more consistent and transparent rostering process. According to the young workers' own accounts, as well as improving individual workers' ability to plan around their work (an instrumental outcome), the effect of having collectively acted to secure more respectful treatment from their managers was a sense of camaraderie and pride, pride in themselves and in the kind of workplace they had created. Thus, in addition to improving work conditions, action had achieved what McDonalds' 'Corporate People Promise' could not, workers who were happy to come to work and who were committed to each other (their work group) and to their work, but perhaps not to McDonalds. In research conducted with members of UNITE in 2007, there was strong support for the critical role of these group-based evaluations. A sense of both respect from the union and pride in its achievement significantly mediated the relationship between members' participation in union action and their intentions to participate in the future (Blackwood and Louis, 2009).

The second example comes from the human services sector where the overwhelming public support for bank workers in a NZ Westpac campaign was given much of the credit for winning the dispute. Although this was explained by union leaders in terms of the political leverage achieved through brand damage (instrumental concerns) these same union leaders also spoke of the boost to members' pride and confidence in themselves as powerful agents in the workplace. This was seen as arising from members' belief that the union campaign was serving broader community values and had the support of their co-workers, customers, and the general public (Blackwood and Louis, 2009). In their subsequent Better Banks campaign, Finsec countered the divide and rule strategy of the banks, producing a common in-group identity that aligned bank employees across the sector with the broader community interest of quality service and debt reduction, against the greed and social irresponsibility of the banks. This appeared to reflect some understanding that the stress workers may experience in response to not being able to live up to the organisation's values is about more than simply inadequate resources and conflicting demands. For those in front-line jobs there may be a dissonance or conflict between the community values workers were told they share with their employer and the reality of their work where the requirement to increase productivity was seen to produce anti-social outcomes. The social-psychological consequences of campaigns such as these for how workers understand themselves and their union is deserving of further study.

Strategies in pursuit of the things workers value

The focus of practice and research around capability development is directed towards transforming individuals so they may adapt to the needs of organisations in a changing world. In this sense it looks backwards to social arrangements and structure. But, fundamental to human nature is our orientation to the future. We are able to conceptualise how we want our organisations and indeed our world to be. This suggests a very different understanding of skill development. One where through the social power that flows from social identity people can assert a contrary view. This is always the greatest challenge for low-status or low-power groups, whether it is unions in partnership with industry, or groups of workers within an organisation or union.

Social psychologists examine the range of strategies we adopt to combat the negative consequences of low-power or status. The most common strategies identified (Tajfel and Turner, 1979) are (a) social mobility where the individual believes they can improve their position through personal effort; and (b) social creativity where a group seeks to enhance status through comparison on non-status relevant dimensions that favour the group (e.g., we may be lower-paid, but we have better social relations). Neither of these strategies threatens the social order, and accordingly they are actively supported by high-status groups (e.g., merit-based promotions and strategies for reframing 'dirty-work': Ashforth and Kreiner, 1999). The pursuit of a social change strategy where group members act collectively to change the group's outcomes (or status) is contingent on identifying with the low-status group and believing that (a) this low-status position is illegitimate; (b) the boundaries between the two groups are impermeable; and (c) there is an alternative to the structural relationship (Tajfel and Turner, 1979). This is supported by a large body of research on collective action that shows the crucial factor is a shift in causal attributions for lack of success from internal attributions (e.g., insufficient knowledge, skills, and networks as emphasised in skill development approaches) to external attributions, such as economic factors and illegitimate practices, that implicate group membership (Kelly and Breinlinger, 1996; Kelly and Kelly, 1994).

In one sense, the above beliefs are the property of individuals predisposing them to particular readings of context. They can also be conceptualised as properties of a politicised identity in that they constitute normative beliefs about how one's group relates to another group and the possibility for change, providing both understanding and agency (Simon and Klandermans, 2001). But it is in a specific context that people perceive matters in group terms and where questions about the legitimacy of an intergroup relationship and the potential for one's group to have an effect on that relationship arise. Rather than the alternative ideological versus instrumental routes to action, widely supported in the industrial relations literature, this implicates the contextual activation of a behaviourally-relevant group where people's values and goals, as well as their beliefs about what constitute appropriate courses of action, are understood at the group level (Turner et al, 1987). In support of this, longitudinal research revealed that independently of their union-related beliefs, people engaged in union activity where their perception of an inter-group context of threat and in-group norms supporting such behaviour made it meaningful to do so. Moreover, these perceptions of the social context qualified the role played by people's union-related beliefs in ways that differed depending on whether the studies were conducted during periods of industrial stability or conflict (Blackwood, 2007b).

Implicit in current debates around union strategy and tactics, are beliefs about the stability of people's belief-systems versus their social-contextual specificity and openness to influence and change. These beliefs map onto competing theoretical approaches within social psychology, for investigating collective behaviour. On the one hand are value-expectancy theories which have tended to privilege individual-level explanations and produce static rational-actor models that favour servicing models (Klandermans, 1992). Research informed by such models is cited in the industrial relations literature as providing support for the ascendancy of selfish individualism, the demise of ideology, and an argument for servicing approaches (e.g., Klandermans, 1984, 1986). On the other hand, more recent theoretical developments influenced by the social identity perspective suggest a more dynamic and genuinely social-psychological model (Simon and Klandermans, 2001; Simon et al, 1998). According to this perspective, by individuating workers' interests, approaches associated with the servicing model (and the business unionism model) actively de-politicise the employment relationship and produce the demise in ideology and action. Thus, more recent research focuses on the processes through which social movement-related beliefs (whether conceptualised in terms of the legitimacy and stability of intergroup relations or ideology and collective agency) come to be deeply held and constituent of a politicised identity. Of course, such deep convictions are not a priori of experience but are formed in the crucible of political experience where political organisations provide the leadership and opportunity structures for sense-making, in conversation with those who share a common fate. Thus we come full circle in our very brief social psychological tour of the production of understanding, agency and motivation.

Collective bargaining outcomes

Both legislation and collective bargaining outcomes are important markers of unions' institutional level success. They might also be conceived as important markers of the extant and emerging normative expectations of workers (and their employers) around the kinds of lives we expect to be able to lead (Barry, 2004). Notwithstanding ongoing contestation around the parameters, NZ employees have basic legislated provision around minimum wages, leave, occupational health and safety and so forth (Blackwood, 2007a). These legislated minimum standards signal the normalisation of societal-level expectations around work, an agreement on what constitutes a decent working life to which all members of a society are entitled. It is in the contestation around both the parameters and the activation of these minimum standards and around emergent areas of public concern that we see the mobilisation of social power for the transformation of not only workplaces, but of the broader society, of what is valued and of what is required to realise those values. Areas of emergent concern can be observed in parental and domestic leave provisions, employee consultation and representation, and training and skills development. More nascent are provisions that address work-life balance (e.g., TOIL, working from home arrangements and tele-working for mainly professional workers). As the 'baby boomers' approach retirement a new category with a powerful voice has come into view, that of the older worker (Blackwood, 2007a). Around the corner, we might anticipate that another set of interests will emerge from the increasing levels of public concern around environmental sustainability.

The point of examining emergent areas of concern for our institu-tions, both our legislators and our unions, is that underlying these institutions are group-based interests and that it is the political con-testation over interests that influences outcomes. From this perspec-tive who has collective voice and who does not is central to how our organisations and society will continue to be transformed. Much of the focus has been on the struggle between employers and employ-ees in terms of conflict over values and interests. But also acknow-ledged is that there are distinct sets of values and interests for different groups of workers and at times these may be in conflict. As one parti-cipant observed in our focus groups around the developing human capability framework, one worker's valuing of a clean office requires that a low-paid cleaner works unsocial hours. Further on the matter of work-life balance there is little evidence of voice around the feast-famine experience of employment for many non-standard workers. And this is the challenge for unions. As much as an appreciation for diversity, the notion that different groups might have different values, is required of our work organisations, it is perhaps more urgently required of our unions. It is our unions that can provide the leadership and the opportunity structures for the emergent power of workers identifying shared values and interests and acting collectively in their pursuit.

Summary and conclusion

The creation of social identities are indeed important, whether it be unions and employers united around the interests of New Zealanders; management and workers united around a work organisation's inter-ests, or unions united in the pursuit of workers' interests. Within all of these superordinate groups there are sub-groups that exist in relations of status and power to each other. When the exercise of this power is seen to be illegitimate and fails to validate all subgroup identities on dimensions that are valued by those groups the project is undermined. Thus, current theorising and research (e.g., Haslam et al, 2003a) suggests that the challenge is to produce the structures and processes that can genuinely involve all groups in the identification and valorisation of both shared and distinct sets of values and interests. This is a dynamic process, a negotiation that is neither wholly bottom-up nor top-down. Much of the research and practice in relation to diversity in organisations and the voice mechanisms that are associated with the high performance work place or democratisation of unions only partially recognise this, what is frequently ignored are the consequences of power differences and the concomitant failure to facilitate low-status group's organisation and articulation of values and interests. Reflecting on similar concerns, Heckshcer (1988, p.177) suggests what is needed is a new kind of unionism, one that 'replaces organisational conformity with coordinated diversity' through an appreciation of new fault lines of union solidarity. To end, the developing human capability framework which begins from an engagement with workers about what they value in their work and the factors that impinge on achieving this, is as much a tool for unions as it is for work organisations. Because of their distinct function, the challenge for unions is how they work with different groups of workers in both the identification of new fault lines that reflect workers experiences and the development of shared understandings and agency that can be mobilised to enhance their collective outcomes.

References

Ashforth, B.E. and Kreiner, G. (1999) 'How can you do it?: Dirty work and the dilemma of identity', *Academy of Management Review*, 24, 413–434.

Australian Government (2008) Australia 2020 Initial Summit Report. Available at www.australia2020.gov.au/initial_report/index.cfm

Avolio, B.J. and Gardner, W.L. (2005) 'Authentic leadership development: Getting to the root of positive forms of leadership', *Leadership Quarterly*, 16, 315–338.

Baccaro, L., Hamann, K. and Turner, L. (2003) 'The politics of labour movement revitalization: The need for a revitalized perspective', *European Journal of Industrial Relations*, 9, 119–133.

Barry, M. (2004) 'Re-conceptualising labour market regulation in Australia and New Zealand', *Labour, Employment and Work in New Zealand*, Proceedings of the 11th Conference, pp.383–391.

Blackwood, L.M. (2007a) 'The scope of collective employment agreement bargaining in New Zealand', *The Employment Agreement* (26) VUW.

Blackwood, L.M. (2007b) 'Social contextual influences on union participation: A group processes approach to explaining collective action', *PhD Thesis*, University of Queensland, Australia.

Blackwood, L.M. (2008) 'Revitalization of the New Zealand union movement', *Unpublished manuscript.*

Blackwood, L.M. and Louis, W.R. (2009) 'Political action: Social contextual factors in winning hearts and minds'. Paper presented at the *European Association of Social Psychology, Medium-sized Meeting on Collective Action and Social Change*, July 3–6, Groningen.

Boezeman, E.J. and Ellemers, N. (2007) 'Volunteering for charity: Pride, respect, and the commitment of volunteers', *Journal of Applied Psychology*, 92(3): 771–785.

Borgerson, J.L., Escudero-Magnusson, M. and Magnusson, F. (2006) 'Branding ethics: Negotiating Benetton's identity and image', in Schroeder, J. and Salzer-Mörling, M. (eds), *Brand Culture*, London and New York: Routledge, pp.171–185.

Bruins, J.J., Ellemers, N. and de Gilder, D. (1999) 'Power use and status differences as determinants of subordinates' evaluative and behavioural responses in simulated organizations', *European Journal of Social Psychology*, 29, 843–870.

Cornelissen, J.P., Haslam, S.A. and Balmer, J.M.T. (2007) 'Social identity, organizational identity and corporate identity: Towards an integrated understanding of processes, patternings and products', *British Journal of Management*, 18, S1–S16.

Department of Labour (2001) Workforce 2010. New Zealand Government.

Drury, J. and Reicher, S. (2005) 'Explaining enduring empowerment: A comparative study of collective action and psychological outcomes', *European Journal of Social Psychology*, 35, 35–58.

Duck, J.M. and Fielding, K.S. (1999) 'Leaders and subgroups: One of us or one of them?', *Group Processes and Intergroup Relations*, 2, 203–230.

Ellemers, N., De Gilder, D. and Haslam, S.A. (2004) 'Motivating individuals and groups at work: A social identity perspective on leadership and group performance', *Academy of Management Review*, 29(3): 459–478.

Ellemers, N., Van Rijswijk, W., Roefs, M. and Simons, C. (1997) 'Bias in intergroup perceptions: Balancing group identity with social reality', *Personality and Social Psychology Bulletin*, 23(2): 186–198.

Feinberg-Danieli, G., Lafferty, G. and Kiely, P. (2007) Employment Agreements: Bargaining Tends & Employment Law Update, 2007/2007. IRC, VUW, Wellington.

Frege, C.M. and Kelly, J. (2003) 'Union revitalization strategies in comparative perspective', *European Journal of Industrial Relations*, 9(1): 7–24.

Frege, C.M. and Kelly, J. (eds) (2004) *Varieties of Unionism: Strategies for Union Revitalization in a Globalizing Economy*, Oxford: Oxford University Press.

Haslam, S.A., Postmes, T. and Ellemers, N. (2003a) 'More than a metaphor: Organizational identity makes organizational life possible', *British Journal of Management*, 14, 357–369.

Haslam, S.A., Eggins, R.A. and Reynolds, K.J. (2003b) 'The ASPIRe model: Actualizing social and personal identity resources to enhance organizational outcomes', *Journal of Occupational and Organizational Psychology*, 76, 83–113.

Haslam, S., Platow, M., Turner, J., Reynolds, K., McGarty, C., Oakes, P., Johnson, S., Ryan, M. and Veenstra, K. (2001) 'Social identity and the romance of leadership: The importance of being seen to be "doing it for us"', *Group Processes & Intergroup Relations*, 4(3): 191–205.

Haslam, S.A., Powell, C. and Turner, J.C. (2000) 'Social identity, self-categorization, and work motivation: Rethinking the contribution of the group to positive and sustainable organisational outcomes', *Applied Psychology: An International Review*, 49(3): 319–339.

Haslam, S., Turner, J., Oakes, P. and McGarty, C. (1992) 'Context-dependent variation in social stereotyping: I. The effects of intergroup relations as mediated by social change and frame of reference', *European Journal of Social Psychology*, 22(1): 3–20.

Hatch, M.J. and Schultz, M.S. (2002) 'Are the strategic stars aligned for your corporate brand?', *Harvard Business Review*, 79: 2.

Heckscher, C.C. (1988) *The New Unionism*, New York: Basic Books.

Heery, E. (2002) 'Partnership versus organising: Alternative futures for British trade unionism', *Industrial Relations Journal*, 33(1): 20–34.

HM Government, Cabinet Office (2008) *Realising Britain's Potential: Future Strategic Challenges for Britain*, The Strategy Unit, Feb 2008. Available at www.cabinetoffice.gov.uk/strategy/

Hogg, M.A., Hains, S.C. and Mason, I. (1998) 'Identification and leadership in small groups: Salience, frame of reference and leader stereotypicality effects on leader evaluations', *Journal of Personality and Social Psychology*, 75, 1248–1263.

Hyman, R. (1999) 'An emerging agenda for trade unions? Labour and Society Programme', *International Institute for Labour Studies*, ILO.

Kelly, C. and Breinlinger, S. (1996) *The Social Psychology of Collective Action: Identity, Injustice and Gender*, London: Taylor & Francis.

Kelly, C. and Kelly, J. (1994) 'Who gets involved in collective action? Social psychological determinants of individual participation in trade unions', *Human Relations*, 47, 63–88.

Kelly, J. (2004) 'Social partnership agreements in Britain: Labor cooperation and compliance', *Industrial Relations*, 43(1): 267–292.

Klandermans, B. (1984) 'Mobilization and participation in trade union action: An expectancy-value approach', *Journal of Occupational Psychology*, 57, 107–120.

Klandermans, B. (1986) 'Perceived costs and benefits of participation in union action', *Personnel Psychology*, 39, 379–397.

Klandermans, B. (1992) 'Trade union participation', in Hartley, J. and Stephenson, G.M. (eds) *Employment Relations: The Psychology of Influence and Control at Work*, Oxford: Basil Blackwell, pp.184–199.

Kochan, T.A. and Osterman, P. (1994) *The Mutual Enterprise: Forging a Winning Partnership Among Labour, Management, and Government*, Harvard Business School Press.

Leach, C.W., Ellemers, N. and Barreto, M. (2007) 'Group virtue: The importance of morality (vs. competence and sociability) in the positive evaluation of in-groups', *Journal of Personality and Social Psychology*, 93(2): 234–249.

Leary, M.R. (2005) 'Varieties of interpersonal rejection', *The Social Outcast: Ostracism, Social Exclusion, Rejection, and Bullying*, New York: Psychology Press, pp.35–51.

Leary, M.R. and Baumeister, R.F. (2000) 'The nature and function of self-esteem: Sociometer theory', in Zanna, M.P., *Advances in Experimental Social Psychology*, 32, Academic Press.

Levesque, C., Murray, G. and Le Queuk, S. (2005) 'Union disaffection and social identity: Democracy as a source of union revitalization', *Work and Occupations*, 32(4): 400–422.

Mael, F.A. and Ashforth, B.E. (1992) 'Alumni and their alma mater: A partial test of the reformulated model of organizational identification', *Journal of Organizational Behaviour*, 13, 103–123.

Maslach, C. (2003) 'Job burnout: New directions in research and intervention', *Current Directions in Psychological Science*, 12(5): 189–192.

McCallum, R. (2002) 'Trade union recognition and Australia's neo-liberal voluntary bargaining laws', *Industrial Relations*, 57, 225–251.

Meyer, J.P. and Allen, N.J. (1997) *Commitment in the Workplace*, Thousand Oaks, CA: Sage.

Milkman, R. and Voss, K. (eds) (2004) *Rebuilding Labor: Organizing and Organizers in the New Union Movement*, Ithaca, NY: ILR Press.

Peetz, D. (2002) 'Decollectivist strategies in Oceania', *Industrial Relations*, 57, 252–281.

Platow, M.J. and van Knippenberg, D. (2001) 'A social identity analysis of leadership endorsement: The effects of leader ingroup prototypicality and distributive intergroup fairness', *Personality and Social Psychology Bulletin*, 27, 1508–1519.

Reicher, S.D. (2004) 'The context of social identity: Domination, resistance, and change', *Political Psychology*, 25, 921–945.

Reicher, S., Haslam, S.A. and Hopkins, N. (2005) 'Social identity and the dynamics of leadership: Leaders and followers as collaborative agents in the transformation of social reality', *Leadership Quarterly*, 16, 547–568.

Reicher, S.D. and Hopkins, N. (2001) 'Psychology and the end of history: A critique and a proposal for the psychology of social categorization', *Political Psychology*, 22, 383–407.

Schaufeli, W. and Enzmann, D. (1998) *The Burnout Companion to Study and Practice: A Critical Analysis*, CRC Press.

Simon, B. and Klandermans, B. (2001) 'Politicized collective identity: A social psychological analysis', *American Psychologist*, 56, 319–331.

Simon, B., Loewy, M., Sturmer, S., Weber, U., Freytag, P., Habig, C., Kampmeier, C. and Spahlinger, P. (1998) 'Collective identification and social movement participation', *Journal of Personality and Social Psychology*, 74, 646–658.

Simon, B., Lucken, M. and Sturmer, S., (2006) 'The added value of respect: Reaching across inequality', *British Journal of Social Psychology*, 45, 535–546.

Smith, H.J. and Kessler, T. (2004) 'Group-based emotions and intergroup behavior: The case of relative deprivation', in Tiedens, L.Z. and Leach, C.W.

(eds), *The Social Life of Emotions*, New York: Cambridge University Press.

Sturmer, S., Simon, B. and Loewy, M.I. (2008) 'Intraorganizational respect and organizational participation: The mediating role of collective identity', *Group Processes and Intergroup Relations*, 11(1): 5–20.

Tajfel, H. and Turner, J.C. (1979) 'An integrative theory of intergroup relations', in Worchel, S. and Austin, W.G. (eds), *Psychology of Group Relations*, Monterey, CA: Brooks Cole, pp.33–47.

Taylor, D. and Doria, J. (1981) 'Self-serving and group-serving bias in attribution', *The Journal of Social Psychology*, 113(2): 201–211.

Turner, J. (2005) 'Explaining the nature of power: A three-process theory', *European Journal of Social Psychology*, 35(1): 1–22.

Turner, J.C., Hogg, M.A., Oakes, P.J., Reicher, S.D. and Wetherell, M.S. (1987) *Rediscovering the Social Group: A Self-Categorization Theory*, New York: Basil Blackwell.

Tyler, T.R. and Blader, S.L. (2000) *Cooperation in Groups*, Philadelphia: Psychology Press.

Van Knippenberg, B., van Knippenberg, D., De Cremer, D. and Hogg, M.A. (2005) 'Research in leadership, self, and identity: A sample of the present and a glimpse of the future', *Leadership Quarterly*, 16, 495–499.

van Zomeren, M., Spears, R., Fischer, A.H. and Leach, C.W. (2004) 'Put your money where your mouth is! Explaining collective action tendencies through group-based anger and group efficacy', *Journal of Personality & Social Psychology*, 87, 649–664.

Videla, N.P. (2006) 'It cuts both ways: Workers, management and the construction of a "community of fate" on the shop floor in a Mexican garment factory', *Social Forces*, 84(4): 2099–2119.

Wegge, J. (2000) 'Participation in group goal setting: Some novel findings and a comprehensive model as a new ending to an old story', *Applied Psychology*, 49(3): 498–516.

Winterton, J. and Winterton, R. (1989) *Coal, Crisis, and Conflict: The 1984–85 Miners' Strike in Yorkshire*, Manchester: Manchester University Press.

Yukl, G. (1989) 'Managerial leadership: A review of theory and research', *Journal of Management*, 115(2): 251–289.

Zickar, M.J. (2004) 'An analysis of industrial-organizational psychology's indifference to labor unions in the United States', *Human Relations*, 57, 145–167.

Part III
Concluding on Capability

10
A Framework for Developing Human Capability at Work

Jane Bryson and Paul O'Neil

In Chapter 2 we made the case for broadening debate from narrow understandings of skill, and organisationally instrumental notions of capability, to the wider concept of human capability. We explored human capability as characterised by people having the substantive freedom to achieve 'beings and doings' that they value, leading a life of value to them. Applied to an employment setting this focuses attention on the social arrangements that lead to the ability of people to achieve things they value. This concluding chapter reports on an attempt to identify the conditions for the optimal development of human capability in New Zealand workplaces. Our research specifically examined influences on these conditions at three levels: institutional, organisational and individual. These conditions are summarised in a framework which is aimed to be of assistance to workplace practitioners in shaping social arrangements which develop human capability. This framework is informed by our reflections from case study interviews; first that institutionally coordinated industry or region-wide responses to product or service markets and commitment to quality jobs are all important contributors to capability, as are clear policy/regulatory signals of acceptable practice. Secondly, that organisations are not fully mobilising the tacit knowledge of production processes which workers possess and this is hindering the capability of workforces. Thirdly, that at the individual level human capability was also about the freedom to live a life that was personally perceived as valuable, and that the capability to perform work for an organisation was merely a means towards that end. In designing this framework we have built upon Sen's approach to human capability by first establishing what it is that workers want in a job which would add to their human capability. At the level of institutions, the organisation, and the individual the drivers and barriers to the achievement of human capability are then identified. The implications of this framework for actors influential in workplace change are then discussed.

Drivers and barriers to developing human capability in New Zealand organisations

As part of the research programme outlined in Chapter 2, qualitative research into human capability in New Zealand organisations was undertaken. This research involved interviewing workers, managers and owners in organisations across four sectors: wine production, furniture manufacture, mental health services, and in the arts sector as part of a research strand examining Maori businesses and Maori workers. Interviews were also conducted with education providers, and a range of industry representatives and stakeholders for each case study. In total approximately 200 interviews were conducted in over 30 organisations. Case studies based on these interviews have been reported separately (Blackwood, Bryson and Merritt, 2006; Bryson, Mallon and Merritt, 2004; Bryson and O'Neil, 2009; Bryson et al, 2006; O'Neil et al, 2008; O'Neil, Bryson and Lomax, 2008). This chapter briefly outlines the themes on human capability which these interviews and case studies suggest for New Zealand organisations.

Examination of all the case study interviews utilised an analytical frame of drivers and barriers to human capability development. Drivers were interpreted as those factors which actively catalyse the development of human capability, and barriers as those factors which stop or constrain people from developing or achieving their capability. Barriers, of course, may simply be the lack of driver factors, but they can also be active barriers which prevent capability development even in the presence of drivers. These two categories were further subdivided according to the level at which they were reported as occurring: a) institutional, i.e., factors related to broader systemic arrangements in society such as policy, legislation, regulation and social attitudes; b) organisational, i.e., factors related to practices within organisations; or c) individual, i.e., factors personal to the makeup of an individual.

What we found in our case studies were a variety of workplace, industrial and sector contexts where the principles of production flexibility with a concomitant focus on quality and cost competitiveness were everywhere in evidence. The dominant driver of these production principles were the uncertainties of competition forced upon producers in an open economy. In the private sector, this drive came from competing in export markets, as with wine production; and competition from imports, as with furniture manufacture which was focused on the New Zealand market. In the public sector, as with mental health services, these production principles were evident and driven by state agencies which were aiming to achieve both efficiencies in the way public resources were spent together with a responsive delivery of quality public good outcomes.

Evident across the case studies was the widespread practice of outsourcing to contractors and subcontractors to manage production flexibility. This acted as both a driver of and a barrier to, capability development. Within the arts sector, most workers were subcontracted, and often the key function within the 'core' firm delivering the final product was project management of this diversity of subcontractors. Much of the work which was now contracted out had previously been done 'in-house' and outsourcing was being used as a deliberate strategy to manage uncertain demand and to economise on costs by externalising them through competitive supply. Similarly, in the state sector, a large proportion of community-based mental health care was supplied on a competitive tendering basis by non-government organisations to the District Health Board funder. Again, this network of subcontractors was a deliberate strategy by the District Health Board to manage changing demands for public heath services and to economise on costs. Across the case studies the great majority of these subcontractors were small firms and often were owner/operators. Aside from retaining a management function within the 'core' firms in order to coordinate production, core firms also retained key people with firm specific skills that were difficult, if not impossible, to purchase through contracting.

The organisations in these case studies were also broadly similar in the spheres of work organisation and of employment relations where the organisation of work and of human resource management (HRM) practices, whether they existed formally or informally, were often being used to reinforce management and owner control, and were not being used to mobilise the tacit knowledge of the production processes which workers held. Human capability development, both individual and collective (the workforce), and the potential to perform, was thus constrained by the inability or unwillingness of owners and managers to mobilise worker knowledge. Whilst the principles of knowledge, multi-skilling and worker self-regulation offer considerable synergies in support of production, it is clear that many owners and managers are more comfortable with the legally ensconced, hierarchical command structure to resolve the real problems and tensions in organising cooperation and productivity in the labour process.

The circumstances where workers and workforces could and did use their knowledge and discretion in the production process were often where management control could be mediated through the autonomy over work which a trade or a profession conferred on workers. Entry into trades such as cabinet-making or professions such as nursing is controlled by the trade or profession itself, and in some cases regulated by unions. The level of skill in the trade or profession is thus governed internally as is the culture, particularly with regard to how to engage in cooperative work. In our cases, trades people and professionals in their work offered their knowledge, were inherently multi-skilled, and worked in self-regulating teams, because they could and desired to out of professional pride.

The majority of workers however had little formal opportunity to use discretion in their work. Tacit knowledge was relied upon as the silent contributor to workplace productivity, but formally the organisation of work and the definition and control of tasks was a responsibility of management and accepted as such. Where participation was sought, it was largely to provide a rationale to justify the role for management to make decisions, and not one of joint-participation in decision-making. This seems to run counter to the findings of Boxall and Macky (Chapter 7 of this volume). They report relatively high levels of employee empowerment in their NZ sample. However, they also report that other high involvement work processes, such as communication and voice, were not as evident. Indeed they conclude that this relative empowerment is related to supervisory style rather than a systematic approach to participation by workplaces.

When one looks across each sector and its network of core and subcontracting firms, the labour market structures appear as a series of interlaced labour market segments in which there is a strong tendency towards dualism. That is, whilst there are sectoral variations, jobs are allocated across primary and secondary sectors. In the primary sector are the better jobs in the labour market – those which offer relatively high wages, secure employment and some form of career progression through an internal market. Formal skill levels in this sector are high and the organisational capability – often enhanced with Information and Communication Technologies (ICTs), is well advanced. In the secondary sector are the least desirable jobs – those with relatively poor wages and working conditions in which the threat of unemployment is constant. Jobs in the secondary sector are also associated with small firms that have little organisational capability and are technologically backward. In our case studies it seemed that there was also a difference in social composition between the two sectors as well, with the secondary sector dominated by Maori women and the young, whilst the primary sector is the domain of pakeha and new immigrant, prime-aged professionals and tradespeople. These findings coincide with those reported by Paul Spoonley in Chapter 5 of this volume.

However, the antithesis to this somewhat bleak managerial and workforce picture also emerged across our cases in a variety of forms. Institutionally the presence of industry-wide responses to economic and other pressures often encompassed a concern for capability. Hence industry strategies acted as drivers and served to ameliorate the tendency to very short-term focus of many of the organisations we visited. Organisationally two things were key to determining the practiced business strategy and culture in relation to human capability. These were the beliefs and motivations of the owner or general manager, and the practices of line managers and supervisors. People in these different tiers of management significantly influenced the organisation culture around human capability by virtue of their beliefs and actions. There were employers interviewed, even from very small organisations, who simply had a belief in developing the next generation of workers in their profession, trade or industry. Similarly many workers identified a key supervisor or employer in their working lives who had actively encouraged or supported them as important.

The cases also showed the power of proactive individual behaviour to enhance the achievement of human capability. Workers who had the awareness, confidence and interest to ask, make time, shape the work environment to suit their needs, were more likely to get the capability opportunities they desired. Access to, and take up of, opportunities through work were positively influenced by proactive individual behaviour. Individuals are not without some agency in most work situations, the question is whether they exercise it or not. Interviews with workers revealed that numerous factors determine this including awareness of rights and possibilities in work and life, issues of identity (cultural, occupational, etc), confidence and self-efficacy (see also Blackwood Chapter 9 in this volume). These in turn are linked to educational and family experiences, presence of role models or supportive facilitators at work and outside of work.

We compared themes from our case studies with insights from recent New Zealand research focused on quality of employment and what New Zealanders want from work. A useful literature review by Johri (2005), for the Department of Labour identified that New Zealand employees valued the interest and challenge of a job, but also 'quality of management, management recognition of employee merit and effort, training and development opportunities, work-life balance, and relationships with colleagues. Pay and job security also mattered' (p.3). In the New Zealand Values Study (Rose, Huakau and Casswell, 2005), when rating issues of most importance in choosing a job, people gave high priority to 'doing a job which gives them a sense of accomplishment, allows them to balance work and life commitments and having an employer who recognises their skill development and contribution to the organisation' (p.30). However, some of these priorities differed according to age and educational level. For instance young people (18 to 24 years) were more concerned about income, and those with lower educational levels were more concerned with income, job security and congenial colleagues. In a related vein, most recently the 'National Conversation about Work' being conducted by the Human Rights Commission (2009) throughout New Zealand has found that issues about pay, workload and hours of work, childcare, health and safety, career progression, non-traditional ways of working, seasonal employment, and management of diversity, have all featured as employer and employee concerns in achieving fairness and equality at work.

These findings echo the views expressed in the course of our empirical research, and directly relate to issues of developing human capability. For instance, those in precarious employment or low-quality jobs are more likely to be women, young, an ethnic minority, and less-skilled and less-educated (Spoonley, Chapter 5 in this volume; Tucker, 2002), thus, relative to other social groups, have less capability to live the life they value. However, we found that for some, non-standard employment is not a problem and reflects their capability preferences. For example, registered nurses in the non-government segment of the mental health sector have relatively precarious employment because of contract funding compared to permanent colleagues in the District Health Board doing the same job, but choose this principally because it frees them from shift work. In another example, a small number of seasonal workers reported preferring the flexibility to pursue other activities (hunting, fishing, hiking) in the off-season. But for many of those in precarious employment, their potential life options were severely constrained by being in such employment. For example, in another New Zealand case study on precarious employment, some employees felt they could not, or were not aware they could, bargain for improvements in pay and conditions of work, had no control over work, and were unable to see how they could improve the quality of their life in the present job or in alternative employment (Web/LMPG, 2004). For such workers therefore, human capability – the possibility of choosing the kind of life they valued, was severely constrained by the precarious nature of their employment.

Other than our own study, there is little empirical work in the New Zealand context which specifically identifies and concludes on both the drivers and barriers to human capability development in employment. Thus by comparing our case studies with other New Zealand workplace research we were able to confirm a number of common drivers and barriers to human capability development.

From case study themes to building a framework

The framework of conditions driving or undermining human capability (see Table 10.2) was developed by a series of iterative steps. As stated above, from our qualitative research involving interviews of individuals in organisations we had formed some working hypotheses of drivers and barriers to the development of human capability. We then applied Sen's capability approach by drawing on a list of capabilities formulated by Vizard and Burchardt (2007) in order to establish a normative base of the capabilities it is reasonable to expect to achieve through employment/work. This list was discussed with a range of focus groups in order to identify the type of workplace practices which supported their achievement. Finally, we combined these with the case themes to arrive at a framework which was tested with further focus groups. Below we discuss these two phases: i) the capabilities achieved through work, and ii) the final framework.

What capabilities could be achieved through work?

In order to build a framework exploring the conditions underpinning developing human capability in New Zealand organisations, we needed to clarify what human capabilities could reasonably be expected to be achieved through work. As discussed in Chapter 2 the focus of Sen's capability approach is on the expansion of substantive human freedoms in the form of human capabilities, thus inherent in the approach is equality in human capability. Nevertheless, what ought to constitute a capability list is contestable. Sen himself has been reluctant to endorse a specific list of capabilities.

> The problem is not with listing important capabilities, but with insisting on one predetermined canonical list of capabilities, chosen by social theorists without a general social discussion or public reasoning. To have such a fixed list, emanating entirely from pure theory, is to deny the possibility of fruitful public participation on what should be included and why (Sen, 2004, p.77).

In contrast, Nussbaum has argued that Sen's position in relation to the formulation of capability lists is too vague and that both the theoretical development and practical application of the capability approach requires the endorsement of a specific capability list. On the basis of this critique, Nussbaum has developed a list of central human function capabilities (see Nussbaum, 2000, pp.78–80), which has been adopted for many empirical studies on the capability approach. Nevertheless, as Burchardt (2006), Vizard (2007) and Vizard and Burchardt (2007) discuss, various concerns have been expressed about the broad nature of Nussbaum's capability list – 'relating to the substantive content of the list, the focus on philosophical derivation, and the lack or absence of democratic legitimacy and participation' (Vizard and Burchardt, 2007, p.33). Alkire (2007) argues that a strength of the capability approach is the wide range of methodologies adopted in order to arrive at lists of capabilities. She goes on to synthesise a set of categories to guide the development of such lists.

Vizard and Burchardt (2007) draw on Alkire in their development of a methodological framework for the Equalities Review in the United Kingdom which was a precursor to the establishment of the Commission on Equality and Human Rights. This framework combined two approaches to the development of capability lists: pragmatic consensus and deliberative/participative methods. Vizard and Burchardt (2007) invoked the United Nations Declaration of Human Rights as the basis of a 'pragmatic consensus' for reaching agreement on the nature and scope of a capability list. To these authors, this declaration serves as a pragmatic starting point to develop a capability list because:

> it has the advantages of drawing upon established processes of international consensus-building around the central and basic freedoms that are of value in human life and that are at least in part deliberative and democratic (rather than being purely of an 'expert' or 'technocratic' nature) (p.11).

The capability list that they developed on this basis was then subjected to deliberative consultation with interested and affected parties.

We decided to draw upon the final capability list which Vizard and Burchardt (2007) developed as our pragmatic starting point for a capability list for developing human capability in New Zealand organisations. This list included the capability to: a) be alive, to live in physical security and to be healthy; b) be knowledgeable, to understand and reason, and to have the skills to participate in society; c) enjoy a comfortable standard of living, with independence and security; d) engage in productive and valued activities; e) enjoy individual, family and social life; f) participate in decision-making, have a voice and influence; and g) be and express yourself, have self-respect and know you will be protected and treated fairly by the law. We presented this set of capabilities to members of a series of targeted focus groups representing a broad spectrum of employers and workers. These human capabilities were discussed with groups in terms of their desirability, and the job conditions or other factors that would facilitate or hinder their achievement. The responses to these questions were collated and are presented in Table 10.1.

The table works from left to right. In the left-hand column is the basic set of human capabilities drawn from Vizard and Burchardt (2007) which we propose is what human capability development aspires to as an end. If individuals can have these freedoms, they are in a position to choose those achievements they value, which we propose is an appropriate end-point of economic and social development.

The relevance of the concept of the capability approach, as we have developed it, lies in the idea that mobilising the economic capabilities of individuals is not simply a process of them receiving the necessary financial resources through a money or social wage so as to exploit their endowments. Rather, the institutional framework of the market needs to be examined in order to establish how far it facilitates or constrains the potential of individuals to lead the kind of life they value.

Our approach to examining how workplaces facilitate or constrain this human capability development was to identify what workers want in a job that would facilitate this freedom. Column two of Table 10.1 presents our findings to this question. What is notable in these findings is that the information found from the focus groups is already well-known as what constitutes quality work. A more complete list of what constitutes quality work as drawn from the literature is presented in Column three of Table 10.1 for comparison.

Many reports, articles and books expound on the elements of good workplace practice contained in Table 10.1 (see Chapter 2, and Boxall and Macky Chapter 7 in this volume). However, debates abound over how these are implemented, for example: best practice HRM versus best fit HRM approaches, hard versus soft regulation for employment standards and protections. But, regardless of approach, flaws are found in patchy uptake by employers of good workplace practices. What is seldom explored is what drives and constrains the reality of workplaces and the practices therein. Rarely is this viewed from the normative base of a human capability perspective. Table 10.1 provides this base, and an essential foundation for building the framework of the conditions driving and undermining human capability development in New Zealand organisations.

Table 10.1   Capabilities and Work

Capabilities (from Vizard and Burchardt, 2007)	Worker capability: What workers want in a job (from focus groups)	Workplace characteristics which facilitate human capability (from case studies and literature)
The capability to be alive, to live in physical security and to be healthy	Work that is safe and healthy in the short and long term. Workplace free from harassment and unfair discrimination.	Safe and healthy workplace: • removal of traditional exposure factors • regard for impact of: organisational change on working conditions; intensification of work; working hours; age; employment status; gender differences. Freedom to voice concerns. Access to health services. Minimal stress at work. • Job design: job rotation; work teams.
The capability to be knowledgeable, to understand and reason, and to have the skills to participate in society	Work that lets you develop your skills and abilities. Work where you receive the training you need to do the job effectively. Work where the communication is good among the people with whom you work. Work that uses your skill, knowledge and experience. Work hours that let you participate in the community.	Ongoing training and development. Collective rights to deliberation, consultation, involvement in organisational change. Positive intrinsic work: • offered initiative opportunities, • employer interest in work, • promotion over time, • opportunity for advancement and challenge.

Table 10.1   Capabilities and Work *– continued*

Capabilities (from Vizard and Burchardt, 2007)	Worker capability: What workers want in a job (from focus groups)	Workplace characteristics which facilitate human capability (from case studies and literature)
The capability to enjoy a comfortable standard of living, with independence and security	Work that pays well. Work where your job security is good. Work where the people you work for treat you with respect.	Positive extrinsic job characteristics: • decent pay, • hours of work to meet needs, • place of work meets needs. Freedom against unjust dismissal. Job and income security: • permanent employment status, • social support to reconcile job flexibility with job security (flexicurity).
The capability to engage in productive and valued activities	Work that is interesting. Work where the people you work with are friendly and helpful. Work that gives you a sense of accomplishment. Work where you receive recognition for work done. Work where your chances of career advancement are good.	Positive intrinsic work characteristics: • offered initiative opportunities, • employer interest in work, • promotion over time, • opportunity for advancement and challenge. Flexible working-time arrangements. Equitable pay and work arrangements. Adaptation to older workers.

Table 10.1 **Capabilities and Work** – *continued*

Capabilities (from Vizard and Burchardt, 2007)	Worker capability: What workers want in a job (from focus groups)	Workplace characteristics which facilitate human capability (from case studies and literature)
The capability to enjoy individual, family and social life	Work that allows you to balance your work and family and personal life.	Positive extrinsic and intrinsic job characteristics. Work schedules: • shift work; compressed work week; flexible hours; work hours preference. Flexible working-time arrangements: • length of, flexibility of, and predictability of working hours; organisation of 'urban' times; adaptation to life cycle. Sick/bereavement/annual leave rights. Adaptation for older workers.
The capability to participate in decision-making, have a voice and influence	Work that allows you freedom to do your job. Work where you can choose your own schedule within established limits. Work that allows you to participate in decision-making. Work that allows you to form and join civil organisations and solidarity groups, including trade unions. Work that allows you to participate in the local community.	Structures which facilitate worker voice. Job design. Union presence. Positive employer (supervisor)-employee relationship. Positive employee-employee relationships.

Table 10.1 **Capabilities and Work** – *continued*

Capabilities (from Vizard and Burchardt, 2007)	**Worker capability: What workers want in a job** (from focus groups)	**Workplace characteristics which facilitate human capability** (from case studies and literature)
The capability of being and expressing yourself, having self-respect and knowing you will be protected and treated fairly by the law	Work where the people you work for treat you with respect.	Know and express/defend employment and human rights. Continuing education.

What drives and undermines developing human capability in New Zealand organisations?

Table 10.2 presents our findings of those factors which facilitate or constrain the development of human capability, and the conditions in which this occurs. These findings are drawn from the case studies and from the focus group discussions in response to the Table 10.1 capability list. A draft of the framework was tested with further focus and discussion groups. The framework presented in Table 10.2 is the result of this final feedback.

The framework firstly outlines key institutional factors underpinning developing human capability in New Zealand organisations. At the broadest level these are: the economic setting; the role of the state/public policy; educational arrangements; and cultural/ideological legacies. Each of these four institutional factors is broken down to more detailed constituent sub-factors and examples are provided of different conditions in which the factor either drives or undermines capability. Likewise two key organisational factors are labelled: philosophy of economic and working life; and, key structures and practices. The second is made up of more detailed sub-factors. At the individual level four key factors are described: attitude, confidence and self-efficacy; educational experience; perception of work arrangements and culture; and, life, capability and experience beyond work. At this level there are no constituent sub-factors.

The framework clearly illustrates how in some circumstances a factor may act as a driver while in others it may undermine capability. All the chapters in this volume report on the influence of different practices at different levels. For instance, Mayhew's Chapter 4 illustrates through a cross country comparison the impact of different institutional arrangements on the profile of low paid work; Boxall and Macky (Chapter 7) observe that some high performance work systems are baseline institutional requirements of workplaces in some countries, and not in others; and at the individual level Dalziel's Chapter 8 reports that young people's career choices are changeable and are influenced by the information available and other factors.

Implications of the influences on developing human capability framework

As discussed in Chapter 2 the aim of this research project was to produce a framework or model of human capability development that was of practical benefit to practitioners and policymakers in the fields of industrial relations, human resource management, and management generally. This framework is summarised in Table 10.2.

The framework is useful and unusual for at least two reasons: 1) it builds on a clearly articulated normative base (in the form of human capability) rather than unacknowledged embedded ideologies, and 2) it attempts to present a comprehensive systemic view of the influences on human capability in work and employment.

It is important to reiterate the philosophy behind the framework – that human capability is about people being able to function in doing the things they value. Such capability ought to be the end point, or purpose, for individuals and groups engaging in productive activities. It thus includes, but goes beyond, capabilities to work towards organisational goals. Drawing on Sen's human capability approach, we define human capability as the capability to choose a set of beings and doings that an individual values. We express this substantive freedom to choose as the capability set in Table 10.1, a set which is derived from the United Nations Declaration of Human Rights (Vizard and Burchardt, 2007).

From this philosophical position, the relevance of the framework for practitioners is as a tool to closely examine the institutional and social structures within and around the workplace so as to establish how far they can go to facilitate or constrain the potential or freedom of individuals to achieve their desired functioning as human beings. The framework is not a 'one model fits all' framework. Rather, it assists those in organisations involved in their particular workplace contexts to recognise the full scope of human capability and the factors that are likely to drive or constrain it. It is also a framework around which parties with different interests, particularly unions and employers, can debate and discuss the wider opportunities and threats on human capability which are posed by particular workplace change proposals.

The framework encourages discussion on how to mobilise the discretionary efforts of workers through the organisation of work and its regulation. There was evidence through the case studies of widespread application of flexible principles of production. However these were very much still 'work in progress' because organisations were focused primarily upon transferring the uncertainties of flexible production and seeking lower costs by outsourcing work previously done

Table 10.2 Framework of Influences on Developing Human Capability in New Zealand Organisations

	Conditions in which the factor …	
Type of institutional factor	… drives human capability development	… undermines human capability development
Economic setting *Nature and state of the product market (especially increasing competition)*	Multi-employer, collective responses (industry or region) tend to enhance human capability. For example: through ITO's or other industry/sector groups or government initiatives focused on specific sectors.	Uncoordinated, fragmented responses are associated with a spiral downwards in human capability.
Nature of the labour market e.g., excess demand for labour or particular classes of work	Managers can promote the development of human capability in such jobs as an enticement to attract scarce workers.	If care is not taken under-staffing (due to insufficient skilled labour available) tends to squeeze out the time needed for orderly on the-job development of capability.
Nature of the legal form of employment (e.g., full-time permanent, part-time, fixed-term, short-term, casual, temporary)	Quality, permanent jobs can provide the stability needed around which to plan and provide the development of human capability. Institutional norms which endorse industry and organisational practices of contracting out/outsourcing arrangements which require skill or development standards to be met, e.g., in mental health provision, has driven up-skilling (and consequent increase in individual confidence, choice and capability).	Non-permanent, non-full-time employment is usually associated with limited interest in or commitment to developing human capability. Contracting out of service provision can also lead to limited investment in capability development, and constraints on career pathways.

Table 10.2   Framework of Influences on Developing Human Capability in New Zealand Organisations – *continued*

Type of institutional factor	Conditions in which the factor …	
	… drives human capability development	… undermines human capability development
Geographic setting (i.e., issue of non-metro localities)	Local cohesion can be a resource which facilitates the goodwill necessary to get coordination between employers, education providers and workers/ potential workers.	Problem of distances and lack of critical mass can constrain possibility for developing human capability.
Role of the state/public policy *Publicly defined standards*	By providing clear signal of acceptable practice (through legislation and regulation) can promote development of human capability.	If reduced or set too low can reward rogue behaviours and give unfair advantage to self-interested/short-term strategies, e.g., the level of minimum wage, the level of standards for health & safety.
Public funding	Can be used to provide rewards and recognition to good performers.	If there are insufficient funds it can lead to under-provision of service.
Policy concerning indigenous community	Latest arrangements (e.g. promoting self-reliance, reclaiming tino rangatiratanga [Maori sovereignty]) can nurture situations that promote human capability.	Traditional model of welfare/income support alone can foster dependence and undermine self-reliance.

Table 10.2   Framework of Influences on Developing Human Capability in New Zealand Organisations – *continued*

	Conditions in which the factor …	
Type of institutional factor	… drives human capability development	… undermines human capability development
Educational arrangements *Infrastructure*	Proper apprenticeship support nurture this form of skill formation.	Hard to have apprenticeships without appropriate institutional support, e.g., non-aligned or no incentives for ITOs, providers, employers and trainees.
Integration of different elements	Where it occurs it fosters human capability development, e.g. , the stair-casing of industry training builds capability (particularly for those with poor secondary school experiences); formal, structured learning drives broader understandings and capability development, and establishes professional networks.	School and other influences on job choice which discouraged or failed to encourage students into certain occupations or industries. Where links are poor (e.g., in dismembered competency standards) undermines the development of human capability (e.g., no understanding of whole processes only of discrete parts).
Sensitivity/engagement with local conditions	Nurtures high human capability, e.g., existence of regionally-based publicly-funded education providers who operate with input from the community.	If absent, means the development of human capability is not as advanced as would otherwise be.

Table 10.2 Framework of Influences on Developing Human Capability in New Zealand Organisations – *continued*

	Conditions in which the factor …	
Type of institutional factor	… drives human capability development	… undermines human capability development
Cultural/ideological legacies (***especially of goodwill and cohesion***)	Social attitudes which are supportive of education, work, and skill development. Recognition and awards for good employer practices, coordinated by agencies such as EEO Trust, HRINZ, etc. Improving asset base of iwi especially as result of Treaty grievance settlements. Partnership between Maori organisations and agencies especially in social services providing employment and skill development.	Social attitudes which eschew post-compulsory education and some types of jobs. Lack of acknowledgement by employers of Maori cultural knowledge that is drawn on in the workplace.

Table 10.2 Framework of Influences on Developing Human Capability in New Zealand Organisations – *continued*

Type of organisational factor	Conditions in which the factor …	
	… drives human capability development	… undermines human capability development
Philosophy of economic and working life	Encompassing approach (a) Ethical, sustainable approach (b) Maori philosophy of 'production for use' Management belief in goals of the organisation, facilitating team work and reflective practice. Supportive employers, managers, supervisors were consistently cited as key drivers of human capability development. Long-term view of the business and developing human capability, in Maori organisations this was sometimes expressed as a vision of iwitanga with iwi economic self-determination.	Mainstream 'commercial' visions based on a definition of value defined by the extent it can be bought, sold and turn a profit. In corporates, a board or a senior management team which prioritises shareholder return ahead of workforce development. In SMEs the beliefs/values of the owner or general manager can work either for or against human capability development. In all organisations a short-term focus of business owners and business strategy can seriously undermine capability development for the business and the industry. Absence of management of the relationship between employer and employee, and between employee and employee. A focus on the employment relationship as purely transactional, for example, just wages, hours of work and leave arrangements.

Table 10.2 Framework of Influences on Developing Human Capability in New Zealand Organisations – *continued*

Key structures and practices

Scale of operation	Larger workplaces often have critical mass and scale to offer DHC.	Small size of organisations presents some practical barriers to training and career development (financial, no one to fill in, time constraints). Although there are alternatives (which some organisations pursued)
Work organisation & design	Pay systems, particularly those that were skill related were cited as an important incentive to increase skills (as long as the design of the job gave the opportunity to use these skills). Additionally, fair pay in general allowed workers to live the lives they desired. Work design and practices drove capability. In particular practices which enabled developing an understanding of a whole process and where one's own job activities fit.	Work design focused on efficiency and targets at the expense of innovation and personal development. Tension between drive for profit through employees meeting targets and work/life balance. Management – performance management based solely on efficiency of production and outputs. Unwillingness to confront and manage poor performance. Lean staffing levels. Lack of trust of employees and autonomy in the job (within limits), e.g. in standardised production models, and in micromanaged performance target models.

Table 10.2 Framework of Influences on Developing Human Capability in New Zealand Organisations – *continued*

Skill formation arrangements	Importance of a balanced team – mix of experienced with inexperienced workers for effective workplace learning, mentoring and sharing of capability. Appropriate resourcing and infrastructure drives quality and capability. For instance, the organisation paying study fees, and providing paid time off work for study; good staffing levels to allow this. Occupations – recognition of certain work areas as worthy occupations with certain skill needs and broader capabilities (e.g., mental health nursing and community mental health work). Professional standards and competency assurance mechanisms.	Managers/supervisors who are unable or unwilling to share their capability (between individuals and between organisations), or who take a narrow employee control focus rather than a more expansive employee development/facilitation focus. Deliberate strategy to poach, not train. Lack of support (in workplaces and in professional training) for use of Te Reo [Maori language] or Maori values impacts on Maori capability and non-Maori capability in a Maori environment. Perceived inequalities in professional development and promotion processes in some organisations.
Workplace [industrial] relations and cultures	Social or other treats for workers were noted, both in large and small organisations, as important motivators. Good customer and supplier relations led to greater sharing of capability and continuous improvement. Unions having sufficient density and adopting a partnership approach with a desire to engage with employers not just on pay and conditions but also on capability related issues (e.g., productivity, service to users, etc).	Perceived inadequacy of organisational induction processes in some organisations. Lack of mechanisms for genuine employee input. For example, consultation aimed to endorse or improve management decision-making and not to increase worker participation in decision-making. Lack of open communication or transparency of information. An organisational culture which discourages questioning. Absence of active union presence in many workplaces without alternative voice mechanisms was, for some, a barrier to any focus on capability. 'Good people as custodians of bad practice'.

Table 10.2   Framework of Influences on Developing Human Capability in New Zealand Organisations – *continued*

Type of individual factor	Conditions in which the factor …	
	… drives human capability development	… undermines human capability development
Attitude, confidence and self-efficacy	Attitude was consistently reported to drive capability. In particular the willingness and desire to learn, and interest in the work. Aspiration to improve one's lot in life or that of one's family. Personal beliefs and values and interests influence career choice and desire to foster personal development and well-being. Proactive individual behaviour was a key driver. The desire to continue learning and developing through experience and to proactively shape the work environment or ask for the development in order to achieve this.	The absence of confidence, motivation, or no way to access it. Poor attitude to work, and to capability development. Lack of awareness, confidence, proactivity or organisation-based self-esteem of workers thus unwillingness to push for improvements in the workplace.
Educational experience	Qualifications and up-skilling opportunities give confidence to be capable. Poor schooling experiences and lack of literacy, both undermine capability development.	

Table 10.2   Framework of Influences on Developing Human Capability in New Zealand Organisations – *continued*

Perception of work arrangements and culture	Clarity about your job, where you fit, relevance of skills, enjoyment of job, self-awareness and a supportive team.	Lack of role clarity, and staff who do not know their own jobs or how they connect to the work of others. Thus, for example, the ability to work as a team or collegially is compromised. Mode of employment, i.e., differential status and rights depending on whether one is a permanent full-time, part-time, casual, fixed-term or contractor. Worker ignorance of employment rights and responsibilities.
Life, capability and experience beyond work	Networking and links to the community enhance capability, as do a role model or encourager (often 'someone like me' who has done well).	Other priorities outside of work were seen by some as barriers to capability development at work. However, for many these priorities were the drivers of living a life that they desired.

'in-house', and by constructing sub-contracting arrangements with peripheral firms for parts of production. There was, in contrast, little evidence of organisations actively constructing the internal organisation of work and its regulation in order to mobilise the discretionary effort of workers. Whilst outsourcing and externalising employment relationships may be an appropriate short-term competitive strategy, it is not the optimal long-term route towards the high-value, high-wage, high-skill economic situation governments are seeking through current policy arrangements. The optimal competitive route, which is also the route which optimises the development of human capability as we have defined it, is through actively organising work and employment relations which produce good quality jobs. The human capability framework opens up these two sides of mutual interest. On the one hand it provides the narrative for a business case for good quality jobs, and on the other hand, it provides a rationale for unions or other workplace forms of democracy, to participate in workplace decision-making towards good quality jobs.

Through the provision of good quality jobs and work environments, organisations improve upon their role as capability enhancing institutions in society. The framework provides important balance to a picture dominated by human capital and resource-based views at the expense of human capability. It does this by articulating a much needed action-guiding moral base for management, and particularly human resource management, decision-making. Our research has demonstrated that other than legal compliance as a clear driver of capability development and organisation behaviour, there is no accepted set of principles guiding employers. Management and HRM practice are largely buffeted along on the tide of 'best practice', personal beliefs, or meeting the demands of a business strategy, where the needs of business survival and shareholder prosperity often outweigh other considerations. Hence, as observed in the framework, good managers and supervisors find themselves in the situation of being 'custodians of bad practice'. The capabilities underpinning the framework, and their drivers and barriers, facilitate a questioning and rebalancing of the norms currently driving business decisions and behaviour.

As is evident from the framework in Table 10.2, the state plays a deep role in facilitating human capability development at all levels, but particularly at the institutional level. At the same time, such state influence on developing human capability is also driving (and to a degree constraining) the development of good jobs which in turn underpins the productive potential of flexible production. Such state intervention in the form of an extension of social rights into the workplace is conventionally thought of as entailing economic costs which must be weighed in the balance of the social gains expected. However, from the perspective of the framework, such state interventions are also an investment in and provide much of the social support to realise the productive potential of new forms of work organisation. As such, the framework opens the space for policy-makers to consider the appropriate role of social policy which complements economic policy (see: Barnard et al, 2001; Salais and Villeneuve, 2004).

Human contributions to society are not solely through work, and organisational contributions to society are not solely economic. A rebalancing to focus institutions and organisations not only on financial wealth, but also on the commonwealth of social well-being, and the arrangements which enhance its achievement, is long overdue.

References

Alkire, S. (2002) *Valuing Freedoms: Sen's Capability Approach and Poverty Reduction*, Oxford: Oxford University Press.

Barnard, C., Deakin, S. and Hobbs, R. (2001) 'Capabilities and rights: An emerging agenda for social policy?', *Industrial Relations Journal*, 32(5): 464–479.

Blackwood, L., Bryson, J. and Merritt, K. (2006) *Furniture Manufacturing Industry*, Discussion Paper, Developing Human Capability Research Project, Industrial Relations Centre, Wellington, Victoria University of Wellington.

Bryson, J., Mallon, M. and Merritt, K. (2004) 'Opportunities and tensions in New Zealand organisations: The individual and the organisation in development', *Labour, Employment and Work in New Zealand*, Proceedings of the Eleventh conference, Victoria University of Wellington, pp.15–21.

Bryson, J., and O'Neil, P. (2009) 'A workplace view of drivers and barriers to developing human capability', *New Zealand Journal of Employment Relations*, 34(1): 62–76.

Bryson, J., Pajo, K., Ward, R. and Mallon, M. (2006) 'Learning at work: Organisational affordances and individual engagement', *Journal of Workplace Learning*, 18(5): 279–297.

Burchardt, T. (2006) *Foundations for Measuring Equality: A Discussion Paper for the Equalities Review*, Case/111, Centre for Analysis of Social Exclusion, London: London School of Economics.

Human Rights Commission (2009) National Conversation about Work, New Zealand Regional reports, accessible at: http://www.haveyoursayaboutwork.org.nz/reports/

Johri, R. (2005) *Work Values and the Quality of Employment: A Literature Review*, Wellington: Department of Labour.

Nussbaum, M. (2000) *Women and Human Development*, Cambridge: Cambridge University Press.

O'Neil, P., Bryson, J., Cutforth, T. and Minogue, G. (2008*) Mental Health Services in Northland*, Discussion Paper, Developing Human Capability Research Project, Industrial Relations Centre, Wellington, Victoria University of Wellington.

O'Neil, P., Bryson, J. and Lomax, H. (2008) *Maori Organisations*, Discussion Paper, Developing Human Capability Research Project, Industrial Relations Centre, Wellington, Victoria University of Wellington.

Rose, E., Huakau, J and Casswell, S. (2005) *Economic Values: A Report from the NEW Zealand Values Study 2005*, Centre for Social and Health Outcomes Research and Evaluation & Te Ropu Whariki, Auckland, Massey University.

Salais, R. and Villeneuve, R. (eds) (2004) *Europe and the Politics of Capabilities*, Cambridge: Cambridge University Press.

Sen, A. (2004) 'Capabilities, lists and public reason: Continuing the conversation', *Feminist Economics*, 10(3): 77–80.

Tucker, D. (2002) *'Precarious' Non-Standard Employment: A Review of the Literature*, Labour Market Policy Group, Wellington: Department of Labour.

Vizard, P. (2007) 'Specifying and justifying a basic capability set: Should the international human rights framework be given a more direct role?', *Oxford Development Studies*, 35(3): 225–250.

Vizard, P. and Burchardt, T. (2007) *Developing a Capability List: Final Recommendations of the Equalities Review Steering Group on Measurement*, Case Paper 121, Centre for Analysis of Social Exclusion, London School of Economics.

Web/LMPG (2004) *Report of Exploratory Case Study Research into Precarious Employment*, Centre for Research on Work, Education and Research Ltd in association with the Labour Market Policy Group, Wellington: Department of Labour.

Index

Note: The page numbers in bold denote illustrations.